THE GENTLE PERSUADER

THE GENTLE PERSUADER

A Biography of James Gladstone
Indian Senator

HUGH A. DEMPSEY

Western Producer Prairie Books
Saskatoon, Saskatchewan

Cover painting by Nicholas de Grandmaison
Cover design by McKay Goettler Design
Printed and bound in Canada

The publisher acknowledges the support received for this publication from
the Canada Council.

Western Producer Prairie Books is a unique publishing venture located in
the middle of western Canada and owned by a group of prairie farmers
who are members of Saskatchewan Wheat Pool. From the first book in
1954, a reprint of a serial originally carried in the weekly newspaper *The
Western Producer,* to the book before you now, the tradition of providing
enjoyable and informative reading for all Canadians is continued.

Canadian Cataloguing in Publication Data

Dempsey, Hugh A., 1929–

    The gentle persuader

    Includes index.
    ISBN 0-88833-208-4

1. Gladstone, James, 1887–1971. 2. Kainah Indians –
Biography. 3. Indians of North America – Canada –
Biography. 4. Legislators – Canada – Biography.
5. Canada. Parliament. Senate – Biography. 6. Indian
Association of Alberta. I. Title

E99.K15G43 1986   971.004'97   C86-098072-3

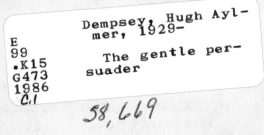

CONTENTS

v

PREFACE

James Gladstone was the first treaty Indian to be appointed to the Senate of Canada. This recognition in 1958 was the culmination of a lifetime of work among his people, beginning with his own family on the Blood Reserve, and growing from there to his tribe, to the Indians of Alberta, and finally to a national concern for legal and economic equality of Canada's native inhabitants. Providing leadership to a people who were suspicious and hostile to those who counselled for change, he often was far in advance of both Indians and the government as he sought the franchise, Indian involvement in education, liquor rights, and equality under the law.

As a junior newspaper reporter, I first met Gladstone at an Indian Association of Alberta meeting in Edmonton in 1950 while he was presiding as president of that body. I was tremendously impressed with his quiet but forceful leadership, and was even more attracted to his daughter Pauline, whom I later married. Over the next twenty years, Gladstone and I were more than just father-in-law and son-in-law; we were friends. Through his dedication, I was drawn into the Indian movement, writing petitions, drafting resolutions, and eventually serving as honorary secretary of the IAA.

During this period, long before Gladstone's senate appointment, I had a sense of his place in history, his role in shaping the destiny of Canada's Indians. Accordingly, on our travels to IAA meetings, trips to Indian reserves in search of oral history, and our extended visits back and forth, I gradually recorded his life story, from the time he ran away from Mountain Mill at the age of six until he became a part of the Indian movement. Other people—family, friends, former classmates, Indian agents— also shared their experiences with me so that by the time he was appointed to the senate I had already taken on the role of his Boswell. Similarly, during his years in the senate, my wife and I acted as his unofficial secretaries, speech writers, and confidants, giving us a rare insight into the man and his mission.

Perhaps impartiality becomes almost impossible under these circumstances but, as a historian, I have tried to balance his strong points with his weak and his successes with his failures. Anything less would have been a disservice to the man for in understanding his shortcomings, one can more accurately measure his achievements.

Many people have assisted in this project, and next to the late senator himself, my wife Pauline heads the list. Not only did she share the exciting years of the IAA movement with me, but she criticized the manuscript—and praised it—even as she was re-typing it. The other children of Senator Gladstone read the manuscript to catch mistakes and offer comments. Lucy Swite, in particular, had many stories to tell, while the comments of Fred and Horace Gladstone, Nora Baldwin, and Doreen Hendra were appreciated.

Much thanks also are due to my late mother-in-law, Janie Gladstone, for her recollections, to the late Jack Gladstone, the senator's uncle, who helped sort out the family tree, and to his widow Reita for her knowledge. Also to Harvey and Marge Buckmaster, who enabled me to find seclusion for writing in their foothills cabin. Other people who helped in various ways were the Hon. Ralph Steinhauer, Douglas Harkness, John Samson, Howard Beebe, Clarence and Vicky McHugh, Dave Crowchild, Bertie Patterson, Mrs. Hilda Bradshaw, Ralph D. Ragan, Charlie Edgar, Suzette Eagle Ribs, and many others from the Blood tribe, the IAA, and the community at large. I also wish to thank my children—James, Louise, John, Leah, and Lois—who have patiently seen this book come to life about a grandfather whom they knew and loved.

Institutions which have been generous with their time and help have been my own organization, the Glenbow Museum in Calgary, the Public Archives of Canada in Ottawa, and the Indian Affairs branch of the federal government. The senator's voluminous records and Janie's detailed diaries proved to be a vital source of information; these were inherited by my wife and me upon the senator's death in 1971, and after Janie passed away seven years later.

As this book, in part, deals with the history of the Blood Reserve, I also submitted the manuscript to Roy Fox, the head chief, and his council, for their approval.

CHAPTER ONE

THE RUNAWAY

Jimmy Gladstone was seven years old.

A near-waif who usually lived with his grandfather, he was playing beside the house in the late spring of 1894 when his cousin Nellie drove up. In the back of the wagon was her young brother Alex, a playmate of Jimmy's.

Cousin Nellie was a Roman Catholic, and a fanatic about her religion. While the Gladstones originally had been Anglicans, almost the entire family had been converted, thanks to the efforts of Father Albert Lacombe. He had known the family in the fur trading days and later built a mission at Pincher Creek, a few miles from the Gladstone enclave at Mountain Mill. About the only ones who had not converted were the old Scottish patriarch of the clan, William Gladstone, and the three grandchildren who had been raised under his roof. One of them was young Jimmy.

Nellie was on her way to St. Joseph's Industrial School for native children at Dunbow, just east of High River, where Alex was starting classes. It occurred to her that if she took little Jimmy along, he would be enrolled and beyond the reach of his grandfather and the Anglicans before anyone could stop her. She invited the boy to join Alex so they could "go for a ride" and soon they were on the old stagecoach route to Fort Macleod. They stopped in the town for a day to visit with a half-breed family named Murphy, and then set out on the hundred-mile wagon route to Calgary, where Nellie wanted to do some shopping for her brother's entrance into school.

The early spring had been a memorable one in the district for its heavy rains and the floods which had coursed downwards from the foothills to the plains. Then, unpredictably, the clouds had fled before the westerly

1

winds and when Nellie set out in June, many farmers already were fearful of drought. Along the Macleod–Calgary trail, the ruts were deep from the wet spring, but now the prairies were dry and a powdery dust hung in the air as the wagon bumped and creaked along its tortuous path.

About a mile from Calgary, there was a half-breed camp where Nellie knew she would find relatives and friends. The little village tried to glory in the name of Rouleauville, but everyone simply called it "The Mission." An assortment of half-breed cabins, a hotel and a few stores and houses were clustered around the Catholic church or amid the cottonwoods that marked the twisting path of the Elbow River. Here the tired travellers rested and exchanged the latest news and gossip. Only a year earlier, Nellie's father, Billy Gladstone, had died in Calgary. He had been the official interpreter for the Mounted Police, a man who could speak seven languages including Gaelic, and was one of the most respected men in the community, Indian or white. His sudden death had been a shock to everyone, and now Nellie was seeing his old friends for the first time since the funeral.

After she had bought a few personal items for her brother, Nellie turned south again until her wagon creaked over the hill and down the dusty side road that led to the Dunbow school. Nestled on the flat at the mouth of the Highwood River, this institution had been a center for the work of the Oblate order since 1885 and was now under the direction of Father Claude.

The students had been dismissed from their classes and were waiting for dinner when the wagon and its three occupants arrived. With dusky faces, their hair cropped close to their heads, and their bodies shrouded in grey military-like uniforms, the boys crowded around the new arrivals. Jimmy recognized one of his cousins and excitedly jumped out of the wagon to greet him. The cousin, in turn, happily offered to show him around. Isolated as they were from the main transportation trails, the most frequent visitors the students saw were parents from the nearby Blackfoot Reserve who came and camped in the trees until the Mounted Police drove them away.

While Jimmy and his cousin wandered through the playing fields and farm buildings, Nellie kept Alex firmly in tow as she went to see Father Claude. They assembled in the principal's office where the priest prepared the necessary admittance papers, one set, as expected, for Alexander Gladstone, and another as an added bonus, for James Basil Gladstone.

Entering a boy in a mission school could be a painful experience. Once out of the family's hands, he was the property of the church and would be home only infrequently for the next twelve years. By then he would be eighteen, a man with an education and good Christian background. To Nellie, that meant he would be a good Catholic, and in her view, no sacrifice was too great for that end. After she had signed the documents, Nellie kissed her brother goodbye, patted a couple of cousins on the head, and turned her wagon towards home.

Jimmy was still with his cousin exploring the shoemaker's room above the carpentry shop when the school bell rang for dinner. Like a hare, his cousin darted down the stairs, calling out that they were going to eat. Jimmy followed him out into the bright sunlight and had raced part way across the grounds when suddenly he stopped.

Straight ahead of him was the forbidding main building of the school. To the west was a thin trail of dust rising from Cousin Nellie's wagon as it climbed the hill. Only then did he realize that he had been left behind; Nellie expected him to go to school. Surprised by the sudden change of events, Jimmy nevertheless was not alarmed. Rather, he was angry at the way he had been unceremoniously dumped at the mission and realized that he had only moments to decide what to do. One way led to the Dunbow School—a life of grey buildings, grey walls, and grey clothes. The other pointed to a wagon, rolling free and unrestrained across the green prairies towards his home, while overhead the sky was blue and the clouds were a billowy white.

There was no real question in the boy's mind. Turning his back on the residential school, the little seven-year-old determinedly trotted along the trail towards the hill—and freedom.

After all, it wasn't the first time he had been away from home. A year earlier, he had hidden in a sleigh and ended up spending the winter in the cook's shack at a winter logging camp. Now he was on his own again. As he loped along the road, he hoped to catch the wagon before it reached the top of the hill, but a little boy cannot run very fast and by the time he had left the river valley, his cousin was no longer in sight. Still not frightened, he followed the trail as it led westward to link up with the main road between Macleod and Calgary. He wasn't really worried as he knew there was a place about twelve miles from the school where Nellie had stopped to pick wild turnips and to stay overnight, so he expected she would be there again. However, when he saw some men putting ballast on the newly built railway, he remembered that its southern terminus was the town of Macleod, so he abandoned the wagon trail, thinking he would make better time going along the track.

By now he was getting hungry and the coarse gravel of the railway bed was hard on his moccasined feet. After a few miles, the weary boy rested near a fence and, seeing a settler's house a short distance away, he went over and in a mixture of Cree and English, he begged for some food. The woman was sympathetic; taking a thick slice of bread, she spread it generously with butter and sprinkled brown sugar over the top of it. Jimmy had never tasted anything so delicious in his life.

By sunset, he had walked several more miles and was out on the open prairie when he saw some large square tents ahead. It was a small construction camp and the men who had been putting the ballast on the tracks were just getting off work. No one objected when the little native lad drifted into the cook tent and shared supper with them. They were a friendly crew, mostly Italians, and that night they found a place for him in the bunk tent. Next morning, after breakfast, the bright-eyed boy was given a ride on a hand car that was taking some men to their jobs farther south. When they stopped, he began walking again but had gone only a few miles when he encountered another crew and got a ride with them. Then, alternately walking and hitching rides all day, he reached another construction camp at nightfall where again he was fed and given a bunk. It was all an exciting adventure and not until the evening of the third day did he finally get to Macleod.

Jimmy expected that Nellie would stop to visit the Murphys on her return trip, but when he reached the log house on the north side of town, he was surprised to find that she had not yet arrived. Somewhere between St. Joseph's school and Macleod he had passed her. After telling his adventures to the surprised family, Jimmy dashed outside to play with the Murphy children and spent the next three days enjoying himself. Nellie finally appeared. She had stopped to pick berries along the way.

The woman greeted the sight of the tousle-headed little boy with a mixture of apprehension and fear. She had expected an argument when she got back to Mountain Mill, but she believed that once the boy was in the Catholic school, the fiery old grandfather would hesitate before trying to remove him. But here was the boy already on his way back home and no amount of coaxing could induce him to return to the bleak mission.

The next day, when the wagon finally rolled into Mountain Mill, Grandfather Gladstone was waiting. He had learned that the boy had been spirited away and, although thankful he was back, he was furious with the kidnapper. Angrily he took the boy and loudly declared that he would never be permitted to enter another Catholic institution. He had raised Jimmy himself and he would remain an Anglican, even if most of the other children had converted to Catholicism.

With his favorite grandson back with him, Gladstone realized that his victory might be only temporary unless he took some alternative action. He knew that Nellie was a zealot and would not abandon her proselytizing efforts; at the same time, he understood that the boy needed an education.

At his first opportunity, old Gladstone went to Pincher Creek to see a friend, a wealthy rancher named F. W. Godsal. That year, the rancher had donated money for new Anglican mission buildings on the Peigan Reserve and an earlier contribution had helped the church to erect a school, boys' home, and church on an island adjacent to the Blood Reserve. The facility had been opened by the bishop that spring.

Godsal explained that this school was primarily for Blood Indians but because it wasn't on the reserve, the church had more leeway than it did at a reservation school. He promised to contact the bishop to see if young Jimmy and his brother Steve could be admitted. A short time later, satisfactory arrangements were made, and the boys were told that they would soon be registered as students in the Anglican mission. Jimmy was no more anxious to enter an Anglican school than he had been to stay in the drab buildings at St. Joseph's, but he loved and respected his grandfather so he never questioned the decision.

As the wagon taking him to school rolled away from Mountain Mill, tears streamed down Jimmy's face as he said goodbye to his relatives and his home. He had no way of knowing it at the time, but he was turning his back on a questionable future where children of mixed ancestry were shunned, often relegated to a marginal existence with little opportunity for education or advancement. In its place, he was being taken away from white and Metis society and was being cast among one of the most warlike Indian tribes in North America. He had no way of knowing that this would ultimately lead him into a life of dedication to a people he had never seen before that day when he finally went to school. And the choice had been made because of his love for freedom and an even greater love for his grandfather.

Young Jimmy's grandfather, William James Shanks Gladstone, was born in Montreal in 1832, the son of William Gladston and Eleanor Shanks. In later years, an *e* was added to the family name.

The family had come from Berwick-on-Tweed, Scotland, only four months before William's birth and his father had opened a blacksmith shop. It was said that William senior was a second cousin of the prime minister of England.

At the age of sixteen, William Gladstone, Jr. entered the service of the Hudson's Bay Company as an apprentice and for the next fourteen years he worked as a boat builder and carpenter at Rocky Mountain House, Fort Assiniboine, Fort Pitt, and Edmonton House.

During this period in the West, most fur trade employees took native wives and were married either by the "custom of the country" or by one of the missionaries. In the 1850s, William met an attractive native girl named Harriet Leblanc whose father Louis was a longtime employee of the company and for a time had been in charge of Rocky Mountain House. Part Cree and part French, Louis had married Angelique Vallee, who was part Santee Sioux.

Gladstone was a staunch Anglican but his bride-to-be had been baptized a Catholic and, as no Anglican missionaries had visited the fort, Gladstone—or "Old Glad" as he came to be known—reluctantly agreed to have a Catholic wedding. The priest, Father Albert Lacombe, who later became a good friend of Gladstone, insisted that if he was to perform the rites, Old Glad would need to turn Catholic or at least he must consent to raise his children in the Catholic faith. Old Glad refused and when he threatened to marry the girl by the "custom of the country," the priest finally agreed to the service. According to family tradition, Lacombe said he could not wear his Catholic vestments for the service.

"I don't care if you don't wear anything," William replied with a chuckle, "just as long as you marry us."[1]

Harriet married William at Edmonton House on May 4, 1855, and during the next seven years she shared his hardships and saved his life on at least two occasions. The first occurred en route to Fort Assiniboine when he broke through the ice of a lake. Harriet, who was in the dog sleigh, heard his cries for help and, with the aid of a long rope tied around her waist, she was able to rescue him. The second incident took place in 1861, when everyone was starving at Rocky Mountain House. An American prospector got into an argument with William over food and was about to shoot him when Harriet, who was standing nearby, used an axe to knock the pistol out of his hand.

During these difficult years, Harriet lost all the toes on one foot when she became lost in a blizzard. As a child, Jimmy loved this kindly old woman who hobbled about the house. She was the one who taught him to speak the Cree language.

In 1864, the Gladstones went to Montana with a party of prospectors. There William worked as a carpenter in Fort Benton until 1870, when he was hired to build a fort at the confluence of the Belly and St. Mary's rivers in southern Alberta. Later dubbed Fort Whoop-Up, this post served as the center for whiskey trading activities in western Canada for the next four years. When he received the contract, Gladstone hired forty half-breed helpers and by the autumn of 1870 they had the fort ready for occupancy. William lived there for the next four years as fort carpenter, building furniture, completing construction work and adding new buildings as required. During this time his children became friends with a young English-speaking Blood Indian who had been adopted by one of the traders and given the name of Joe Healy.

Joe was later to figure prominently in the Gladstone family, but at the time he was simply a unique young man who could speak both Blackfoot and English and was able to teach some of his language to the carpenter's children.

After the North-West Mounted Police came to the West in 1874, Fort Whoop-Up was closed and William was hired to build many of the structures in the new town of Fort Macleod. After operating a carpenter shop there for a few years, he found the Mounted Police village too demoralizing for his children, so in 1879 he moved to the solitude of the foothills west of Pincher Creek. He chose a location on an unnamed creek where there was good hunting and fishing for the family. It was here he hoped to raise his children and grandchildren in a healthy moral environment away from the settlements. While he failed with some of his own children, grandson Jimmy became an apt pupil, learning to love the valley and the kindly old patriarch who was his grandfather.

In 1881, the destruction of the last buffalo herds meant that the nomadic Indians were obliged to settle on their reserves and build houses to replace their worn tepees. Accordingly, the Indian Department established a mill just downstream from Gladstone's house and made arrangements for him to help with the carpentry work. Eventually, the small stream was named Mill Creek and the community became Mountain Mill. Upstream, one of the tributaries was named Gladstone Creek while the peak nearby was called Gladstone Mountain.

Old Glad's house was a small log structure nestled in the valley of the creek, hugging a tree-dotted slope that angled down to the water below. With two rooms and a lean-to, it had dovetailed corners and snug-fitting logs as mute testimony of the carpenter's skill. From the doorway, one could see the towering ridges of the Rocky Mountains just a few miles to the west, while eastward the rolling foothills gradually gave way to the prairies beyond.

By the 1880s, most of Old Glad's four boys and six girls had either grown up or had died. Bill, the oldest, had married a Metis girl named Mary Samat, while another son, Robert, had married Azilda Jervais. The two younger boys were born in the 1880s, Harry remaining unmarried while John later married the Widow Tourond and, after her death, Reita Hughes.

Of the girls, Elizabeth, Sarah, Prudence, and Ellen all died before they were five years old. Mary, another of Old Glad's daughters, married Peter McEwan, a former member of the North-West Mounted Police. Like others in the extended Gladstone clan, the McEwans settled in the Pincher Creek area at the confluence with South Fork. In fact, in the 1880s, Gladstones could be found scattered throughout the district. Immediately downstream from Old Glad was Fred Pope, a former Mounted Policeman who had married Harriet's half sister Maggie. Farther south, near Twin Butte, were some of Billy Gladstone's children, while nearby was Harriet's brother Cornelius, who had changed his surname from Leblanc to White; then there was Harriet's sister Victoria, who married William McClure and later moved to Montana. And most of Old Glad's surviving children lived in the area as well.

Old Glad also had a child whom he named Harriet, after his wife. She was the mother of young Jimmy. Born at Rocky Mountain House in 1859, Harriet married a Metis named Basil Laurence in 1879 and in the following year they had a son, George. When that union broke up, she moved in with a Fort Macleod liveryman named James Kennifik and in 1882 they had a daughter named Caroline.

Harriet was a lively girl and very attractive, perhaps too attractive for her own good. Hard drinking and good times seemed to be the most important parts of her life, but it threw her in with a tough crowd of half-breeds and coarse frontiersmen who were frequently before the judge on charges of intoxication, gambling, or brawling. In 1883, Harriet had separated from her second husband and seemed destined for a life of continuing adversity when her fortunes suddenly changed.

When the Indian Department decided to close down its mill, the plant and timber berths were acquired by Senator Peter McLaren, a Conservative politician from Lanark, Ontario. He hired a manager but also sent out his nephew, James Bowes, as foreman, with the hope that he would eventually take over the whole operation.

Shortly after his arrival, Bowes fell in love with Harriet and she found the young easterner particularly attractive. Old Glad happily gave his blessing to the courtship and was pleased to observe that his daughter had cast aside her rough companions and was settling down quietly at Mountain Mill. However, problems began to arise when Bowes seemed unable to grasp the complexities of the milling operation. The company had both a lumber mill and grist mill at Mountain Mill as well as another mill and lumber yard at Macleod. Senator McLaren had held out high hopes for his sister's son and, during his periodic visits to the West, he berated the young man for not applying himself more attentively to his work.

It was about this time that Harriet became pregnant. Bowes told her frankly that he wanted to marry her but he was just barely holding his job at the suffrance of his uncle. If he now embarrassed the eastern family by marrying a native girl, he was afraid that he would be out of work and be forced to go back East alone. So, much to the disgust of Old Glad, Harriet left the Gladstone roof and went to live in a common-law relationship with the mill foreman.

When no minister was available, Old Glad could countenance a marriage in the "custom of the country," and he could even forgive Harriet's passing involvements during her unmanageable years, but he saw no justification for this relationship. He liked Bowes and found him an easy man to work with, but he was disturbed by his lack of aggressiveness when dealing with his influential uncle. In fact, Bowes proved to be a chronic worrier, too insecure to stand up to McLaren or to break away on his own.

Their first child, Steve, was born in 1885, at the beginning of a relationship which lasted for more than a decade. Their three other children were Jimmy, born on May 21, 1887, and christened James Basil, followed by Lucy, born in 1890, and Helen, born in 1894. During most of this period, the children were raised by their grandparents and, at the insistence of Old Glad, they all took the name Gladstone.

During the 1880s, Bowes' insecurity and failure to receive the appointment as mill manager finally caused him to suffer a mental breakdown. He was committed to the West's only asylum in Brandon, Manitoba, where Harriet accompanied him and regularly travelled back and forth to visit him. This proved to be a mistake, for on one of her trips she ran into her old crowd and became enamoured with a flamboyant young man named Charlie Northwest, alias Charlie Young. They settled in Macleod where the wild Metis was in and out of jail on charges ranging from intoxication to horse stealing.

"He was a rotten character," recalled a member of the Gladstone family. "He was a heavy drinker, a thief, and no good. He was finally arrested for stealing a team of horses from an old Peigan Indian at Brocket and was given five years in Stony Mountain Penitentiary."[2]

Harriet never returned to Bowes, even though he was released from Brandon and spent the rest of his life back at Pincher Creek, where he died in 1924. Instead, she followed Charlie to Regina, visiting him while he was awaiting trial and then drifting to the nearby reserves along the Qu'Appelle Valley or periodically staying with her parents back home.

Harriet's four children never really knew their various parents when they were small. Their kindly grandfather and patient Cree-speaking grandmother were the only folks they remembered. The cabin where they were raised was usually crowded with children, both Old Glad's boys and the grandchildren who needed a home.

"The earliest event in my life that I can remember," recalled James Gladstone, "is my old grandmother thumping around the house with her cane." To him, his grandparents were the center of his existence, and they gave him a home, love, and guidance.

Life at Mountain Mill was usually lively, particularly when the logging season was in progress. Half-breeds came from Pincher Creek to work in the camps while Indian hunters who roamed the foothills often settled nearby. The sounds of the Red River jig, the resonant beat of the drums, and the music from square dances and reels filled the valley with sounds as variable as the people who lived there.

The most frequent Indian visitors to Mountain Mill were the Stoneys, whom Old Glad had known in the fur trading days. He often gave food to the hungry and traded with the Indians if they had been successful in their hunts. On one occasion, a passing hunting party had a sorrel colt which had a lame foot. The Indians realized it could not travel and they could not wait for the foot to heal so they traded it to Old Glad for a hundred-pound sack of flour. In the end, it turned out to be a good deal for Gladstone, as the sorrel proved to be an ideal pet for the children and foaled seven of the best saddle horses in the district.

In this mixture of cultures at Mountain Mill, young Jimmy learned to look after himself. He was neither shy nor timid and was often involved in youthful pranks which occurred around the cabin. He also spent considerable time with his grandfather, who bestowed a love and affection upon the boy which no one else seemed willing to give.

Old Glad had watched with sadness as his children had ventured into the changing world of the prairies. His eldest son had become a successful interpreter for the North-West Mounted Police but he wondered what the future held for the others, and his grandchildren, who had little opportunity for the kind of education or training they would need in the emerging West. Young Jimmy, the liveliest of the lot, was a particularly bright boy who often climbed on the old man's knee to hear his stories and homey philosophies. No one, least of all Old Glad, would have ever dreamed that this ragged little boy who spoke a faltering mixture of English and Cree could ever hope to rise beyond the destiny which seemed to lie before him and his people.

But Jimmy was developing basic habits that centered around honesty, hard work, and reliability. There was no doubt that these came directly from his old grandfather, a man who embodied the basic Christian work ethic.

Perhaps it was his grandfather's influence, or maybe it was his schooling, but Jim Gladstone remained a devout Christian all his life. Every night he knelt by his bedside to pray, regardless of whether he was in a log house or, in later years, in an expensive hotel. His interest centered around his church and whenever he had a decision to make, he often turned to the Bible for an answer. He was familiar with the Indian religion and even became part of the Sun Dance encampment, but his true beliefs were focused upon Christianity. He was not dogmatic about being an adherent to his church; he simply followed a way of life in which he believed.

Old Glad's efforts to have Jimmy admitted to the Anglican mission in 1894 provided the chance the boy needed to forge a meaningful life for himself. His grandfather had provided the means; he had to do the rest himself.

CHAPTER TWO

SCHOOL DAYS

St. Paul's Anglican mission was established in 1880 by the Rev. Samuel Trivett to serve the Blood Indians, one of the tribes of the Blackfoot nation. For a number of years the mission had consisted only of a crude log church and house, with educational facilities being limited to a number of day schools in the various Indian camps. In 1894, a new set of buildings had been erected, including a mission house, boys' home, a church, and outbuildings. For the first time, the church was able to offer residential facilities in its attempts to Christianize the tribe.

The day schools had not proven to be as successful as the missionaries had hoped, for the lessons of the day seemed to be forgotten when the pupils returned to their cabins and tepees. Often the main reason the boys came in the first place was for the rations of hardtack and soup which were given at lunch. The missionaries were convinced that the only way they could ever hope to Christianize and educate the Indians was by taking them away from their home environment and keeping them in virtual bondage from the ages of about six to eighteen.

Most parents were loathe to give up their children; consequently many of the first students at the residential school were orphans or the children of progressive chiefs who saw the value of the white man's education. When F. W. Godsal approached the bishop about admitting Gladstone's grandsons, the school had less than two dozen students in a structure designed for seventy. The combination of a low enrollment plus Godsal's philanthropic assistance to the church overcame any reluctance about admitting the two boys.

When Old Glad received the news, he took Jimmy and Steve to Pincher Creek where their sister Caroline was working in a local clothing store. After the two boys were fitted with new clothes they said goodbye to her for the last time, never dreaming that she would be dead of a passing sickness before her seventeenth birthday. The family then set out on the long wagon ride to the Blood mission. Within a few miles of each other were the Indian agency, the Methodist mission, and the new Anglican buildings on the adjacent island of Omuksini. This time Jimmy did not try to run away but, as his uncle recalled, "The kids were crying so hard when we left them behind that I felt bad all the way back home."[1]

For the first few days, life at the mission was a traumatic experience for the boys. Accustomed to seeing the docile Stoney hunters near Mountain Mill, they were unprepared for the tall fierce-looking Blood warriors who came to the mission to visit the children or to beg for food. They carried guns, wore their hair long, dressed in leggings, breech-cloths and blanket coats, and most had wide leather belts, brass-studded scabbards and double-bladed knives. The women were invariably clad in blankets over their cotton or skin dresses, and were festooned with brass wristlets, rings, and necklaces. Their hair, either braided or hanging loose, was usually divided down the middle, with a streak of vermillion paint emphasizing the parting.

They seemed a strange and fearsome sight, but Jimmy soon discovered that they were a proud yet friendly people who were particularly fond of children.

If their fellow pupils at the mission were antagonistic towards the two little foreigners, Jimmy was unaware of it. Steve was a timid boy, so the others did not bother him, but the outgoing Jimmy was soon part of the group and a willing participant in their pranks and games. At the time of his admission, most of the boys had been there for just a few weeks and had learned only a few words of English. Jimmy, on the other hand, could speak English and Cree, but no Blackfoot. Yet their communication through smiles, fumbled words, and signs was relatively trouble free, due in part to their mutual knowledge of a sign language which was universal among the Indians of the plains. The right index finger to the mouth meant "hungry"; the hand drawn in a cutthroat fashion across the neck meant "Cree"; and across the face at eye level meant "Blood." Within a few weeks, Jimmy had picked up enough Blackfoot to converse in their tongue and before the end of the year he had become proficient in the language.

The principal in charge of the mission and school was the Rev. Frank Swainson. Using Ontario textbooks, he organized the classes so the boys studied the basics for a week at a time, followed by a week in which they went to school half days and worked on the mission farm for the other half. Besides providing a source of food for the mission, the farm became a means of teaching the boys about proper agricultural methods. A practical farmer, Jack Yeomans, showed them how to cut and plant potatoes, build root houses, sow and harvest grain, and many other things which would be useful to them in later years.

Although Jimmy got along well, his first weeks at St. Paul's were not without problems. As a new arrival he became the center of attention for the school's two bullies. Whenever the weather was good, the supervisor assembled the boys and took them for a walk around the island. At one end, where the tree growth was particularly dense, the Bloods traditionally placed their dead. They did not believe in underground burial, so the bodies were wrapped in blankets and put on platforms in the forks of trees. Over the years, many of these platforms had rotted, causing the bones and burial objects to tumble to the ground. The boys were in mortal fear of the place, but the supervisor insisted on taking them along a pathway which led through the heart of the trees to the tip of the island.

One day, not long after Jimmy's arrival, the students were walking through the burial ground when the boy was suddenly seized by the two bullies and hurled into the bushes among some fallen scaffolds. The first time it happened, Jimmy was terrified and he rushed back to the pathway. Heartened by their success, they repeated the trick several times, but after the first frightening experience, Jimmy found that nothing happened to him and his fear was replaced by curiosity. Poking around the burials, he saw a number of skulls and this gave him an idea for getting even.

"On one of our daily walks," he said, "I picked up two skulls from the graves and smuggled them into the dormitory. When it was dark, I tied one of them above Arthur's bed and another over Sydney's. Then I went back to bed and waited.

"At night, the boys used to make cigarettes and pass them around from bed to bed. I heard the boy next to me rolling one. When he struck the sulphur match there was a moment's silence as he stared at the skull, then he shouted, *Noo-aw!* [Look out!] Arthur woke up and the first thing he saw in the flickering light of the match was the skull staring down at him. He didn't say a word; he just passed out. Right across from him, George LaChappelle also fainted, but Sydney wasn't scared at all.

"When the supervisor came in, I pulled the covers over my head and pretended I was asleep. He took the skulls away and no one ever found out who was responsible. But Arthur must have guessed, because from that time on, he stopped bullying me and we became good friends."

During this period, the staff concentrated upon teaching English to the students, for until they could communicate, none of the other lessons were practical. They even offered weekly prizes of five, ten, or fifteen cents to those who spoke the best English. Interestingly enough, Jimmy never won the prize but was punished on several occasions for speaking Blackfoot when he was learning the language. At this time, he was amused to hear the boys trying to speak English. On one occasion the supervisor caught two boys near the boundary fence, which was against the rules. As the supervisor approached, one student, who was up in a tree, shouted: "Me good boy. Me not outside fence. Me upstairs tree. Him outside fence."

After the first few weeks, Jimmy settled easily into the school routine. He was a bright student and with his knowledge of English he was often far ahead of the other students—at least until they had mastered their grammar. He was a willing worker and whenever he got into trouble, it was usually the result of boyish pranks.

In the six years that he lived at St. Paul's, Gladstone gradually took on the culture of his fellow students. Blackfoot was used to the exclusion of all other languages when they were out of earshot of the staff, and the long story-telling sessions in bed at night or out in the fields during the day gave him a good grounding in the history, religion, and beliefs of his fellow students.

But he was disturbed that he was not actually one of them. As the years passed, he lost touch with his relatives at Pincher Creek and more and more he looked upon the students and their families as his people. But his curly brown hair and blue eyes marked him as someone different and, in the eyes of many of the Bloods, he was automatically treated with suspicion or hostility. The fact that he was part Cree only exacerbated the situation, for that tribe was traditionally one of the Blood's bitterest foes. Practically no intermarriage had taken place between them.

One exception was Bull Shield, a minor chief of the Bloods and leader of the Scabbies band. He learned through his son that a Cree-speaking boy had been admitted to the school and came to visit him at his first opportunity. It turned out that Bull Shield had taken a Cree wife and had lived with that tribe for several years. Cree was initially the common language between the man and boy, but when Jimmy became fluent in Blackfoot, that was the language they used.

In many ways, Bull Shield was like a surrogate father. When the chief's son Joey was admitted to the school, he commenced a friendship with Jimmy that lasted throughout their lives. Just as in the nomadic days when a young man took a companion to travel with him to war, so had the Bloods carried this practice into their reservation life. Soon after Joey came to the school, the two boys decided they would become comrades. Like Jimmy, the young Bull Shield boy was lively and intelligent. The pair made a good team; both were prone to mischief and pranks, but basically were good students and willing workers.

This friendship gave young Gladstone a direct line into the Blood community. Now he had a kinship with the other Bull Shield boys, and whenever the parents came to call, he joined the family group. Since Bull Shield lived just across the river, his visits were as frequent as the teachers would allow. The fact that he was a chief and a respected member of the tribe meant that his acceptance of the boy eased the hostility that the Bloods usually felt towards intruders.

While Jimmy was developing from the age of seven to his early teen-aged years, he gave little conscious thought to his status. The other students were Blood Indians; he was not. The others had legal treaty status; he had none. The Bloods were there by right; he was there by suffrance. But to young Jimmy, he was simply a student at a school where his fellow students felt that the outside world was as strange and alien as he did. Any incidents of discrimination on the part of the Bloods were ignored, none being open or flagrant enough to cause anything more than a momentary twinge. Similarly, the discrimination shown by whites on the rare occasions that the students were off the reserve was an experience to be shared with his friends as part of the accepted domination of the white man. Whether Indian agent, ration issuer, missionary, Mounted Policeman, or storekeeper, the white man always took the role of the authoritarian whose influence on the economic survival of the tribe implied a natural superiority, as though between master and servant. The Bloods did not consciously believe it, but they had no choice but to accept it.

During this period, the Bloods were just beginning to emerge from more than a decade of economic stagnation. Prior to the extermination of the buffalo, they had been free nomadic warriors who controlled the vast territory of southern Alberta. But when that shaggy beast had been destroyed by avaricious hide hunters, the Indians were forced to settle on their reserve. With a population of almost three thousand at the signing of Treaty Number Seven in 1877, their numbers had gradually dwindled until, by the time Jimmy entered school, they numbered about fifteen hundred.

In the first few years, the government had tried to introduce farming, or more correctly, large-scale gardening. Plots of turnips, potatoes, and grain were sown along the river bottoms by Indians who were anxious to provide food for their families. But a combination of government mismanagement, a distaste for scratching the earth like chickens, and the growing dependence upon rations as a source of sustenance gradually turned the efforts into little more than a make-work program to keep the Indians busy.

In the year of Jimmy's enrollment, however, the government at last listened to head chief Red Crow's plea for cattle, and a foundation herd was acquired when some of the leaders exchanged their horses for the animals. In many ways, herding cattle was not unlike following the buffalo and before Jimmy left school, the Indian herds had increased to more than thirty-five hundred animals. During this same period, individual Indians began to buy their own mowers and fill hay contracts while, at the north end of the reserve, a man named Black Horses started a coal mine, hiring Indian teamsters and miners.

The situation at the mission changed drastically during these years as well. A girls' dormitory, hospital, and rectory were added to the grounds, creating a neat square with a playground in the middle. Most of the students learned to speak reasonably good English while others excelled in writing. The traditional Indian games of mud-ball fights, archery, and spin top were replaced by football, cricket and hockey when the required equipment was sent out by the various missionary societies and women's auxiliaries in England or eastern Canada.

These were happy years for Jimmy. His friendship with Joey Bull Shield flourished and when he was about ten years old, resulted in him receiving an Indian name. At that time, all students were registered under their official names but, following the age-old practice of the tribe, they were given personal names of their own. Both boys and girls received such names when they were born, and those for the girls remained with them for life. With the boys, however, the names were temporary and, as they approached manhood, they were expected to earn adult names.

Jimmy, of course, had no opportunity to get an Indian name at birth but one day, when he was sitting in Bull Shield's tepee, the chief announced that he was going to give him a name. Bull Shield rattled through a half dozen names in Blackfoot and asked the boy to pick one.

His choice was Many Guns, *Akai'namuka,* a name that stayed with him for the rest of his life. In later years he was given two other names, Running Wolf, *Issoyo'komuka,* and Bear Chief, *Ninoh'kyio,* but everyone persisted in calling him Many Guns.

The Rev. Arthur Owen was appointed principal of the school in 1897. By this time, Jimmy was a tall ten-year-old whose proficiency in English and Blackfoot came to the new missionary's attention. As he had not yet mastered Blackfoot, Owen took the boy with him to interpret when he went to the camps to visit parents of his students or to seek new candidates. He would usually offer prayers in parents' tepees and try to explain to other families why they should send their children to school.

During these years, the tuitions for Jimmy and his brother Steve were not charged to the government, as they were for the Indian students. The boys were there either at the generosity of the Anglican church or through fees paid by Mr. Godsal. In any case, in 1899 a problem arose regarding their status and the boys were informed that they would have to leave—at least until the problem was resolved.

While Steve willingly returned to Mountain Mill, twelve-year-old Jimmy had no wish to leave the Blood Reserve which had become his home. The situation was resolved when L. H. Wood, a missionary teacher on the reserve, offered to provide room and board for the boy in exchange for his services as an interpreter and babysitter for his children. Arrangements were made for him to attend a special school that was provided for children of Indian Department employees.

There were about ten other children in the class, including Kate and Edith Wilson, daughters of the Indian agent, and those from the Deane-Freeman and Patterson families. This was the first time Jimmy had been educated with white students, but because their parents worked for the Indian Department and they lived on the reserve, they shared an intimacy with the Indians that would have been lacking elsewhere.

Wood lived in the old mission house which the Methodists had abandoned when they left the reserve. Although situated only a short distance from St. Paul's, it operated independently, as Wood carried out parochial work in the various camps. When he was not attending school, Jimmy went along to interpret and to help distribute clothing sent by Ontario women's auxiliaries.

During the summer of 1899, Jimmy saw his first Sun Dance. This was the annual festival of the Blackfoot people in which they reaffirmed their faith in the Sun spirit. They gathered in one huge camp for the better part of a month, each religious society taking its turn to perform its rituals, pray for the sick, and seek spiritual guidance for the future of the tribe. The culmination of the Sun Dance occurred when a holy woman supervised the erection of a large shelter of tree branches and leaves in which the final prayers took place.

All the years that Jimmy had been at the residential school, the summer festival had been out of bounds to the students. Not only did the missionaries consider it to be pagan, but they believed that the large encampment with its lax supervision was a breeding ground for licentiousness and immorality. To counteract any desires that the students might have about attending the rites, the government sponsored a mammoth sports day which the pupils were permitted to attend.

Now that Jimmy was living with the Woods, he had no such restraints. His actual attendance, however, was accidental and fraught with excitement. It started when his riding horse, Shamrock, strayed from the mission. Jimmy tracked it for some fifteen miles, finally roping it near the village of Glenwoodville. There he turned loose the horse that he was riding and mounted Shamrock for the ride home.

When he crossed the river ford near Standoff, he saw that the Sun Dance was in progress at the base of the Belly Buttes and decided to ride over that way. From a distance he could see that it contained more than a hundred tepees and was at least a quarter of a mile in diameter. As he was riding through the last coulee to the camp, he was suddenly attacked by a mounted party of Black Catchers, a secret warrior society which guarded the grounds. To relieve their boredom, the members watched for lone Indians coming to the ceremonies; if they could capture them, they either demanded a payment or took part of the person's equipment or clothing.

Realizing what was happening, Jimmy quickly wheeled his horse around and galloped down the coulee towards the river with the Black Catchers hollering and whooping in pursuit. After a run of about two miles, the boy finally reached the dense cottonwoods and willows along the Belly River and managed to elude his pursuers. Had he not been mounted on Shamrock, he probably would have been caught. Although he still wanted to visit the Sun Dance camp, he did not go back, as he was afraid the warriors might be lying in wait for him.

In the autumn of that year, the Woods decided to leave the reserve to go farming and, as Jimmy's status still had not been settled, he was again in danger of having to leave the reserve. The constant insecurity of his situation was of considerable worry to the boy, and more and more he envied his friends in school who were safe in the knowledge that as Blood Indians they had a place to stay and, more important, they had a host of relatives who would always look after them. Jimmy had reached the point where he thought like an Indian and felt like an Indian but was in a state of limbo between being a resident of the reserve and having no legal right to be there.

About this time, another teacher named Napier Hardiman needed someone to look after his children while his wife was in hospital so he arranged for Jimmy to be sent down to his mission school at the mouth of Bull Horn Coulee. Now, although he sometimes attended Bull Horn day school with the Blood children, he was really an employee who served both the school and the Hardimans. During the entire winter, he was treated like one of the family and in turn he worked hard to please them.

Mr. Hardiman knew that very few of the Indians wanted to attend school and the only reason they came was to be fed. As a result he devised a schedule which took the needs of both the students and the mission into consideration. First thing in the morning, he rang the school bell and when the pupils were in place, he closed the doors and took roll call. He taught them all morning, with Jimmy usually in attendance, sometimes as a student but often as an interpreter.

At noon, the students were let out for a break while Hardiman and Jimmy prepared lunch. When it was ready, Jimmy carried a big iron pot full of beef broth into the classroom while the teacher carried in a barrel of hardtack. By this time, the pupils were waiting hungrily for their food and, when all were in their seats, the doors and windows were locked and roll call taken again. Any students who had not been there in the morning were ejected, while the rest were each given a tin cupful of broth and a hardtack. After they had eaten, Hardiman taught for the rest of the afternoon.

Had this routine not been followed, the children would have run away immediately after they had been fed. Instead, Jimmy stood guard at the door until classes resumed to be sure than none of them escaped.

Among the students were two boys that he came to know well in later years—Tom Three Persons, the famous bronc-riding champion of the Calgary Stampede, and Jack Low Horn, later a holy man.

In the spring of 1900 when Jimmy was thirteen, arrangements finally were made for his re-admission with Steve to St. Paul's school. After extended discussions with Indian agent James Wilson, Ottawa officials agreed to educate the boys with funds provided by the Department of Indian Affairs. Although the brothers still had no legal status as Indians, at least they were recognized as residents of the Blood Reserve.

Indian agent Wilson was agreeable to the idea of giving them full treaty status but before any action could be taken, he discovered that their mother, Harriet, had applied for half-breed scrip. By this action, she was willing to surrender any rights she might have as a native in exchange for a document worth 160 acres of land or $160. She could also apply for scrip for any of her minor children and investigation determined that she had done so on behalf of Steve but not for Jimmy. At this time she was living with Charlie Northwest again and could not even remember Steve's first name, calling him Albert Bowes.

Her action effectively prevented Wilson from seeking treaty status for either of the boys until the matter was resolved. In the spring of 1901, he received a circular from Ottawa indicating that "the Minister has decided that applicants for scrip who are living on Indian Reserves as Indians should be paid annuity instead of scrip . . ."[2] However, no reference was made to the Gladstone case which was still pending.

Finally, late in 1902, the half-breed commissioner wrote to Wilson, asking him about Harriet's claim and attempting to determine if treaty money was being paid to an Albert Bowes, or Gladstone. Wilson responded by indicating that there was no such person, but that both James and Steve were attending St. Paul's at government expense.

The matter was finally resolved when the Half-Breed Commission decided not to permit Harriet to claim scrip on behalf of her children. This left the way clear for James Wilson to conclude the necessary treaty arrangements. Unfortunately for the boys, however, the news came to the agency just after James Wilson had resigned. He was replaced by Robert N. Wilson, who was strongly opposed to admitting any more persons into treaty. "The Department's suggestion to legislate in this connection," he wrote, "is twenty-five years too late so far as this agency is concerned." Instead, he was willing, as he stated, to leave such persons "drifting about the country pariah-like, acknowledged by neither whites or Indians."[3]

Neither of the Gladstone names was put forward by Wilson in 1904 when he was told that the government was considering changing its policy regarding non-status children. He was asked to "kindly report, at an early date, the number of such children within your Agency" and also to recommend "as to what in your opinion would be the best and fairest mode of dealing with such cases."[4]

Wilson was a complex man. Originally a member of the North-West Mounted Police, he became an Indian trader and opened a store at Standoff. There he became proficient in the Blackfoot language and took a great interest in the customs and traditions of the tribe. He wrote articles for anthropological journals, attended religious ceremonies, and collected artifacts for eastern museums. As an Indian agent, he often enforced government decrees with compassion and later provided support to the tribe in battling those who tried to force the surrender of reserve lands.

Yet he was a man who rode roughshod over the tribal council, tried to depose unco-operative chiefs, and coldly refused to recommend Gladstone for treaty status when Ottawa asked for his suggestions. As an amateur ethnologist, he wanted to keep the tribe as pure as possible. Jim came to know Wilson well in later years and considered him a friend, but for years the agent was to stand in the way of the boy's dream of becoming a Blood Indian.

A number of changes had taken place at the mission while Jimmy was away living with the Hardimans. Instead of staying in school all year round, arrangements had been made for some of the students to go to a summer camp on Pass Creek, in what was later to become Waterton National Park. In addition, such games as croquet and baseball had been added to the list of activities.

There were fifty-one students at the school; almost half of them were girls. Their teacher, Miss Jenny Wells, had proven to be something of a miracle worker. An elderly woman who had retired from church work in Ontario, she became utterly devoted to the girls in her charge and they in turn adored her. She was strict, yet treated them as though they were her own and her students soon became known as "Miss Wells' girls." In later years they became the leaders on their reserve. Their husbands were economically successful and the girls themselves insisted on having the kinds of homes, clothing, and social graces that one would find in any white community.

Mr. Owen, who was still the principal of the school, had expanded the facilities and added new programs to the curriculum. The boys still spent part of their time in the fields, while the girls worked in the garden and kitchen. The school also had a carpenter shop and butter-making room. The six cows provided plenty of milk and up to fourteen pounds of butter a week. Like the surplus of vegetables produced in the garden, anything that could not be used was sold.

A little more than a year after Jimmy's return, his brother Steve went back to Mountain Mill for good. Harriet had written to say that she wished "the lad sent home to assist her and allow the husband to work out for a living."[5] In exchange for Steve, she offered to send her youngest daughter Lucy, who had just turned seven. Jimmy was pleased with the arrangement for, although he was fond of his older brother, Steve was quiet and, while not retarded, he experienced learning problems. Lucy, on the other hand, was a bright vivacious little girl whose personality was much like Jimmy's. Even though he hardly knew her when she arrived at the school, she soon became one of his favorites. Perhaps the fact that she was a little sister he could protect gave him a sense of family that was lacking for him on the Blood Reserve. Although he felt at home with the Bloods, a sense of identification with his Mountain Mill family was important to him throughout his life, even when some of his relatives rejected him for "turning Indian."

However, Jimmy and Lucy were not at the same school for very long. Late in 1902 when Jimmy was fifteen, an appeal was sent to the mission seeking students for the Calgary Indian Industrial School. Jimmy was one of two students to respond.

The school, properly called St. Dunstan's Industrial School, was located four miles southeast of Calgary; it had been opened by the Anglican church in 1896 to provide industrial training to senior Indian students. While it was possible for a pupil to come directly from his home to the school, almost all had been attending residential schools when they were recruited. A number of students who had been at St. Paul's when Jimmy arrived were now there. Other students were from the Blackfoot, Peigan, and Sarcee Reserves—a total of thirty-four when Jimmy got there.

The school was located on a half section of land bordering the Bow River, with large open areas for gardens, grain, and a soccer field. The site for the industrial school was selected far enough away from any Indian reserves so that pupils could be raised without the influences of family, Sun Dance, and other distractions. Rather than emphasizing classroom study, it provided training in farming, carpentry, and printing. The latter was not so much a practical trade which could be used on reserves as it was a means of developing a distinctive Blackfoot alphabet. A set of syllabics had been designed by missionaries who hoped it would permit Indians to have written communication with each other in their own language.

The school achieved a high level of success during its ten-year exist-ence, many of its graduates becoming self-sufficient farmers and leaders on their reserves. The school was financed by the Indian Department and, as was the case with schools on the reserves, the annual grant was dependent upon the size of the enrollment. As a result, the principals on the reserves did not appreciate the periodic "raids" upon their student populations. After all, the residential school principal was obliged to go into the Indian camps to plead with parents in order to obtain students. The loss of senior students—usually the brightest and most helpful ones— meant a loss of funds unless their places could be filled from the reserve.

Mr. Owen was angry when Jimmy and another student, Norman Nice Cutter, said they wanted to go to Calgary Industrial. He tried to talk them out of it, but when both remained firm, he prepared the necessary transfer papers and arranged for transportation on the train to Calgary. On the appointed day in January, 1903, he drove the boys to the station near Macleod.

When the boys reached the industrial school, they discovered that the principal, the Rev. George H. Hogbin, was on a leave of absence with typhoid fever. Acting in his place was Archdeacon W. F. Webb. "We met at the door," recalled Gladstone, "and disliked each other from the very beginning."

In the next few weeks, he tangled with the acting principal on several occasions. One of Jimmy's main complaints was that he had come to the school to learn a trade. When the appeal was sent to St. Paul's, the prospective students were told they could learn carpentry but once at the school, they discovered that there was no instructor for the subject. Jimmy was put to work in the laundry and if he had any extra time, it was spent in the kitchen washing dishes.

Like the principal, Jimmy caught typhoid fever about three months after his arrival at the school. After a few days in a Calgary hospital, he was returned to the school's temporary hospital ward where he was placed on a convalescent's diet. He was back for only a short time, however, when he became involved in a students' strike.

The demonstration arose after the laundress missed a pair of moccasins and accused the pupils of theft. When the acting principal heard about it, he put all students on bread and water until the guilty one confessed. In turn, the boys refused to attend classes unless they were properly fed and instead wandered aimlessly around the school and district. In the hospital ward, Jimmy's diet was also replaced with bread and water, so he got up and joined the strikers.

One of the students got the idea of going home. Why stay in school if there were no classes and no food? About twenty-five boys, Jimmy among them, set out at dusk and walked all night. By morning they had travelled about twenty-five miles and just as the sun was breaking over the horizon, they came within sight of the village of Okotoks. Two or three of the boys wanted to go into the town to buy food, but Jimmy protested.

"We can buy all we want from the farmers," he said. "If we go into town we'll probably get caught."

But the students were hungry, so two of them went ahead to find out if anyone was looking for them. They came back a short time later with the news that they had met a half-breed who promised to take them to a Cree camp on the other side of town where they would be fed. He said the Indians had just come back from a hunt and had plenty to eat.

By this time, Jimmy was weak and giddy from the long walk, the lack of food, and the effects of the typhoid. He joined the other boys as they walked over to the half-breed's tent, but before he got there he became dazed and feverish, collapsing in the arms of one of his fellow students. They carried him the rest of the way to the tent and only after he regained consciousness did he learn that their "benefactor" was really a Mounted Police scout. Instead of going to a Cree camp, the strikers were taken to the local police detachment where they were fed before being put on a train back to Calgary. No punishment was meted out to the group, partly because the bread and water edict was indefensible. More importantly, the laundress had found her moccasins where she had misplaced them under a pile of magazines in her room.

When Principal Hogbin returned in the spring, Archdeacon Webb had compiled a long list of black marks against young Gladstone. However, when Hogbin called Jimmy into his office, he threw the paper into the fireplace without reading it and said he wanted the boy to start with a clean record. Jimmy explained that he had come to Calgary to learn a trade but had spent all his time in the laundry. In response, Hogbin arranged for him to be transferred to the printing shop, where his work included turning out the monthly Anglican diocesan magazine, as well as Masonic rules of order, church notices, and other bulletins.

Jimmy was popular with the Hogbins and as the principal's wife was fond of travelling, he often acted as her driver. Whenever she went to town, he was relieved of his regular work and was off with the buggy. Besides acting as driver, Jimmy also looked after the Hogbin children. On one occasion, he had taken one of the daughters, Hilda, for a ride when the horse was suddenly spooked. As it galloped uncontrollably towards the school, Jimmy skillfully guided it into the lane that led to the main buildings. Then, as the Hogbins and a number of students watched in alarm, he had the animal almost under control when it veered sharply, upsetting the rig and dumping them both under the horse's feet. Miraculously, neither was hurt, although, as Hilda recalled, "Daddy never could figure out how Jim and I were not killed."[6]

One of the most popular extracurricular activities at the school was soccer, a sport which gave the school an enviable reputation. Within a few months of its opening in 1897, the school had invited the Calgary fire brigade for a match. Although the Indians lost this first game, a reporter noted that "the brigade found out that they had considerable of a job on their hands, the Indian boys being fleet runners and not handling the ball too bad."[7]

By the time Jimmy came to the school five years later, they were in a league which included the fire brigade, city police, railway workers, brewery staff, and two professional teams, the Albions and Caledonians. The rough sport appealed to the Indian students and they soon had one of the best teams in the league.

His two and a half years in Calgary Industrial were of great benefit to young Gladstone. Not only had he matured under a staff of devoted teachers, but he had established lifelong friendships with Indians from the Blackfoot, Sarcee, and Peigan Reserves. When he received his discharge in June, 1905, shortly after his eighteenth birthday, he was given a certificate as evidence that he had reached Standard V— approximately grade VIII—and had become a "farmer and excellent printer."[8]

He was now ready to face the world, but whether as an Indian, a half-breed, or a white man, he did not know.

CHAPTER THREE

A WANDERER

Nine other boys were discharged when Jim Gladstone left school in June of 1905. Among them were his close friends Cecil Tallow and Mike Mountain Horse who, like the others in the group, immediately went back to their reserves. However, because Jim's treaty status had not been resolved, he decided to find a job in the Calgary area. He was hired as a handyman at the Craighurst Farm, not far from the school, where his task was to milk cows and help get the calves ready for the fat stock show in the fall. When this was finished, the rest of the crew was laid off, but Jim had proven to be such a good worker that the owner, C. W. Peterson, offered to keep him on for the winter of 1905–06 for off-season wages of fifteen dollars a month. Instead, he went to Calgary to buy his first suit of clothes and then headed back home to the Blood Reserve.

During the time he had been away, a number of changes had taken place, both with his family at Mountain Mill and on the reserve itself. His brother Steve had settled into life at Mountain Mill and made no attempt to keep up the friendships he had made at school; to him, St. Paul's had simply been a place where he had been forced to go to become educated. Jim's sister Lucy, on the other hand, was one of the brightest students in her class and had made many friends among her fellow students.

The situation on the Blood Reserve was more complex. Most Indians still relied upon rations for survival, although a few cattle owners were relatively self-sufficient. But haying and coal mining provided most of the employment which was available on the reserve. The only bright spot was the development of a sugar beet industry among the Mormon communities east of the reserve. Indians found ready work there at cer-

25

tain times of the year, topping and hauling beets to the refinery at Raymond. In 1905 they earned $2,182.25 in the fields, which was the largest single source of off-reserve income.

The cattle industry was developing rapidly, with Indian-owned herds increasing from a few hundred at the turn of the century to almost five thousand by 1905. In the latter year alone, nine hundred calves had been branded and $11,000 worth of beef sold.

These impressive figures had not gone unnoticed among the politicians, who saw great personal advantage if they could gain access to the Blood grazing lands. As a result of some machinations among Liberal stalwarts in Ontario, arrangements were made in 1903 for the McEwan Cattle Company, of Brandon, Manitoba, to run seven thousand head of cattle on the Blood Reserve for ten years, at an annual rate of $5,000.

At that time, the going rate for leases, even those negotiated by the Indian Department, was for 2 cents an acre, but critics estimated that the McEwan deal was closer to 1¼ cents an acre. Not only that, but the expanding Indian herd now had to share the reserve with those of the lessee. Investigation indicated that the whole deal had been engineered by Peter Ryan of Toronto, a Liberal organizer who had earlier arranged the biggest private timber deal in Canada. According to reports, Ryan and another politician, Charles Beck, had visited the Blood Reserve and then, with the help of cattle magnates Gordon, Ironsides and Fares Ltd., arranged for the McEwan company to get the lease and stock it with cattle supplied by the combine. Later, when there was a falling out among the group, Ryan and Beck sued the two ranching companies, claiming they were "entitled to a forty per cent interest in the net profits of a certain ranching enterprise on the Blood Indian reserve, leased by the Dominion government to McEwan."[1]

One of the reasons the Bloods had agreed to the deal was that T. Page Wadsworth, for years the inspector of Indian reserves in the West, had come to the reserve and convinced them that it was a good business arrangement. Only later did the chiefs learn that Wadsworth had resigned from the Indian Department before his visit and was employed by the McEwan Cattle Company. When they found they had been victimized, and that there were other ranchers willing to pay more money for smaller numbers of cattle, the Bloods protested, but to no avail.

These kinds of problems were to occur time and again on the reserve, but not until such persons as Jim Gladstone became senior members of the tribe could anything be done. Traditionally, the control of the reserve was vested in the Indian agent and the chiefs. The former was there by government decree, the latter as lifetime appointments, sometimes as a result of elections and sometimes not.

R. N. Wilson, who became Indian agent in 1903, was enthusiastic about the McEwan lease as he saw the income as a means for the Bloods to progress. His plans included purchasing heavy equipment to bring large areas of the reserve under cultivation and to encourage the Indians to leave their little garden plots along the river.

By this time, Gladstone was eighteen years of age, tall, husky, with a square determined jaw, curly brown hair, and blue eyes that twinkled with mischievousness when he smiled. He had forgotten the Cree language over the years, but had become equally comfortable with either Blackfoot or English. He had developed a fondness for reading, and was constantly perusing the local newspapers, farm journals or—when he could get them—books and novels. He also had his own Bible, presented to him at school, which he read regularly.

While he had been in Calgary, Jim had thought constantly about the Blood Reserve. The mission school had provided him with a home during his growing years and the reserve had given him his friends and comrades. Joey Bull Shield was like a brother to him, and the Blackfoot language was his second tongue. But Wilson saw Gladstone as just another outsider who was trying to get on the reserve. The agent's attitude prevented Jim from getting treaty status, but it did not keep him away from the reserve, for this had become his home.

The few years of living with the teachers had made him realize that his residence on the reserve was tenuous at best, but at the same time, it made him appreciate just how much he believed that he belonged there. It worried him that some shadowy figure far away in Ottawa could ultimately decide his fate by a simple stroke of the pen. Jim was old enough to know where he wanted to be, and that was on the Blood Reserve.

When he returned there from school, he immediately went to see his sister Lucy at St. Paul's. There he spoke with the new principal, Rev. G. E. Gale, and was pleased when he was offered the job of farm hand for the winter. Actually, his duties were varied. There were no real farm duties in the winter, so he acted as teamster and helped out as boys' instructor and girls' supervisor. He sat with the girls at their table during meal times but, as much for his own protection as anything else, he gave most of his attention to his little sister.

Among the girls that Jim came to know at the school were Janie Healy and Minnie Akers, both about thirteen years of age. Janie didn't like him at first but that really didn't matter, for supervision was so strict that boys seldom talked to the girls.

Although he was not fond of Principal Gale, Jim managed to get along with him until the spring. As long as he did his work, the principal left him alone. Then, one day, Jim made the long trip to the coal mines and forgot to take a bucket of axle grease with him. The wagon could not make the return trip without being greased and Jim was not prepared to ride horseback all the way back to the mission, so he bought a can of grease at the mines for fifteen cents.

When he got back, Principal Gale was furious. He claimed that Jim should have borrowed the grease from an Indian and then returned it on his next trip. Furthermore, he placed the blame for the unauthorized expenditure squarely on the boy's shoulders and refused to refund the money to him. When the argument continued, Gale fired Gladstone and ordered him off the premises. Some of the other staff members, Miss Wells and Miss Denmark in particular, offered to pay Jim out of their own pockets, but he wouldn't take it. Instead, he left the mission and angrily stalked off to Macleod.

This was the first time he had ever been on his own away from the Blood Reserve. However, during his visits as a teamster during the winter he had come to know a few merchants in town and went to them looking for work. When he heard that Doctor Milburn had a laboring job, he immediately applied and was told to go out to the Milburn farm, about five miles east, where he was hired to dig a well. It was back-breaking work and when the task was finished, Jim was paid the contract price for the job.

Back in Macleod, he heard that the local livery man, James Grant, needed a man so he hurried over to the livery barn and was signed on as drayman and tankie. At this time, Macleod was a town of some fifteen hundred people. At its west end were the neat rows of barrack-like buildings which marked the headquarters of the Royal North-West Mounted Police. A railway to Calgary had been built in the 1890s but when a line was extended from Lethbridge, the railway promoters located the station a half mile south of the town where they laid out the village of Haneyville. By this action, they hoped to draw the merchants away from Macleod and thus profit by the sale of lots. However, they had not counted on the loyalty of residents to their old historic town, and Haneyville remained a desolate railway station surrounded by the windswept prairies.

Wind! That was a term often used in Macleod. The stories were legion of the adventures and experiences of residents with the constant, dreary, heavy winds that seemed to rise out of the Crow's Nest Pass and sweep through the gravelled streets of town.

Macleod's main street consisted of a line of old stores and shacks—erected in 1883 when the town moved to the site—combined with more recent brick and sandstone structures. The Hudson's Bay Company, Queen's Hotel, and the Grier Block were among the most imposing structures, but the overall appearance of the place was distinctly depressing.

"We cannot help but comment on the dirty, filthy and disgusting appearance of the streets, lanes, vacant lots and back yards," commented the Macleod *Gazette* in 1906. "It is bad enough that we are obliged to exhibit to strangers the ghastly appearance of the shacks on Main Street and around the business centre of the Town without having to add to that exhibition the filth and dirt which has been accumulating on the places mentioned."[2]

The population of the town was equally diverse, ranging from the elite who lived in the fine two-storey houses with bay windows in the southeast part of town to the half-breed community in shacks along the river. There were Chinese laundrymen and cooks, Japanese whores, one-time American whiskey traders, eastern Canadian and European merchants, and a number of men whose pasts were best forgotten. And always conspicuous were the red-coated Mounted Police from the nearby barracks and the blanket-clad Bloods and Peigans who were constantly in town shopping, selling, or bartering their goods.

In such a polyglot mixture, Jim Gladstone, the blue-eyed boy of Cree-Scottish-French descent, who spoke Blackfoot, was not out of place. He would have preferred to be home on the reserve, but he knew he had to find work and Macleod was the closest settlement to the Blood camp. He already knew some of the people in town, such as the Murphys, and was close enough to visit his old grandfather at Mountain Mill from time to time. Even his mother Harriet dropped by to see him on her infrequent trips home from Regina. However, there were two people he didn't see: his father, James Bowes, whom he never really knew and for whom he shared his grandfather's antagonism, and Senator Peter McLaren, who made periodic visits to his lumber yard in Macleod but chose to ignore the fact that his nephew's son lived in the native community.

Reporting for work at Grant's livery, Jim was given a bed in the company bunkhouse and for the next several months he labored from dawn to dusk as a teamster. The heavy work was done alone, whether delivering a piano to Charlie Reach's home, steam coal to the power house, or groceries to the merchants. Most of this work meant driving to Haneyville station, unloading the goods from a boxcar, and hauling it a mile and a half back to town. One of his regular customers was the Macleod Hotel which received a full wagonload of beer kegs every day from Calgary. Jim's experience in hauling this load later gave rise to an incident which became an oft-told highlight in his colorful career.

One day while he was hauling beer he got a bright idea. He went into one of the stores in town, bought a corncob pipe and gimlet, pulled the bowl off the stem, tossed it away, and stuck the rest in his shirt pocket. The next time he picked up a load of beer, he let the horses take their time. He got out his 'tools,' drilled a hole in one of the casks with the gimlet and stuck the stem into the hole. Using it like a straw, he sucked out all the beer he wanted. When he was finished, he whittled a plug, stuck it in the hole, and rubbed the whole thing over with dirt. Nobody could ever tell the difference.

Jim probably would never have been found out had he not picked up a load of whiskey one hot August day. He had gone to Haneyville station for a shipment of dry goods, but when they didn't arrive, he loaded eighteen barrels of Scotch whiskey instead. It was quite a load for a two-horse team so the outfit moved slowly on its way back to town. En route, Jim mused how nice a sip of whiskey would be, and figured if the gimlet and pipestem worked on beer casks they would do just as well on Scotch. He drilled a little hole in the closest barrel, took a sip, and then another. Soon the combination of straight whiskey and the hot sun took its effect.

"When I woke up," said Gladstone, "I was in the sample room of the hotel. It was right behind the bar, and I could hear a crowd in there. I thought it was kind of funny because the bar was usually pretty empty on a weekday."

He was ashamed to go out the front door, as he would have to go right through the bar, so he tried to use the side door, but it was padlocked. So he walked quickly out the front way and was headed for the street when the bartender called him back.

"Can't stay very long," Jim told him. "I've got to get back to work or I might lose my job."

"You can always get a job right here," laughed the bartender. Then he brought out a bottle and poured Jim a drink. "Here," he said. "You look a bit sick. Try this."

After the drink, Jim felt a lot better so he decided to see Tom Wilton, the owner of the hotel, to find out what kind of trouble he was in. Wilton was a big, gruff-speaking man. As soon as the young teamster walked in the door, Wilton handed him his gimlet and pipestem.

"It's okay," he said. "You brought in a lot of business when the team stepped in front and everybody saw you sprawled unconscious and spreadeagled over the barrels. Just don't try it too often."

Jim learned later that a crowd of people had followed the team down the street, some thinking he was dead and others that he was sick. When they discovered that he was simply drunk, they had loaded him on their shoulders and merrily carted him into the bar. Once inside, many of them decided to stay, giving Wilton an unexpected boost in business on a quiet day.

On Saturdays, Gladstone usually took over as relief tankie, delivering water to the homes and stores in town. There were no waterworks and few wells, so most of the drinking water was taken from the river and delivered for twenty-five cents a barrel. The boss tankie, a morose man named Joe St. Luke, had not been popular with his customers because of dirty barrels and poor service. Young Jim, on the other hand, was a friendly, happy person who got along with everyone.

Most of the residences in Macleod took a barrel of water three times a week. Once a month, the barrels were dumped and scrubbed, although Jim usually did this whenever he found an empty barrel.

When Christmas came, Jim had become so popular that his water customers gave him gifts of mittens, underwear, and other items, while the boss tankie got practically nothing. In anger, St. Luke quit and Jim was given the job with a $5.00 raise, bringing him to $40 a month. At the end of the first month, he turned in $75 more than his predecessor, giving rise to the suspicion that not all the previous collections had been accounted for. With Jim there was no doubting his honesty—then or ever.

The winter of 1906–07 that Jim worked on the water wagon was one of the worst on record for local ranchers. The season started badly with late fall rains which froze the ground and made foraging difficult for the cattle. This was followed by one blizzard after another which blew out of the north, driving chilled and weakened cattle before it. The prairies were overstocked that winter and ranges that once were wide open were now cut up by miles of barbed wire fences.

The results were disastrous. Cattle wandered with the storm, piled up against fences or along the railway right-of-way, and perished. Sixty percent of the cattle in the Calgary area, 50 percent in Lethbridge, and 25 percent in Pincher Creek died that winter. Many ranchers were completely wiped out as animals hopelessly tried to find shelter in coulees and even in towns to escape from the relentless winds and blizzards.

"One day in January," observed a journalist, "the citizens of Macleod saw what appeared to be a low, black cloud above the snow to the north, which drew slowly, draggingly until it was seen that a herd of thousands of suffering range cattle were coming from the north, staggering blindly along the road allowance in search of open places in which to feed. A steady, piteous moaning filled the air as the suffering creatures drew close, feeble, starving, skinned from the knees down by sharp snow-crusts and by stumbling and struggling to arise, hair frozen off in patches—naked, mangy steers, tottering yearlings, and dying cows. Straight into the town this horde of perishing brutes slowly crawled, travelling six and eight abreast, bellowing and lowing weak, awful appeals which no one was able to satisfy.

"They were Bar U and other Northern cattle, and their numbers were so great that it took over half an hour for them to pass a given point. Right through town they dragged themselves—exhausted animals dropping out every minute to fall and die as they lay, the route through town being marked with a string of carcasses—past the hotels, the stores, the staring people on the sidewalks, out into the blackness of the prairie beyond."[3]

During that winter, after the first storms struck, Jim carried a chain behind the water wagon, and on his return trips he hauled dead carcasses down to the river and left them at the town dump. Every trip was marked by the dragging of at least one carcass of an animal that was huddled up against the side of a building or trapped on the wires of a fence. Before he was finished, he had hauled at least a hundred frozen and pitiful creatures out of town.

Relief came for the surviving cattle and the residents of southern Alberta on February 9, 1907, when a chinook blew in. Early that morning it had been thirty-five below, Fahrenheit, and by two o'clock water was running in the streets.

Something about the sudden change in the weather affected Jim. That morning, Grant had scolded him for some minor infraction and by afternoon he suddenly had the urge to quit. Instead of going for his next load of water, he turned the team into the livery, tossed the reins to a surprised boss and said, "Here, you drive." Grant was so surprised he didn't say a word.

On that day, there was joy in Jim's heart for just being alive. The warmth of the chinook winds, the gracefully curved arch in the west that separated the grey clouds from the clear blue sky, the feeling of slushy snow underfoot, all made him feel that life in the town was too confining for a country boy. He just wanted to get back to the reserve.

During the time that he was in Macleod, he had not lost touch with the Bloods. One of his problems had been to constantly refuse Indians who wanted him to buy liquor for them. Although he enjoyed a drink himself, he saw how many men who associated with Indians eventually found bootlegging to be a profitable enterprise. As long as government regulations made it an offense for Indians to buy, possess, or consume alcohol, he would not be a party to the illicit trade.

One important visitor to Macleod during the winter had been Crop Eared Wolf, the head chief of the Blood tribe. He had come to town to see a lawyer, Colin McLeod. Lacking an interpreter, he had sought out Jim, who outlined the chief's problems to the barrister. The chief had learned that the government intended to force a land surrender vote on the reserve and he wanted to block it.

Yielding to political pressure from the Mormons, the government had decreed that the Indians must vote on surrendering 2,400 acres between the railway line and the town of Cardston and throwing the land open for settlement. Crop Eared Wolf was violently opposed to giving up a single foot of the reserve. He went back home to organize a campaign to offset the promises of Indian Department negotiator J. A. Markle and agent R. N. Wilson that every man, woman, and child on the reserve would receive a $10 gift as a result of the surrender.

The final vote on the reserve was 109 to 33 against surrendering, but it wasn't the last time that land hungry settlers would be trying to acquire parts of the Blood Reserve.

"This dusky gentleman [Crop Eared Wolf] has missed his vocation," said an irate editor of the Macleod *Gazette* after the vote was finally taken. "He should have been a politician. He personally canvassed every vote on the reserve. Some he scared, others he coaxed, and others he induced to stay away, and he converted a sweeping sentiment in favor of selling into a triumphant majority against, which only goes to show that he is a particularly pig-headed Indian who doesn't know what is good for his people."4

Agent Wilson never forgave those who voted against the project. He appointed three prosurrender men — Running Crane, Many White Horses, and Little Ears — as minor chiefs and launched a bitter campaign to depose Crop Eared Wolf. Soon the chief was back in Macleod to see his lawyer, charging the agent with firing antisurrender Indians from his staff while prosurrender forces were hired and given preference at the ration house. The chief also complained he was "humiliated on every occasion in the eyes of the Indians."5 While no direct action was taken against the agent by the Indian Department, Crop Eared Wolf's spirited attack caused Wilson to curb his repressive actions.

After leaving Macleod in the spring of 1907, Jim went back to the Blood Reserve to renew acquaintances, particularly with Janie Healy and Minnie Akers at St. Paul's. Courtship — if it could be called that — was a strange affair in a residential school setting. Normally, boys and girls were not permitted to talk and never allowed to be alone together. So a secret smile, a surreptitious note, or a nod of the head was sometimes the only communication possible. Of course, because Jim was an ex-pupil who was visiting his sister, he was treated differently, but any discussion with either Janie or Minnie was closely supervised. With Jim now twenty and the girls only fourteen, no thoughts were entertained about any romantic relationship. For her part, Janie did not care for the young man nor the attention he bestowed upon her.

On the reserve, Jim caught up on the latest gossip. He learned that minor chief Running Wolf was gaining the ill will of the tribe for his support of the land surrender proposal. He also found that three ex-pupils had been arrested with another young Blood for horse stealing. They had been taking stock from ranchers near the reserve and selling them to newly arrived settlers at ridiculously low prices. The boys had received varying sentences of up to four years, with the judge making it clear that this kind of transaction could not be compared with the kind of horse raiding which had been condoned in the old days.

Jim also learned that some of the money from the McEwan grazing lease had been used to buy a large steam tractor and a ten-furrow plough to break new land on the reserve. A number of Bloods had shown an interest in going into farming on a larger scale and although the Blood cattle had come through the rough winter very well, some of the younger men believed that farming was a more secure business than ranching.

Jim enquired about work on the reserve but found that nothing was available. However, after looking around he learned that a nearby rancher, Robert Patterson, was advertising for a laborer. Gladstone was hired and for the next year and a half he was in the ideal situation of drawing a regular monthly wage while still being close to his friends on the Blood Reserve. Joe Bull Shield, Cecil Tallow, and Ben Strangling Wolf were among those he saw frequently – often at the school – while Mike Mountain Horse was working only a few miles away as a scout for the Mounted Police at Kipp. He also continued visiting the girls at the school, where gossip was rife as to which girl would eventually get him, Janie or Minnie. Everyone knew the girls had to stay in school until they were eighteen, but when that time came, every effort would be made by the missionary to get them married right away – even before they graduated – so they would not be tempted into marriage with a pagan or, even worse, with a Roman Catholic.

During these years at the Pattersons, Jim was a hard-working, fun-loving young man. He was equally at home with Indians or whites, drank when whiskey was available but made no attempt to seek it out.

Late in 1908, work was slack at the Patterson place so Jim was hired by Frank Tatum, a young rancher who lived nearby. When work there was finished late in the fall, he decided to go to Mountain Mill for a visit. He had not really spent any time with his family since leaving to go to school at the age of seven. Now he was twenty-one and his grandfather was in failing health. Besides, his sister Lucy had graduated from St. Paul's and was back home in Mountain Mill.

By this time, many of Old Glad's children and grandchildren were married and resided in the community, some making a living by working at the mill while others were in the mines. The lively half-breed community which had been a visible part of Pincher Creek and Mountain Mill life had been pushed into the background when an influx of eastern settlers came to dominate the region. As Indian Agent Wilson had predicted a few years earlier, the half-breeds were becoming pariah-like drifters, acknowledged by neither whites or Indians. They had no distinctive legal status and many had neither the education nor the skills to compete in the agricultural economy. Instead, they retreated to the bush and tried to eke out a living by trapping, hunting, or working for white settlers.

After Jim had been in Mountain Mill for a couple of months, he learned that jobs were available cutting mine props and ties on the side of the mountain above the town of Coleman. He joined the crew but was with them for only a few weeks when he moved farther west through the Crow's Nest Pass and found employment for the rest of the winter cutting cedar posts near Fernie, B.C. As spring approached, he decided it was time to return to the prairies.

Back in Macleod in April, 1909, he learned that a newly arrived American named Horace Glaze was looking for a farm hand. Seeking the man out, Jim was hired and told that he would be working on a spread not far from the Blood Reserve. The Glazes were from Pittsburgh and Horace had come out ahead of his wife Nora in order to buy the farm.

Jim batched with Glaze at the ranch for a while but then the owner decided to move into Macleod to wait for his wife. He took a room at the Empire Hotel and when he was not living it up with whiskey, he was down at one of the whorehouses with the girls. Jim went to town every day to receive his instructions, but Glaze usually just gave him some money and told him to go and amuse himself.

One morning, Jim knocked on the hotel-room door and a woman answered. It was Nora Glaze. Sternly she told Jim to hitch up the team, that they were leaving for the ranch right after breakfast. Her husband, sitting in the background, was as meek as a lamb. Jim knew that the Glazes were wealthy, but he now learned that all the money belonged to Nora.

Jim worked for the couple for more than a year. During that time, Mrs. Glaze went back to Pittsburgh every three months to collect the rent for the buildings she owned. This amounted to about $100,000 a year. As part of their philanthropic work, the couple provided food and other assistance to St. Paul's mission which was just across the river from the ranch.

In the fall of 1910, Mrs. Glaze finally found out about her husband's periodic escapades with the women in Macleod. Usually when she went back to Pittsburgh he headed straight for the brothels and lived it up until her return. Grim-faced, Mrs. Glaze had Jim drive her in to Macleod where she arranged for a broker named Mathews to sell the ranch and tidy up her affairs.

The couple had grown fond of Jim—Mrs. Glaze in particular—so she invited him to go east as far as New York with them, from which point she would pay his return fare. However, Jim declined. He later heard that they had gone back to Pittsburgh where they obtained a divorce, but subsequently remarried each other. The last he heard from them was news that Horace had joined Pancho Villa's army in Mexico and had been killed.

"I thought a lot of Horace and his wife Nora," said Gladstone. "In fact, I named two of my children after them."

After the Glazes left, Jim was free of any responsibilities so he decided to make another trip to Mountain Mill before winter. When he arrived he found that his grandfather was bedridden and seriously ill, with only Lucy to care for him. Arrangements were made for Jim to work for his Uncle Bob during the winter while he helped Lucy to care for Old Glad.

The old man received almost constant attention from his loving grandson, who read to him and kept him comfortable.

Old Glad had become the venerable patriarch of the community. Grey-bearded and wan, he had spent the last few years of his life writing his memoirs in serial form for the Pincher Creek newspaper and penning letters to the editor. Old Glad had been through the exciting days of the Hudson's Bay fur trade, gold prospecting, lynchings in Montana, and the riotous period of Fort Whoop-Up and the whiskey trade. He also had an amazing memory for names and dates.

He continued to decline all winter, and on April 8, 1911, he died. There was a huge funeral in Pincher Creek, with a cortege a block long following the horse-drawn hearse down the street. Newspapers all across Canada mentioned this venerable pioneer who never had an enemy and was loved and respected by everyone he knew. It is no wonder that he served as such a model and inspiration to the tearful grandson who followed behind the glass-walled hearse.

Jim was now twenty-four and this was the second winter that he had been away from the Blood Reserve. More and more he found himself involved with white people and as long as R. N. Wilson was Indian agent, he knew there was no chance of being admitted into treaty. Without status he could never be anything more than a casual employee of the Indian Department. With the death of his grandfather, Jim began to seriously consider his future. He had grown tired of wandering from one job to another, never really sure where his next dollar was coming from. All that time, he had stayed close to the Blood Reserve, hoping there was some way he could become accepted. The Belly Buttes, the mission school, and the cabins and tepees along the Belly River were the only home he wanted.

Jim went back to Macleod after the funeral and met Frank Tatum who said that he had given up his ranch and was going north to homestead. He said there was land available west of Innisfail, and if Jim came along he would have no trouble filing on a quarter section. If he made the decision to go, however, Jim knew he would be starting a new life in the white man's world and that he would have to give up the idea of ever being accepted as a Blood Indian.

The choice was a difficult one, but at that moment, the route to the homestead offered land and security while the pathway to the Bloods was fraught with uncertainty and no assurances that he could ever make a life for himself on the reserve. He told Tatum that he would go north.

His trunk was packed and at the station when the hotel clerk at the Queen's said there was a man named Colonel Evans looking for him. Jim found the colonel in the bar and learned he was a relative from Montreal. Evans had read in the eastern papers about Old Glad's death and had come west to see that all the funeral arrangements had been carried out. When Evans learned that Jim had looked after his grandfather in those final months, he gave him a hundred dollars, explaining that the family in Montreal wanted Jim to have it for his trouble and for the funeral expenses.

Evans then announced his plans to buy a ranch in the area and asked Jim to help arrange the deal. In partnership with a local man named Jack Graham, Evans wanted to buy a place near the Blood Reserve and asked Jim if he would go out with $200 and get a thirty-day option. The idea of working for a rich eastern relative was appealing, so Jim cancelled his homestead plans and arranged for the option. When he got back to town, however, he found a note saying that Evans had been called back to Montreal on important business; his young cousin was instructed to stay in Macleod at the family's expense until his return.

Jim couldn't just laze around, so while he was waiting he did some ditch digging for the Town of Macleod and helped as a carpenter and day laborer on local construction jobs. Finally, a letter came from Evans saying that his business was taking him to Scotland, but he enclosed enough money to cover Jim's expenses. It was the last time Gladstone ever heard from his rich eastern cousin.

Disgustedly, Jim concluded that if this was what it meant to deal with white people in a search for security, he wanted no part of it. In a complete about-face, he decided that his people were not relatives in Montreal, or Pincher Creek, or Mountain Mill, but the Bloods. Culturally and in his heart, he felt more Indian than white or half-breed, so he was resolved to make the plunge which would commit him to an Indian future.

He decided to get married.

Right up until the time he proposed, there was gossip and speculation as to whether he would choose Minnie Akers or Janie Healy. People thought he had been attracted to both; he had been seen in the company of both girls who, during their school years, were close friends. The indecision was more apparent than real, however, for Jim loved Janie and never had any doubt that she was the one he wanted for his wife. The girls knew, too, but it was part of Jim's wry sense of humor to keep everyone else guessing until the last minute.

Right from the beginning, he had been drawn to the quiet, lithesome Healy girl. In the few occasions when he could visit with her, he found her to be a kind and considerate person who was close to her family and popular with other girls in the school. And she was beautiful too. Jim had held back because Janie was not yet eighteen and there was no way she could be released from school until she came of age. As well, Jim had had to grapple with the problems of his status and his place with the Bloods. However, Janie was no longer indifferent to the persistent and likeable young Gladstone. Early in July, just before Janie turned eighteen, Jim went to the school and proposed to her. There was joy in his heart when she accepted, and together they made plans to be married on July 23, 1911.

CHAPTER FOUR

WITH THE HEALY FAMILY

Janie Healy was a member of one of the most prominent and progressive families on the Blood Reserve. Her father, Joe Healy, or Flying Chief, was the first Blood to become proficient in English and, as a result, was in constant demand by the Indian agency, mission school, and Mounted Police as an interpreter. Flying Chief had been orphaned at the age of fourteen when his parents were killed in a horse raid at a trading post at Sun River, Montana. The two traders, Hamilton and Healy, adopted the boy and John J. Healy named him Joe. Healy sent the boy to school in nearby Fort Shaw, where he learned to speak English, and later they went to Fort Whoop-Up where Joe became good friends with Old Glad.

After the Mounted Police came west and ended the whiskey trade, Joe Healy moved back with the Bloods and settled on the reserve when it was established in 1880. Two years later he married Double Gun Woman and started to raise a family. Because he lived close to the Anglican mission, most of his children were sent to the mission school. The result was a well-educated family that was involved with farming. Christianity was part of their lives, as were medicine pipes, and the Sun Dance.

Healy himself, however, would not agree to be baptized and confirmed by the church until 1918 when he was sixty-three. In the years between, he was an active participant in the medicine pipe rituals and played a significant role in forcing the Indian agent to abandon his attempts to suppress native religion. In fact, Healy was arrested in a test case when he defied the agent. When the matter came to court, the rituals he performed were defined as religious, rather than as those of a giveaway dance which were prohibited under the Indian Act.

In later years, Jim often heard the old man tell about his efforts to preserve the medicine pipe ceremonies. He was impressed by the fact that Healy was an honest and law-abiding person who was friendly with the Indian agent. But when the survival of his people's culture was at stake, no sacrifice was too great, even if it meant gaining the ill will of the all-powerful bureaucrats on the reserve. It was a lesson which Jim would later apply to his own life.

Normally, Healy was a quiet, easy-going man who loved to hunt antelope and visit with his friends. He was a wise, respected man who seemed to be as comfortable with white people as he was with Indians. This sometimes made him suspect in the eyes of his fellow Bloods and he was often derided for trying to "act like a white man." This was a derogatory expression used whenever a tribal member went too far in adopting non-Indian ways. Joe, however, carefully balanced his "progressive" ways with his involvement with the Sun Dance and other native rituals. Because of his progressiveness, he openly welcomed young Gladstone as a prospective son-in-law. He knew the young man to be a hard worker who would look after his daughter and treat her well. In turn, Jim learned from him how to find the delicate line between the Indian and white societies.

This attitude was not shared by Double Gun Woman. Janie's mother was a strong-willed, acid-tongued woman who had already experienced humiliating remarks and jokes about her husband's white man's ways so she had no desire for her daughter to marry a man with blue eyes and curly brown hair. In spite of the fact that she had once had a white husband and her oldest daughter was married to a man who was half white, she was culturally so Indian that she resented any intrusion into her well-ordered life. She had nothing against young Gladstone personally. In fact, she rather liked the boy. It was just that she did not want any of her children marrying outside the reserve, and at that time Gladstone was not a member of the tribe. After the marriage, however, Double Gun Woman's antagonism would have very little effect on Jim, as an ancient taboo frowned upon a mother-in-law speaking to a son-in-law or even remaining in the same room with him.

After he had proposed to Janie, Jim was in high spirits when he found a job as special constable with the Royal North-West Mounted Police in Macleod. As soon as he was on the job, he was issued a navy blue suit decorated with fancy brass buttons and a star with "scout" stamped on it. As he was still single, he was billeted with the other Indian scouts. His duties included taking dispatches to the detachments at Peigan, Big Bend, Kipp, and Standoff, as well as going on patrols of ranches on the reserves with a constable or corporal. He also acted as an interpreter.

At first, he wasn't allowed to go into the canteen where liquor was sold, but when one of the constables saw him in a bar in town, he told the mess manager. A quick check confirmed that he was not a treaty Indian, so he was permitted to eat and drink with the police, which proved to be a mixed blessing. At the end of the first month, he had used the facilities so liberally that his pay cheque came to only twenty-three cents.

Jim Gladstone and Janie Healy were married at St. Paul's Mission on July 23, 1911. Janie borrowed a long white dress and veil from her sister-in-law, *Enimaki,* and with all the Healy clan in attendance, they were wed by the newly ordained missionary, Samuel H. Middleton. Having previously labored on the nearby Peigan Reserve, Middleton was to have a profound influence on the lives of Jim and Janie in the coming years. Signing as witnesses were Joe Healy, his son Johnny, and Janie's closest school chum, Annie White Rider.

Following the service, the couple went directly to the Macleod headquarters where Jim was given rooms in the married quarters. It was a strange and frightening experience for Janie, who had never been away from the school or reserve before, although with Blood scouts and their families posted at the barracks she soon adjusted to the new life. But Jim was anxious to be involved with the reserve again, so when he learned that the agency needed a mail carrier, he got the job. By this time, Agent R. N. Wilson had been replaced by W. Julius Hyde, a man Jim found to be honest and fair in his treatment of the Indians. At first he considered asking him about being admitted to treaty status, but his father-in-law cautioned him to be patient. It would be better if they waited until Hyde knew the young man better.

The agency was only a short distance from the Healys, so Janie was happy with the new arrangement. Much of her time was spent at her parents' place and Jim, too, found his life gravitating around their double log cabin. He enjoyed visiting with his father-in-law and with Johnny, his oldest brother-in-law, who became his friend.

While Agent Wilson was on the reserve, he had been assiduous in bringing about major changes. Since the acquisition of heavy equipment in 1907, more than three thousand acres of land had been broken, with forty families taking it over and planting it to crops. As their efforts bore fruit, the agent added threshing equipment and granaries to the inventory, making machinery available to individual farmers. During the same time, cattle owners continued to expand their herds and, with beef selling at $15 a head, some of the men were faring quite well.

The overall picture, however, remained grim. Most of the people still lived in tiny cabins which they abandoned for tepees or tents as soon as the warm weather arrived. Tuberculosis, measles, whooping cough, and other diseases struck down the very young and the aged, and by 1912 the tribe's population was down to 1,128 persons—a far cry from the 3,071 that had been paid treaty in 1879. And although a few Indian ranchers and farmers were doing well, the majority of Bloods had to line up twice a week for their rations of beef, flour, tea, and sugar in order to survive. The periodic jobs at the coal mines, haying, or picking sugar beets were often the only employment available to the non-farmers.

As one Indian agent observed: "The Blood is a dignified Indian. This self-pride is in many ways a detriment to his progress, giving him a tendency to scorn innovations: yet show a Blood Indian how he can make money, and he will work, but not in a persevering manner. He will not plog doggedly towards any desired end, but rather wishes to proceed too rapidly: his expectations not being realized as soon as anticipated, he sometimes becomes discouraged."[1]

Jim liked the job at the agency and he, in turn, was well liked by the staff. A year later, he had no problem when he asked for a month off so that he could substitute for his father-in-law who was working as a Mounted Police scout in Lethbridge.

His first two weeks in August were routine. Jim's duty consisted primarily of going on patrols with a constable to the Indian camps on the St. Mary's River bottom and in the area around Whoop-Up. This was a center for bootlegging and prostitution, but the place was almost deserted as the Indians were away haying. Not a single arrest was made during that time.

Then, in about the middle of August, Superintendent J. O. Wilson called Jim into the office and told him about a horse-stealing ring which was operating in the area. A month earlier the police had seized seventy head which had been stolen in Sweet Grass, Montana, but the thieves had escaped. They suspected a cowboy named Jean Laliberty so the superintendent wanted Jim, who was unknown in Lethbridge circles, to work undercover and learn who the man's associates were.

During the evenings, Gladstone frequented the bars in the Dallas and Lethbridge hotels where he became friendly with the suspect. Laliberty told Jim that he and his partners were picking up horses in the Lethbridge district and running them across the line. On their return trips they were bringing American horses into Canada and selling them to settlers in the district. In the course of conversation, Jim learned the names of his two accomplices.

After reporting the information to Sgt. Mason, Jim didn't hear anything for several days. Then, when out on a patrol near Raymond, they met three Mounted Policemen who had Laliberty and his partners in custody, together with about twenty-five horses that they had stolen and were taking to Montana. The police had picked up their trail near Milk River and had caught the thieves before they reached the line. Needless to say, Laliberty was surprised to see his barroom pal wearing a badge and riding as a scout with the police.

Jim was detailed to herd the stolen horses until the trial was held, so he drove them through Lethbridge and out onto the prairie on its southeast outskirts. There he discovered a quarter section which had been fenced, but the wires were down and it obviously wasn't being used. He decided that it would be easier to fix the fence and keep the horses inside than it would be to close-herd them all day.

"I didn't have any tools," he said, "but I saw a Blood camp on the outskirts of town a short distance away. When I rode over I found that it was Three Guns' family and when I went inside I saw the whole bunch were drunk. A bottle of whiskey was lying in plain sight. They knew I was a police scout so they looked pretty scared, but I just ignored the bottle and told them I wanted to borrow some tools. They loaned me a shovel and some other things and were only too glad to co-operate. They weren't causing any trouble so I didn't see any reason for turning them in."

After he had repaired the fence Jim turned the horses loose inside and for the next few weeks all he had to do was to drive them out from the barracks' corrals every morning and take them back at night. The hardest part was keeping them under control while driving through the streets of Lethbridge.

After the trial, the horses were returned to their owners and the incident was all but forgotten when the owner of the quarter section came to the barracks to see Superintendent Wilson. He thanked the officer for having the fence fixed and said he didn't mind having the horses graze there as they reduced the risk of fire. Wilson didn't know what he was talking about, so he called Gladstone for an explanation. He wasn't pleased with the information, but no rules had been broken so there wasn't much he could do.

By this time, Joe Healy had returned so Jim returned to his mail carrier's chores at the agency. The only excitement that fall was when the first Calgary Stampede was held and a large contingent of Bloods attended. Jim didn't go, but his father-in-law could not resist the temptation and took a leading role in the parade.

More impressive, however, was the news that Tom Three Persons had won the North American bronc riding championship and a prize of one thousand dollars. Tom was an ex-pupil from the Catholic mission who had later attended Dunbow school. After leaving school, he had made a living breaking horses on nearby ranches and working for Bobtail Chief as a rider. Although Jim knew him well, he did not have much to do with him, partly because of the division between the Anglican and Catholic ex-pupils, but also because Tom hung around with a drinking crowd. In fact, one of the humorous stories going the rounds that year was that Tom, Jack Low Horn, and Calling High had tried to buy a bottle of whiskey from a bootlegger in Lethbridge, but they couldn't meet his price. Finally, one of the trio offered to bring him a woman, and the bootlegger agreed. They went to the camps below the High Level Bridge and borrowed a dress and kerchief which Jack volunteered to wear. He pulled the kerchief right over his face and when he was all dressed he looked just like a woman. The other two took him to the bootlegger and when he handed them their whiskey, all three ran off, Jack hoisting his dress in the air so he could run faster.

By the spring of 1913, Gladstone had been on the reserve steadily for almost two years and thought Agent Hyde understood his situation. With the help of his father-in-law, another application was made for him to be admitted into treaty. When the chiefs asked Agent Hyde to prepare the document and submit it to Ottawa, he did so, including one for Dave Mills at the same time. Both submissions asked that the men be able to "partake and share of all the benefits now and in the future coming to individual members of the Blood Tribe" and was signed by the entire council.[2]

Hyde did as the council requested, but his covering letter was so negative that it made the reply a foregone conclusion. In it he said Mills' father "is married to a Blood Indian Squaw," while Gladstone "was educated at St. Paul's Mission School here and in this way became acquainted with a Blood Indian girl whom he married, but otherwise have [sic] no connection with this Reserve by birth or breeding."[3] As expected, the reply was an outright rejection of the application.

Yet, interestingly enough, while Hyde was willing to thwart Gladstone's chances for treaty status, a day after his letter went to Ottawa he had no hesitation in sending another note to the Horse Shoe Liquor Store in Macleod claiming that "James Gladstone of this Reserve now comes under the provisions of the Indian Act and to all intents and purposes is an Indian."[4] In addition, Hyde made no attempt to remove Gladstone's wife from treaty status at the time of her marriage.

When Jim learned that the Indian agent had opposed his treaty application, he was both angry and frustrated. Hyde had always acted in a friendly manner towards him but he decided he could no longer work for him. So the couple moved into Joe Healy's double log house with the rest of the family and Jim joined the ranks of the unemployed.

When the Sun Dance camp began to gather in July, a Blood named Cross Child asked him if he would run a store for him. It was set up in a twelve-by-fourteen-foot tent on the north side of the huge camp circle. When Jim arrived, he added a counter across the front and soon had it open for business. The camp was a big one, with about seventy tepees and 150 tents. It was the last big Sun Dance where they had to move camp twice, once for the ceremonies of the Old Women's Society and once for the Horn Society. The whole affair lasted for more than a month and a half.

Jim sold a thousand dollars in goods in the first week because he stocked such a wide variety of goods: blankets, carrot and twist tobacco, print cloth, silk, ribbons, bread, canned tomatoes, prunes, raisins, and all kinds of other food. It was the only store in the camp and Cross Child hired a camp crier to go around early in the morning whenever new supplies came in. Jim took the team to Macleod twice a week to get fresh bread and supplies.

The ceremony that year was known as the "Whiskey Sun Dance" because of the large amounts of liquor that were smuggled into the camps. On several occasions, Jim was asked to buy liquor when he went to town, but each time he refused, getting only enough for himself and, interestingly enough, for some of the Mounted Police at Standoff. They were not able to get into Macleod so Jim obligingly filled their orders whenever he went.

The drinking did not interfere with the religious ceremonies at the Sun Dance, but each night Jim took his bedroll and slept on the floor in his store, just in case any drunks tried to break in. The night serenaders—a group which moved through the camp after dark, singing in front of tepees in exchange for food—made a point of serenading him regularly because they knew he had plenty to eat in his store.

After the Sun Dance, Jim stayed with his father-in-law until the following summer. This was as much by choice as it was by circumstance, for Janie was pregnant and wanted to be near her mother. Their first child, christened Lucy Winnifred, was born at the Joe Healy house on November 4, 1913. Her first name was given in honor of Jim's favorite sister.

Just about the time the baby was born, Weasel Fat, the leader of the Scabbies camp, announced that he intended to build a new dance hall and, with the help of his son Maxwell and volunteers, he wanted to have it underway before winter. Jim and a number of other ex-pupils were among those who were ready to offer their services.

When the Bloods first settled on their reserve in 1880, the winter dances had been held in any house large enough to contain a crowd. But where the average cabin might hold a couple of dozen people, it was not uncommon for two or three hundred to show up when news of a dance was circulated. Finally, Running Antelope enlarged his log stable and it served as a passable, but inadequate dance hall for a number of years. The livestock were kept in an adjacent part of the building and sometimes an evening's festivities were interrupted by the bawling of the cattle.

Shortly after the turn of the century, Sweet Grass built the reserve's first dance hall next to his house. It was crudely constructed but far better than the stable and large enough to hold a reasonable crowd. However, when Sweet Grass died the building was torn down, according to custom, so that his spirit would not be able to haunt it. This left the reserve without a hall until Weasel Fat made his announcement. The support of a number of other chiefs was obtained and together they went to the new Indian agent, W. J. Dilworth. He agreed that any Indian who signed a petition could have two dollars of his treaty money set aside to buy building materials for the hall. This included shingles, nails, building paper, and lumber necessary for the doors, windows, and platform. The logs were to come from the timber limit in the mountains and all labor was volunteered by members of the tribe.

Jim worked all winter on the hall, squaring logs, helping with the roof, and putting to use some of the carpentry he had learned while at Calgary Industrial. When it was finished in April of 1914, the hall was an impressive, circular structure with a sloping roof and wooden skylights which could be opened when the heat became too oppressive. It was a well-made building which was to serve the reserve for almost thirty years.

When it was finished, Johnny Healy and some of the other ex-pupils decided that they should have a celebration. Jim had always declined buying liquor for Indians, except for members of his own family, but after a winter of steady labor, he agreed that they deserved a party. With Johnny, he went to Macleod and there he bought a bottle of gin and two large and two small bottles of rye.

What Jim didn't know was that the Mounted Police had learned about his trip. As the pair approached the Little Ears ford, the scout from Stand-off and a Mountie came over the hill. Jim was arrested for illegal possession, but because he hadn't disposed of any of it, they couldn't charge him with supplying liquor to Indians.

Jim was taken to Macleod where he was given a fifty-dollar fine or one month in the barracks. When he could not produce the money, he was put to work cleaning out the stables. A few days later, his old boss, Bob Patterson, heard that he was in jail and offered to pay his fine if he would come to work at the ranch for forty dollars a month. Patterson had been elected as a Conservative member of the legislative assembly in 1911 and spent much of his time in Macleod and Edmonton, so he needed someone reliable at the ranch. In spite of his unenviable position, Jim explained that he was now a married man with a child and could not work for less than seventy dollars a month. Expecting that Jim would change his mind after he spent a few more days in jail, Patterson said he would be back later.

In the meantime, Janie sold one of their horses and raised the money for the fine. Jim had just been released and was walking across the parade square when he encountered the surprised Patterson. Although he had lost the advantage, the politician repeated his offer of forty dollars, but again Gladstone declined and was soon out job hunting once more. There was no work for him on the reserve, so he began to roam, this time with a wife and daughter.

CHAPTER FIVE

OFF THE RESERVE

Since Jim Gladstone had left school in 1905, many changes had taken place in southern Alberta. Settlers by the thousands had poured into the area, until the Indians had become a minority in a land they once owned. In keeping with the attitude of their new arrivals, the government obligingly made regulations to prevent Indians from attending fairs or other celebrations. One reason was that the festivities kept the Indians away from their farms and hay fields; another was that the booming towns considered themselves to be progressive, modern, and forward looking. Except to add color in their parades, they did not want a lot of blanket-clad natives to remind them about the "pioneer" days so recently past.

Calgary and Macleod were two exceptions, but they had to fly in the face of criticism and anger to convince Ottawa that Indians should be permitted to join in their stampedes and fairs.

Feeling less and less welcome in the towns, the Indians tended to remain within the familiar isolation of their own reserves, except when they had money to spend in the stores. As a result, many of the changes in the West passed unnoticed by the native people. All they knew was that the country was filling up with whites and every available quarter section off the reserve seemed to be fenced, broken into cultivation, and occupied.

Jim, of course, was more aware of the economic and political events which were occurring in the country. Unlike treaty Indians, he had a vote and, like his grandfather, he was a strong supporter of the Conservative party. He had supported Bob Patterson when he ran in 1911 and was elated a year later when the Liberals were defeated in Ottawa on the issue of reciprocity.

The boom which followed in the wake of land settlement seemed to create an upward economic spiral which had no end. Real estate promoters in 1910 believed that Calgary would reach a population of one hundred thousand within a couple of years, and even the moribund town of Macleod laid out new subdivisions and sold lots that extended out onto the open prairie. Wages were good, prices were up, and everybody's spirits were high as they floated along on the buoyant economy of the New West. And then, as though Nature wanted to add to the economy from her storehouse of riches, oil and natural gas were discovered at Turner Valley and Bow Island in 1913 and 1914.

Jim had no trouble finding a job as a temporary teamster in Waterton National Park through the help of his old friend John George "Kootenai" Brown. This colorful rangeman had been instrumental in having the park established and was about to retire as its first superintendent. Educated in India, he had served as a scout for the American army before going prospecting for gold. He had arrived at Waterton Lakes in the early 1870s, built a trading post, and stayed. He was married to a Cree woman and had been a friend of the Gladstone family for years. He had hired several of the Gladstone boys at the park, some working there most of their lives. Jim had met the Browns many times and now he had the pleasure of introducing them to Janie and baby Lucy.

Good men were at a premium during the boom period, so Gladstone soon found a more permanent job as a ranch hand for Jacobs and Bradshaw, who had a large spread at Caldwell, near Waterton Park. Jim stayed with the company for the next three years. During the first summer, Janie and Jim camped at Red Rock Canyon, now one of the scenic attractions in the park. Later they moved to the base of Blakiston Mountain where they were closer to the park headquarters and to the trails to Pincher Creek and the Blood Reserve. Living in a tent and using a cook wagon for their gear, they looked after about five hundred head of Jacobs and Bradshaw cattle which were grazing in the park. In winter, Jim usually took the animals out to the Kootenai Ridge, although one year when the area was over-grazed he had to trail them all the way northeast to Whoop-Up.

During this period, Jim was always bothered by the fact that he was not a treaty Indian. This concern was shared by his father-in-law who was even more upset when he learned that his granddaughter Lucy had also been excluded from the rolls. By this time, the Indian agent who had opposed the last application had left and was replaced by W. J. Dilworth. So without his son-in-law's knowledge, Joe Healy raised the matter with the chiefs again. In the spring of 1915 the chiefs approached the agent about a number of young men whom they believed should have treaty status. Dilworth agreed to check on a test case and selected Johnny

Pace, the son of a white trader and Blood mother. The reply immediately came back from Ottawa to the effect "that John Pace is not to be admitted into Treaty."[1] Only if it could be proven that both parents were treaty Indians should the agent seek the concurrence of the tribal council in having a person admitted. With this ruling in hand, Dilworth made no attempt to submit the names of Jim Gladstone, Dave Mills, or the other two applicants.

In spite of his failure to achieve treaty status, Jim was having a good time. As a young man in his twenties, earning a good wage, and having his own camp in the middle of one of Canada's most beautiful parks, he was enjoying life to the fullest. He had grown into a tall, sturdy, square-jawed man who radiated strength and quiet self-confidence. His appearance belied his Indian ancestry, and only when he launched into eloquent Blackfoot did strangers realize that this man was different from the other tanned and wind-burned cowboys they saw in town.

Liquor was easy for Jim to obtain in Pincher Creek and most of the cowboys and park employees he knew were a hard-drinking, fun-loving group. They did not drink steadily, but when they did drink, they often had a real blowout. About the only problem drinkers in the whole area were Kootenai Brown and his wife. Early in July, 1915, for example, Mrs. Brown picked up a bottle of Scotch and drove out to Pass Creek in her high-topped buggy to see Janie and Jim. When she arrived, she found that Minnie Akers was visiting them, so she invited everyone to share her bottle. She had brought along her own cup and drank her whiskey as though she was sipping tea.

"Finally, when she wanted to go home," recalled Gladstone, "I offered to drive her back. She was quite drunk. We travelled along for several miles and were just passing the edge of a gravelly bench when she told me to stop as she had to get out and relieve herself. She got out of the buggy all right, but fell down a long sloping incline at the edge of the bench. It was a grassy slope about thirty feet down. I got out of the buggy to help her, but I slipped and rolled right down the hill too and landed right on top of her. She was a big fat woman and neither of us were hurt."

Kootenai Brown died a year later. Jim and Janie heard that he was slipping fast and went to his cabin, but he had passed away before they got there. His dying wish was for a drink of whiskey and his wife was just opening a flask of Johnny Dewar's Scotch when he expired. Brown had always called his wife *Nichomoose,* which was Cree for "sweetheart," and she remained his faithful companion right to the end.

Just as the economy of western Canada cooled with the onslaught of World War I, so did patriotic fervor begin to heat up. With a wife and daughter, Jim had no intention of joining up, but he noted with interest how the Bloods reacted to the conflict. As soon as they heard that someone across the water was attacking their king, they compared the situation to their old days on the warpath. Other tribes rallied as well and thirty-five hundred Indian lads from all parts of the country fought for Canada in World War I.

One of the first Bloods to enlist was Albert Mountain Horse, who attained the rank of lieutenant and went overseas with the first contingent. He was gassed at St. Julien and died on the way home. His brother Joe also enlisted and was wounded in three different engagements, while another brother, Mike, was wounded at Cambria after capturing a number of German soldiers. Before the war was over, several other Bloods had enlisted. Even one of the old traditional Indians who could not speak English, a man named Bumble Bee, tried to join up but balked at the idea of having his braids cut off.

As a further indication of their support of the war effort, the Bloods subscribed more than $3,500 to the Red Cross. Considering the poverty that existed on the reserve, this was a huge sum of money.

The war years saw the Bloods' land and lease questions come to a head. When the McEwan lease expired in 1913, tremendous pressures had been applied to have the area opened for agricultural leases. Delegations from Lethbridge, Cardston, Macleod and Magrath submitted petitions to Ottawa, claiming that a ten-year lease should not be renewed, but that agricultural leases should be granted as part of a plan "for acquiring that vast and fertile region from its Indian proprietors and adding it to the farming district."[2] Much to the chagrin of local boards of trade, the Bloods made it clear that "nothing on the reserve should be leased except the grass."[3] In particular, the Bloods were opposed to the Mormons acquiring the land, accusing them of permitting bootlegging to go unchecked, throwing their garbage on the reserve, and cutting boundary fences to let their cattle graze on the reserve.

In the end, the government acceded to the wishes of both parties: it refused to renew the ten-year grazing lease, but turned down requests for farming leases. Instead, it increased the grazing fee from the old figure of 1¼ cents per head to three cents a head and approved the grazing of herds without the benefit of specific lease agreements. The politically influential beef trust headed by Gordon, Ironsides and Fares was able to continue running seven thousand head on the reserve at the increased fee while a local firm, Knight and Watson, also was given access. The increased revenue was of distinct benefit to the Bloods and still left plenty of room on the 354,000-acre reserve for their own farming and ranching activities.

In 1916, each time Gladstone crossed the reserve to visit the Healys, he noticed how the Indian herds were increasing, with some of the ranchers becoming relatively prosperous. By that year the Blood cattle herd had increased to four thousand animals, while seven thousand acres of land were under cultivation. A total of $125,000 was brought in by Indian grain crops, including the sale of 65,000 bushels of wheat and 27,000 bushels of oats.

A year later, however, everything changed when Arthur Meighen was appointed superintendent general of Indian Affairs. "That year," stated ex-Indian Agent R. N. Wilson, "marked the abandonment by the Indian Department, so far at least as the Blood Reserve was concerned, of the traditional Canadian policy of Indian administration . . . . The established and successful Canadian policy of advancing the Indians on their Reserve was abandoned in favor of a policy of Indian Reserve exploitation in the interests of covetous white men."[4]

In June, 1917, the Bloods were forced to vote on a proposal to surrender ninety thousand acres of their reserve, consisting of two large blocks of land, one northwest of Cardston and the other at the north end of the reserve between Macleod and Lethbridge.

"The land is the choicest in southern Alberta," said an enthusiastic reporter. "The Lethbridge board of trade has been working for a long time to have all or part of the reserve set apart for bona fide settlers, and the present effort on the part of the government may be the result of the local body's activity."[5]

The government summarized its offer to the Indians in a three-page mimeographed circular which Jim translated for a number of chiefs and farmers who came in. They did not trust the government's interpretation given at an open meeting. According to the proposal, the land would be sold for not less than $15 an acre, bringing in a potential of $1,350,000, of which $175,000 would be placed in a fund for the construction of houses for the old and destitute, complete with furnishings, and stables and sheds for every farmer on the reserve. Another $75,000 would be set aside to break forty acres of land and provide first year's seeding to anyone who wanted to farm, while $75,000 would be used to buy breeding cows and bulls and a further $25,000 for mares and stallions for the use of Indian ranchers. Any remaining monies would go into a trust fund at regular interest rates and would be used to finance all the annual expenses of Indian farmers and ranchers.

Then, as a *pièce de résistance,* the surrender document promised that the interest monies would "be used to supply forever to each member of the band who presents himself on set days at the food distributing stations to receive the following ration: 5 lbs. beef per head per week; 5 lbs. flour per head per week; 2 lbs. oatmeal per head per week; 2 lbs. of one of the following: split peas, pot barley or beans, per week; ½ lb. tea per head per month."[6]

Gladstone was not surprised when the Bloods turned the offer down flat. They had become so suspicious of the word "surrender" that even when arrangements were made to survey an existing trail across the reserve from Cardston to Glenwood, the chiefs would not permit it.

To the government, the rejection of the 1917 surrender vote was only a temporary setback, for they immediately announced that a second vote on the same land, offering the same terms, would take place early in the following year. Then began, according to Wilson, "an official campaign of great pressure" to force the Indians to surrender.[7] Underaged boys were enrolled, votes were bought with tribal funds and official favors, and others were gained by intimidation. At the same time, the government constantly tempted the many impoverished band members with the promise of big money and perpetual rations if the sale went through.

In one instance, an Indian was told: "If you come down here (to the Agency) and vote against the surrender, your family will starve next winter."[8] Another opponent to surrender was offered an appointment to the tribal council if he changed his vote, "a Minor Chief's medal being held up before his eyes during the conversation."[9]

At the same time, all new breaking was halted and farming assistance curtailed while aged and infirm Indians were temporarily denied rations as a threat of what might happen to them if they voted against the measure. Even those Indians who had personal accounts at the agency were not permitted to draw upon them unless they agreed to the surrender.

When election day finally arrived on February 15, Gladstone learned that the faction which favored surrender anxiously went to the polls to cast their votes. Those who were opposed, however, were afraid to show their faces at the agency to vote no, yet were unwilling to go and vote yes. The result was an insufficient number of ballots for a valid election. Undaunted, the government simply postponed the election until February 28 and in the interim "Indians who could not or would not consent to the land sale were black-listed and systematically persecuted."[10]

When the vote was finally held, the surrender was approved, but by then the persecution had become so open and flagrant that the head chief, Shot Both Sides, immediately filed a complaint in Ottawa charging fraud, bribery, and intimidation. He demanded that the surrender not be effected until his charges had been investigated. As a result, the document was never implemented.

If the government officials could not obtain access to the land in one way, they would soon find another. The answer was a program entitled the Greater Production Effort, which proposed placing large areas of western Canadian Indian reserves under cultivation to assist in the war effort. In order to accomplish the patriotic purpose, the Indian Act was amended early in 1918 to give the government the power to grant grazing or agricultural leases on uncultivated land without the consent of the tribe.

Arthur Meighen explained that this dictatorial piece of legislation was required as it was "putting it out of the power of what one may call reactionary or recalcitrant Indian bands to check their own progress by refusing to consent to the utilization of their funds or vacant lands for their own advantage. It is necessary to do so now, particularly, in view of the production campaign that we have under way throughout the Indian Reserves of Western Canada . . . . We do not want to have this campaign entirely at the mercy of the Indian bands themselves. We do not want to have those bands stand in our way."[11]

The immediate reaction of the Indian Department was to claim that the ninety thousand acres which the Bloods refused to surrender was uncultivated and was therefore available for grazing purposes. This was done in spite of the fact that many Indians were dispossessed from their homes by the action and had to move to other parts of the reserve. Some of the white men who obtained leases were friends of the government and, with no fences to hinder them, they heavily overstocked their leases and let their animals run at large.

In the southwestern corner of the reserve, the area taken from the Indians contained prime hay lands and was used as the winter grazing area for the Bloods' own herds. Much of it was soon stocked with sheep, much to the indignation and disgust of the Indians. As cattlemen, they knew that sheep overgrazed any hay lands and that cattle would never go where sheep had been.

In addition to these major leases, given without consultation with the Bloods nor the calling of tenders, the Indian Department also leased six thousand acres near Cardston, which was to be broken and planted to crop. Another five thousand acres were set aside for a farm which the government intended to operate itself, using Indian Department staff. This meant that within the first few months of 1918, the Indian Department had taken away eleven thousand acres of Blood land for cultivation and permitted thousands of cattle and sheep to be poured into the rest of the reserve.

Gladstone was still working for Jacobs and Bradshaw during most of this time, at first looking after the cattle end and, for one season, becoming their sheep herder. Using the company's sheep wagon, he and Janie drifted with the herd as they grazed on the lease south of Caldwell. Unlike some cowmen, Jim had no objection to working with the "woolies," nor was he bothered by their foul smell or their stupidity. A few were lost to coyotes and wolves, but the area was good sheep country with few natural hazards.

The fact that Janie and his daughter Lucy were with him made life more bearable. They had a milk cow and a small flock of chickens which gave them a ready supply of milk and eggs. Whenever they moved camp—which was often—Jim simply scooped up the chickens from their temporary enclosure, loaded them into a gunny sack and, with the cow hitched to the back of the wagon, they were soon on the trail.

When he was not busy with Jacobs and Bradshaw's stock, Jim found plenty of other work in the district. The rush of activity on the Blood Reserve meant that skilled hands were in demand and much of his spare time was spent cutting hay on the Greater Production leases.

In 1916, a son, Lloyd Cecil, had been born, but he lived for less than a year, dying of bronchial pneumonia early in 1917. On April 17, 1918, another son was born. He was named William Frederick in honor of Jim's beloved grandfather.

Living near Waterton, Jim was frequently in touch with his sister Helen, who had married a Metis named Bill Tourond. He also wrote regularly to Lucy, who had married another Metis, Dan Nault, and moved to Fairholm, Saskatchewan. His brother Steve remained unmarried, drifting from relative to relative, or from town to town, picking up casual labor and apparently quite contented with his life. He was a quiet, kindly man who seldom drank and was liked by almost everyone who knew him. On occasion, he came to Jim's camp in the park and remained with him for days or weeks at a time.

Their mother Harriet had spent several years on various reserves in Saskatchewan. In 1918, she decided to return to Alberta and, unable to look after herself, lived with Helen for a while and then came to stay with Jim and his family. While there, she mixed easily with the Bloods, some of whom remembered her from the Whoop-Up days, and later in the year she married a widower named Slap Face.

When Jim learned that his mother was getting married, he built a house for them on Bull Horn Coulee and was pleased that his mother now had a home of her own. Slap Face treated her well; he was a good worker who made most of his money by haying. To him, and others on the reserve, his new wife was known as *Hai'eet*, which was simply a Blackfoot way of saying Harriet.

Ironically, the marriage automatically made Harriet a treaty Indian and a member of the Blood tribe — something that her son had been seeking for half his life.

During the summer of 1919, the repressive situation on the Blood Reserve continued to deteriorate and even though the war was over, the Greater Production Effort went on unabated. Indian farmers discovered that the agricultural machinery which was bought with their tribal funds was no longer available as they were needed for the new government farm. Similarly, farm instructors were not able to advise on agricultural matters as they were working on the newly broken lands. Some Indians were unable to seed that spring while a few went back to the ancient methods of planting their seed by broadcast. Then, when autumn came, no harvesting could be done with Blood-owned machinery until work had been finished on the government farm.

Even more disastrous was the situation with the Blood cattle. Although the animals were individually owned, they were run as a single herd, each animal carrying an ID brand and a number indicating its owner. Whenever an animal was slaughtered for rations or sold, the money was credited to the owner's account.

By the summer of 1919, it was apparent that the south country was in for a dry season. Hay crops were light and the entire Blood Reserve was overstocked with cattle. On the southwestern lease, sheep owners had devised a practice of driving thousands of their animals to drink at the St. Mary's River, which was on the opposite side of the reserve. For days they trailed them slowly across unleased land, the sheep grazing all the way, and then just as slowly drove them back to the lease.

By this time, the Indian agent was becoming alarmed at the grazing situation and reported to his superiors that the reserve was rapidly becoming overgrazed. His report was ignored. In the fall, when about three hundred Indian-owned calves needed to be branded, the government refused to give the authority and when winter came, the unbranded animals wandered with their mothers onto the range. By spring they would be weaned and there would be no way of knowing their owners. In fact, there was no way of telling that they were Indian cattle and they could be branded by any lessee on the reserve.

Then, to add a touch of lunacy to gross mismanagement, the agent was instructed to discontinue using the Bloods' own Cattle Management Fund to buy hay from the Indians; instead, cattle owners were told to look after supplies for their own stock. This meant that two thousand ton's of hay normally put up during the fall would not be forthcoming, and Indians were given the impossible task of riding through the Blood herd to pick out and care for their own animals.

The major lessee, Gordon, Ironsides and Fares, was aware of the potential disaster and pulled its entire herd off the reserve, driving the cattle to new grazing lands on the Milk River and across the Montana border. Even though they were paying for their lease on the basis of their cattle population, no attempt was made to count the stock or check the brands as they left the reserve. However, a number of Blood riders went down to the Milk River country and found twenty Indian cattle in the Canadian herd; they never did check those on the American side.

The removal of Gordon, Ironsides and Fares' stock finally prompted the government to take action. Authority was given to take six hundred head of starving cattle and to sell them before the onset of winter. The animals were rounded up and moved to Cardston but two weeks passed before cattle cars could be dispatched to that town. In the meantime more than a hundred tons of precious hay were fed to them while they waited for the train. They were a skinny, miserable lot of cattle which were eventually bought by Gordon, Ironsides and Fares at their yards in Moose

Jaw and Rush Lake. They averaged only 5¼ cents a pound, whereas healthy animals would have sold for more than twice that amount.

Gladstone became involved in the tragedy in November, 1919, when he was hired as assistant stockman for the reserve. He joined other assistant stockmen who, under Cliff Clark, were trying desperately to save the Blood herd.

An experienced cowman, Jim was placed in charge of the cow camp and his first suggestion was to get the twenty-seven hundred head out of the southeast corner of the reserve. The land had been overgrazed by Knight and Watson's cattle and close cropped by the sheep on their way to water. He recommended moving them to the north end of the reserve to graze in the vicinity of Kipp siding. That way, hay could be brought in by rail if the winter proved to be a bad one. However, Clark had orders to keep the animals in the south and that's where they stayed.

Clark and his crew were with the rest of the stock all winter, performing their pathetic task. The old cows and weak cattle were the first ones to go, and throughout the winter the bawling of starving animals was constantly with them. Each morning, new carcasses were stretched out on the prairies, their legs sticking out like so many toothpicks from gnarled, shriveled-up frames. Even the self-sufficient horses had a hard time surviving that winter, more than six hundred perishing because of the lack of grass.

On May 10, 1920, a savage snowstorm swept across the prairies; it was the last straw. When it was over, more cattle were dead and when Jim went out to see the herd, he was greeted by a pitiful sight. Most of the animals had been chilled by the spring storm and had fallen in their tracks. All over the prairie were mounds of snow marking the carcasses of the dead animals. Sometimes, there was a live calf near its mother's body, the young animal somehow having survived, but now facing certain death. That storm reduced the tribal herd to a pitiful few. There was no hay left on the reserve, so Gladstone and the others spread oats on the prairie but many of the animals had become too weak to eat. They counted more than two hundred new carcasses after the storm.

Interestingly enough, one of Jim's old debts was paid off just after the storm. He had found a bunch of weakened cattle that had drifted in the storm and, using a sleigh, he tried to break trail for them back to camp. However, the snow was two feet deep in places and after the first day his tired team had made only six miles. Next morning they continued the struggle but were out for only a short time when Jim met Three Guns, the Indian whose bottle he had ignored while a scout in Lethbridge. The old Blood promptly offered his own team to hitch in front of Gladstone's animals and in this way the pathway to the cow camp was broken without further trouble. Three Guns refused to accept payment for the use of his team; he just wanted it back when Jim was finished with it.

"Later that month," said Gladstone, "we had a roundup, with only Clark and I as riders. When we went around the Belly River from Standoff to Weasel Fat's bottom, we found twenty-three head of fat cattle that had wintered in the area where I'd suggested we move the whole herd. Those twenty-three head were used for rations and they were the first meat with any fat on them that the Bloods had that year."

Later, Gladstone and Clark went to Cardston to unload some heifers that had wintered at Morley. Of the 400 which had been shipped, only a few came back; the government claimed there were 250, including new calves, but Jim's count was 130. "The surviving cattle were in such bad shape," he said, "that it took us two days to drive them eight miles. During that time another five head died before we could get them to the cow camp."

During that spring, cow hides were selling at between thirteen and fifteen dollars each, so Jim hired two Bloods, Percy Creighton and Yellow Shine, to skin the carcasses which were scattered around the cow camp. The men were to receive fifty cents per animal. When the first pile of hides was sold, the cheque was sent to the Indian agent who dispatched the news to Indian Commissioner W. M. Graham in Regina. The commissioner immediately sent a telegram ordering Gladstone to stop skinning, and to haul the carcasses into the coulees and leave them.

Jim did just that, but at the bottom of every coulee, waiting with their skinning knives, were Fred Mountain Horse, Big Wolf, Sinew Feet, and Green Grass Bull. They skinned the carcasses and sold the hides themselves, realizing that the government would not try to stop them. The Indians knew that the disastrous winter was the result of gross mismanagement on the part of the Indian Department and officials wanted no incriminating evidence, such as the government sale of hides, to reveal the actual losses. Arthur Meighen claimed that the Bloods had started the winter with 3,300 cattle, that they had sold 591 starving animals in the early winter, and were left with 1,309 animals in the spring. That meant a loss of 1,400 cattle, or almost half of the entire herd. Gladstone, on the other hand, said there were only 1,100 left when they made their spring count. Whichever figure is right, the loss was catastrophic and became the basis for several confrontations in the House of Commons.

If the government's intention was, as some people suspected, to destroy the Blood cattle herd and open the way for land surrender, they were partially successful. Although the Bloods continued to raise cattle, their herds never reached the size of those herded just after the turn of the century. A number of the Indian ranchers gave up in despair, selling off their remaining animals to anyone who would buy them. On the other hand, their attitude about land surrender remained unaltered and throughout the history of the reserve, not one acre of ground was surrendered to land-hungry settlers.

As for Gladstone, he was concerned and frustrated all winter. He saw the whole tragedy as a political and economic mess which could have been avoided. Even if they had listened to him in the fall, the losses would have been reduced. More and more, he was becoming familiar with the role of Indian Department bureaucrats in the daily lives of the people. Even if the local agents were good men—which happened occasionally—there were still enough short-sighted and callous decisions coming out of Ottawa to create endless problems. At this point in his life, Gladstone had no ideas about fighting the system, but the winter of 1919–20 made him painfully aware of the catastrophies which could result from poor administration.

In some ways it bothered him that he was actually a part of the system, yet he realized that all of his efforts that winter had been directed towards the interests of the Bloods and not to the government which was paying his wages.

CHAPTER SIX

INTO TREATY

Late in 1919, Gladstone decided to try again to be admitted into treaty. Each time another child had been added to the family, he shared Janie's concern that they were being denied Indian status. By this time, he knew that his future was tied irrevocably to the reserve, so he had virtually abandoned any idea of making a home for himself in the white community. Yet he knew that he could stay only as long as he was employed by the church or the government; otherwise he would be a trespasser and could be ordered off at any time.

Ever since his daughter had married Jim Gladstone, Joe Healy had raised the question with each new Indian agent. As the years passed, the matter became more pressing to him, as his grandchildren would ultimately be affected. Accordingly, when the Indian agent left in 1919 and J. E. Ostrander was appointed, Gladstone and his father-in-law decided to try again.

Jim's desire to become a Blood Indian was not motivated by greed or material self-interest. In fact, the Bloods could offer him very little other than a place to live among a people he considered to be his own. The tribe was poor, government control oppressive, and the opportunities for individual initiative limited. Why, then, become a treaty Indian? It was because he belonged. There was the comfortable feeling of being part of a big family—not just the Healys but the entire tribe. There was a need to be with his friends like Joe Bull Shield and Cecil Tallow, and to be like them. There was the assurance that his wife and children could never be turned away. In short, the Blood Reserve was home and he wanted to be there by right, not by suffrance.

The Bloods knew, of course, that the Indian agent was the "supreme being" on the reserve. But Healy had been to eastern Canada as an interpreter for the chiefs and he had learned that there were men in Ottawa who were even more powerful than their local agent. He also realized that petitions from Indians were seldom considered, but if a white man would act on their behalf, there was more likelihood of something being done.

At their first opportunity, Gladstone and Healy went to see Samuel H. Middleton, the principal of St. Paul's, to see if he would write a letter to Ottawa supporting Jim's petition. Middleton, an Englishman who had entered the holy orders after coming to Canada, had gained the favorable attention of authorities for his part in the war effort. Even before war was declared, he had organized one of the first military cadet units on an Indian reserve and had encouraged the enlistment of boys into active service. Two of his ex-pupils had been wounded in action and one who died was buried at St. Paul's with full military honors.

In the course of his school and military work, Middleton had become personally acquainted with Duncan Campbell Scott, who was deputy superintendent of Indian Affairs, and so, bypassing the Indian agent, he directed the appeal on Jim's behalf right to the top.

"From personal observation," wrote Middleton, "I would strongly recommend that he be made a member of the Blood Indian Band. He married one of my old school girls a few years ago and has since been working off the reserve as a farmer, but owing to the tribal relations of his wife, who is an industrious girl, periodical visits are made to the old people and naturally all the advantages which would accrue from an affiliation with the Indian people are emphasized during each visit. I pointed out to him that by becoming an Indian—legally—he would forfeit his right of franchise, but this apparently he was ready to forego if he were given the privileges of settling on the Reserve and taking up farming as his vocation.

"In character he is steady and progressive—by no means a leader— and owing to having received his education amongst the Indians has more or less imbibed their characteristics. He has a longing to settle on the Reserve and I rather think if he were given that privilege, his influence amongst the young Indians would be productive of progress."[1]

The application sat in Ottawa for the next six months but in March, 1920, while Jim was working to save the Blood cattle herd, the matter was finally referred to the new Indian agent for comment. Perhaps Ostrander had strong personal feelings about Gladstone and the others who had been denied treaty status, or perhaps he was influenced by the fact that the matter came from his superior in Ottawa with the endorsation of the local missionary. For whatever reason, for the first time since Jim left school, he found an Indian agent who was ready to support his application.

"I cannot understand how Gladstone's application should have been turned down," said Ostrander, referring to earlier submissions, "as his mother was a full blooded Indian & the wife of Slap-Face, one of our Indians, who of course was not his father."[2]

Back in 1901, without realizing what she was doing, Harriet had spoiled her son's chances of entering treaty when she applied for half-breed scrip; now, almost two decades later, her marriage to a Blood Indian was proving to be a key factor in considering his most recent application.

"The Chiefs on several occasions, continued Ostrander, "have requested that Gladstone be admitted to Treaty. This man lives on the Reserve all the time with his wife & is a very steady hard-working man. Last summer he was engaged on the Greater Production Farm & proved himself very reliable. So soon as he was through with that work, he was hired by Mr. Clarke, the Stockman, to take charge of the St. Mary's cow camp for the Winter & is very well thought of by Mr. Clarke. I understand he has made his home on the Reserve for the last few years & is a very handy man to have around. I would recommend that he be admitted."

When no reply came from Middleton's letter over the winter, Jim concluded that this had been another fruitless try. He was now thirty-three and wanted to settle down on his own farm. Yet his ties to the Bloods were so close that he could not envision himself living anywhere else. Although comfortable with white people, he thought like an Indian and whenever a perplexing problem arose, he worked it out in his head in Blackfoot, regardless of what language he finally used to express it. His friends were all members of the tribe. And more important, his wife could never be happy living off the reserve. She felt strange among white people and whenever she was away for any length of time, she was homesick and anxious to be back within sight of the Belly Buttes.

In April, 1920, Janie went to the Indian agency to collect her annuity money. Under the terms of the Blackfoot treaty, every man, woman and child was to receive five dollars annually, with the councillors receiving fifteen dollars and the head chief twenty-five. When Janie came home with twenty dollars, Jim realized that he had at last been admitted into treaty, along with their children Lucy and Fred.

When he went to the agency, he was greeted by a good-humored council who cheerfully welcomed him into the tribe. He learned later that one of the chiefs, Little Ears, had gone to the agent when he heard that the matter was being considered and, with the support of another friend, John Cotton, had urged Ostrander to accept.

"You are now one of us," a member of the council laughingly told Jim.

"When you grow older," cautioned Heavy Shield, one of the traditional chiefs, "be sure you help us and not the white people."

Johnny Pace was admitted at the same time as Jim and a short time later, Dave Mills, Harry Mills, and Charlie Blood were given treaty status.

For Jim, the dream of almost two decades had been realized. Ever since he was a student in the mission school he had wanted to become a bona fide member of the tribe. Discouragement had almost sent him away to a homestead but always he had been drawn back. Then, after he married Janie, there was no question that he wanted the Blood Reserve to be his home forever. He was grateful that the people now accepted him, in spite of his curly brown hair and blue eyes, and he was determined to prove that their faith was not misplaced.

As for losing any rights he may have held as a non-Indian, those were unimportant. Legally, he would not be able to drink, but he knew that anyone, Indian or white, could find a bottle without any trouble. Perhaps he regretted the fact that he could no longer vote, but more and more his interest in politics had turned to matters affecting the Blood Reserve. As an individual voter, he knew he was practically powerless against the huge political and bureaucratic machine which controlled the lives of the Indians. And now it was going to try to control his life as well. Perhaps.

Gladstone had joined the Blood tribe just as Canada was ready to sink into a post-war economic slump. Returning war veterans were unemployed and confrontations were taking place between new radical unions and the owners of factories, coal mines, and other industries. Only the farmers seemed to be prospering, wheat having risen from 91 cents a bushel in 1914 to $2.31 by 1920. However, even this burst of prosperity was only temporary, for within two years, poor conditions had pushed the price all the way down to 77 cents. Not until the latter part of the decade would high prices again make farming attractive.

For Gladstone, it was a poor time to start his own farm, but the choice of dates had not been his. If he had had his way, he would have been farming as soon as he was married in 1911. Now, in 1920 and on the brink of crashing prices, he was venturing into his own farm while having a wife and two children to support. At thirty-three, he was a mature, husky man and ready for the challenge. Clad in denim overalls, heavy shirt, and work boots, he looked like a typical sodbuster whose roots were deep in the soil. He felt this way, too, but not until the roots could be planted in Indian soil had he been ready to settle down.

The Blood Reserve at this time was trying to recover, both from the disastrous winter of 1919–20 and from influenza epidemics in 1918 and 1919 which had reduced the tribe's population to its lowest point in history—1,112 persons.

In order to re-stock the Blood cattle herd, more than $21,000 was spent from the tribe's own trust fund in 1920, in spite of the fact that the losses had been due to government mismanagement. In addition, trust monies were used to issue rations of beef, flour, and tea to anyone who needed them, while the elderly and destitute received rice, soap, flannel, and cotton goods. The funds to pay these expenses came from leases and income derived from the Greater Production scheme.

The Bloods themselves had only about 15,000 of their 354,000-acre reserve under cultivation; divided into small family holdings, they provided a basic income for many of the Bloods. In 1920, the farms produced more than a thousand bushels of wheat and fifteen hundred tons of hay. During the entire year, individual Bloods made $20,000 from farming, haying, and selling beef, and another $25,000 working in the coal mines, harvesting sugar beets, working for the Indian agency and schools, and doing chores for neighboring ranchers and farmers. That was less than $45 per capita for the year.

Yet mere statistics could not properly reflect daily life on the Blood Reserve. While most people had given up their tiny cottonwood cabins in favor of larger dwellings, they still moved into tents and tepees in the summer to escape from the squalid confinement made worse by a people who still had not become accustomed to staying in one place. In their nomadic days, it had been practical to leave their wastes for nature to reclaim but on the reserve it simply created a fertile breeding ground for disease.

The standard fare in most homes was beef and bannock, the former usually boiled in a large pot on an iron stove. Tea was the usual beverage and during social visits several pounds of tea leaves were dumped into a pot and boiled until almost black. During the late evening, about midnight, the dancing ceased and everyone enjoyed the black tea and bannock. People brought their own cups and plates, while many old ladies carried little cotton sacks and lard pails to take home anything that was left over. The practice might have seemed amusing to white observers, but these old women were probably on the verge of starvation.

The rations were adequate for the aged and destitute, but when assigning portions, officials did not take into consideration the fact that visitors had to be fed. If an old lady received a call from one of her children or grandchildren, she could not let them leave without some tea and perhaps bannock, or meat cooked with boiled rice. Similarly, if a guest came from another reserve, she would not be permitted to go without a gift, perhaps several yards of precious cotton. As a result, an elderly woman who lived alone often had no food and few clothes. For everyday wear, she had a shapeless cotton dress, plain moccasins, a leather belt with her knife sharpener and awl case attached, and a kerchief. Over it all went a brightly colored blanket which kept her warm in winter and respectably dressed in summer.

The old men, too, dressed in the plainest of garb. A pair of trousers, cotton shirt, plain moccasins and a kerchief around the neck were their main items of dress. Under the trousers, many of the men continued to wear the old-time breechcloth, even if it couldn't be seen. Sometimes, the elderly also wore a head scarf, usually black, and sun goggles to protect the last of their eyesight that was fading with glaucoma or cataracts. Their hair was usually braided for special occasions, but left loose most of the time. For decorations, a man often had shell earrings for his pierced ears, and sometimes a beaded choker. But his main identity as an Indian was in his face: brown, weathered by decades of prairie heat and winter storms, his aquiline nose and high cheekbones retaining an aura of pride that seemed to go with being a Blood Indian.

At the other end of the spectrum were the ex-pupils, many of whom, like Jim, were ranchers or farmers. The girls dressed in modern cotton broadcloth or velvet dresses, their hair decorated with ribbons, and wearing shoes instead of moccasins. The boys had wide-brimmed ten gallon hats, hand-tooled cowboy boots, fancy shirts and jeans or more expensive trousers. They were the dandies of the reserve, who spoke English at every opportunity and actively participated in the reunions, sports programs, and dances held at their respective schools.

In between were the majority of the farmers and ranchers, many of them too young to have been warriors, but who had not attended school. Most of them spoke only Blackfoot and, like the old people, they often were aghast at the styles and actions of the ex-pupils. In dress they ranged from traditional to modern, but usually tended to be more conservative. Although they worked in their fields or with their cattle by day, these same persons were deeply involved with the secret societies, medicine pipe ceremonies, and other rituals of their forefathers. They had no interest in Christianity but were comfortable with their spirit helpers, the power of the Sun Dance, and the religious traditions of the tribe.

One result of mixing these diverse groups was the rise of jealousy, hostility, and misunderstanding. Not only did this take place between the ex-pupils and the older generation, but between ex-pupils of the Anglican mission and those from the Roman Catholic. It also existed between the farmers and non-farmers, the latter believing that farmers received favored treatment at the Indian office—which was true. There was also considerable suspicion on the part of the followers of the Sun Dance religion, who feared that former pupils would disclose secret ceremonies to white people, or obtain religious objects so they could sell them as souvenirs. For their part, most ex-pupils approached the Sun Dance with a mixed feeling of confusion and fear. It was still part of their own heritage and in spite of Christian teachings, they were never very far from their traditional religion.

One of them discovered how perplexing it could be when he attended a Sun Dance. As he sat down for a feast, his mother handed him a large wooden bowl.

"A big six-foot warrior, with a pail of crushed chokecherry broth approached me first," he said. "I held out my bowl; he tipped his pail, emptied about half a pint of broth into it, and moved on. A few seconds later another fellow came along with a pail of rice. Some of this was spilled over my chokecherry broth. The next gentleman had boiled beans, some of which he emptied into my already half-filled bowl. The fourth individual had evaporated peaches in his pail, a portion of which was added to my mulligan. The last man filled my bowl to overflowing with an additional helping of dried apples. I placed this epicurean puzzle in front of me, trying to find the best way out of my dilemma. My appetite being unequal to the mixture in my bowl, I emptied it into a gopher hole on my way to my father's tepee."[3]

When Gladstone entered treaty he was, obviously, soon to become a farmer. Through his work as an interpreter and the role of his father-in-law in protecting native religions from outside pressures, he was generally accepted by the older chiefs and leaders. The main problem was with his racial origin which the Bloods could not overlook. It was not the fact that he had a white father; many young men on the reserve were descendants of whiskey traders. If someone wanted to insult them, they referred to them as *anoki'tapikwex,* or half white men.

No, Jim's sin was not so forgivable: his mother was a Cree. That tribe had been the inveterate enemy of the Bloods for as long as anyone could recall. Two or three families on the reserve, such as the Bull Shields, had Cree ancestry, and no one would ever forget it. They, and Jim, were called *sai-a'pikwex,* or Cree people. In spite of his blue eyes, brown hair, and fair skin, Gladstone was identified for the Indian part of his heritage, and to many Bloods, it was the wrong tribe. This did not mean that he was ostracized, or even that people consciously thought about the matter. It only meant that as long as he acted like everyone else and as long as he did not try to be different from the others in the tribe, his past was ignored or forgotten. But if he should ever do anything to gain the ill will of tribal members, the first thing they would bring up would be his Cree background.

Jim had succeeded in his long quest to become a member of the Blood tribe. Now he realized that he would have to work harder than anyone else in order to be accepted. Previously, some traditional families had looked upon him simply as a fair-haired man who could speak their language. Now that he was legally one of them, they would expect him to abide by their rules and customs or be rejected by them.

After receiving the news that he had been admitted to treaty, Gladstone went to work as usual, but was informed by Cliff Clarke that he was out of a job; he could no longer be in charge of the cow camp. The position entailed signing vouchers and permits, but now that he was a treaty Indian, the government considered that his signature had no legal status.

"You're just like a baby again," laughed the inspector when Jim dropped by the agency to pick up his last pay cheque. Not only was he unable to sign government documents, but as someone who was now under the provisions of the Indian Act, he had to get a permit from the Indian agent if he wanted to sell anything he produced on the reserve—grain, hay, or cattle. At first, this did not bother him, but later it became a sore point and a source of conflict.

Anxious to start farming, Jim learned that part of the Greater Production land which had been broken northwest of Cardston was being made available to Indian farmers. After checking out the area, he discovered that the southeast quarter of section 30 was unoccupied. It was about four miles from town on land that had been badly broken and cropped twice since the Greater Production scheme had started. Returning to the agency, Jim was pleased when he was able to get permission to farm the land.

He was too late for the 1920 season, so he stayed with the Healys all winter. It was during this time that the religious side of Indian life was brought into his own family. A Peigan Indian visiting the double cabin said that he wanted to transfer his medicine pipe tripod to Janie. This was the first time that either Janie or Jim had actually owned a ceremonial object. Janie's only experience with religious rituals had occurred when her father was away from his job as police scout in 1912. As the owner of a medicine pipe, he had both Janie and his wife painted and purified so that they could take the pipe outside each morning and bring it in before sunset. They also were shown how to burn incense to purify themselves before picking up the bundle, and what prayers to recite as they carried it.

In this instance, Janie was not receiving a whole medicine pipe, just the decorated wooden tripod from which it hung. Like the bundle itself, it was a sacred object. A simple ceremony followed inside the Healy home, with seven-year-old Lucy being dressed up and her hair tied together in a foretop which hung in front of her face, just as medicine pipe owners did. The big pot-bellied stove in the center of the room took the place of a campfire as the participants were painted and danced around the circle. The tripod itself wasn't important but the ceremony was another sign that he and his family were being accepted as part of the tribe.

In the spring of 1921 he loaded his family, supplies, chickens, and a tent into a wagon and, with a milk cow trailing behind, they set out for their new farm. With a thousand-dollar loan from the Greater Production trust fund, he was able to buy two work horses, a farm wagon, sulky plough, disk harrow, seed drill, binder, and enough seed grain for his first crop.

As he had observed from his earlier visit, the ground had been poorly broken and almost all of it would need to be partly rebroken when it was cultivated. Selecting a forty-five-acre plot near his tent, he determinedly concentrated his efforts there, and after a spring of backbreaking toil, he succeeded in planting most of it to wheat and some to oats. Grain prices had already tumbled and he worried that he would have a hard time making enough money to feed his family that year, even if he had a good crop. In the summer, he sought credit from one of the merchants in Cardston, but only after the store had been assured by the Indian agent that Gladstone was "very trustworthy & prompt in meeting his obligations" would they extend credit to a treaty Indian.[4]

That fall, Jim's financial situation was grim. His year's work had grossed only $700 in grain sales and by the time he had paid all his expenses he had less than $200 left. Fortunately, he was able to get winter employment as poundkeeper for the reserve. Located near the cow camp on St. Mary's River, the pound provided him with a cozy log house, a regular wage, and special rations issued to tribal employees. His job was to make sure that the Blood Reserve stayed free of foreign stock, particularly near the cow camp where the Blood herd was wintered. Any horses or cattle found wandering on the reserve were impounded and the owners required to pay a fee before they would be released.

The job proved to be filled with adventure, excitement and a few laughs. But, more than anything, it called upon Gladstone to make quick decisions, something he found he could do with ease. He had his own ideas of right and wrong, based more on his knowledge of the Bible than Canadian law. Soon after he had started on the job, for example, the foreman from Knight and Watson's ranch asked if he could use the nearby ford to take his cattle to pastures that the firm had leased on the reserve farther north. Gladstone agreed, but only on the condition that he be warned ahead of time so that the Blood cattle could be herded away from the line of the drive. In this way, none of them would get mixed up with the ranchers' stock on the way north. A permit would be issued when they knew the herd was on its way.

"A little while later," he recalled, "I was riding with Chris Shade when we saw all their cattle coming across the river. The cowboys just drove them onto the reserve where they began to mix with the Indian cattle."

Furious, Jim ordered Shade to impound everything that was not branded. The early winter branding had not yet taken place and there was no way they could tell Indian cattle from those of Knight and Watson. After the unbranded stock had been rounded up, the ranch foreman said he would send a couple of men over to cut out those that belonged to his outfit, but Jim, still angry at the way they had come onto the reserve, said he couldn't do that unless the ranchers got a permit from the Indian agent.

"We knew he couldn't do this," continued Gladstone, "as he had no permit to trespass on the reserve, so we had about fifty of their calves. Although these were supposed to be kept in the pound and later put in the band herd, I decided to distribute them among the Indians to help them get started in ranching on their own. I branded a calf for each cattle owner and gave my best riders two each. Of course, I didn't keep any for myself."

These were the kinds of decisions which sometimes got him into trouble with government officials. Perhaps they weren't legal, but he knew they were right and benefitted the people who needed help the most. Throughout his life, he was more concerned with results than the red tape that was often involved.

In the spring of 1922, the Gladstones were back on the farm but, tired of living in a tent, James bought an old clapboard granary, about ten by twelve feet in size, and hauled it to the site. With a door at one end and a single window, it was home for the next two years. Farm prices were still low, but more land was re-broken and almost a hundred acres put into crop. Their oldest daughter, Lucy, was sent to St. Paul's school that year, so they just had two children at home, four-year-old Fred and his two-year-old sister Nora, who had been born shortly after they came to the farm.

Jim was almost a recluse during the spring and autumn while he devoted his entire time and energy to planting and harvesting. Sometimes a member of the Healy family came to help him and in the fall Janie was usually out stooking, her children not far behind. But in the winter, when they went back to the pound, there was plenty of time for visiting and socializing. More and more ex-pupils were settling on the southwest corner of the reserve, particularly since it was rumored that St. Paul's school would be moved closer to Cardston.

In the autumn of 1923, Jim finally gave up his quarter section of land in disgust, just when he had it all cultivated. For three years, cattle from nearby ranches had been constantly getting into his fields and in the third year, they had caused so much damage he decided to move. Realizing that the west half of section 32 was unoccupied, he applied for that land and when approval was received, he dragged his granary a mile east and set it up at a location which would be his home for most of his life. The other half of the section was farmed by Owns Different Horses and Running Antelope. Three years later, the latter farmer moved out and Owns Different Horses left in the early 1930s, leaving Gladstone with the entire section.

The new farm had some advantages over the old place. First, and most important to Janie, the main trail from Cardston to Standoff ran right past their place. Known as the Blue Trail, it was on the approved automobile route, and once in a while one of the sputtering buggies went chugging down the rutted road. Usually, however, it was a wagon or buggy containing someone from the reserve who dropped in for a visit.

Another advantage was that there was no problem with cattle because the farms lying beyond their place and the grazing area were fenced.

Just as his first farm had been badly broken, so was this one in poor shape. Using a method called backsetting, he turned the sod over and then planted the ground to crop. During this time the sod rotted and when he later turned it back again, it was easy to work into the soil. But it was slow, back-breaking work, and only seventy acres were cultivated in the first year. In the following year he built a small leanto to replace the granary, and in 1925, he had enough money for a crew of Cardston carpenters to build a neat little four-room house, shingled on the outside to keep it cool in the summer and warm in the winter.

Janie loved the place. She put a fence around it, started a garden at the back and even grew flowers along the path that led to the gate. An English woman who saw it a few years later was amazed.

"We went to the Gladstones," she said, "who had the nearest thing to a White man's home that I've seen yet: a *garden path* leading to a verandah!"[5]

Janie was proving to be a great asset to her workaholic husband. Although she had the children to raise and meals to prepare, she was out helping him on the farm whenever possible. And, more important, she was able to drag him away from his work periodically to enjoy himself with friends and relatives. Janie was an outgoing, vivacious woman and loved Jim with a passion. Exceedingly jealous, she would share him with no one, and although he gave her no cause for concern, she reacted strongly if he danced with the wrong woman at a pow-wow or seemed to be enjoying himself too much in female company. But Jim just laughed when she complained; she was the only woman for him, and deep down she knew it.

About this time, the rumors were confirmed that all the services and facilities located on the Belly River would be moved to the Cardston area. This included the Indian agency, Anglican school, Catholic school, and the hospital. The reasons given were that all the buildings were old and needed to be replaced, and that Cardston provided ready access to railroad, telegraph, and other services. Of course, the people of Macleod sent petitions to Ottawa, but being a Conservative town during a Liberal regime meant that they had no particular influence in retaining the multi-million-dollar business provided by the Bloods and the government. If the Bloods had had a choice, they would have continued dealing at Macleod, for they found the people there much more friendly than the Mormons in Cardston. It was not so much that the Mormons were actively discriminatory, but rather that they had such a tightly knit community that there was no room for a Gentile or a Sun Dancer. In their religion, the Mormons were taught that the Indians had descended from the Lamanites, a people who had been rejected by God and cursed with dark skins. Such a philosophy left little room for friendship and equality.

For the Gladstones, the move was a decided convenience. Jim was pleased in 1924 when construction of the Indian agency began two miles north of his farm on the Blue Trail, and even happier a year later when the site of St. Paul's school was located less than two miles west. By this time, both Lucy and Fred were in school, while two-year-old Horace was still at home and Doreen Ruth was born a year later, March 23, 1925.

Jim remained active in church affairs and when the St. Paul's Old Boys' Association was formed, he and Janie became longtime members of its committee. Their main function was to organize an annual reunion during which time ex-pupils made speeches, and visiting dignitaries like the bishop were guests. The day was marked by the presentation of prizes to outstanding students, and a banquet and dance.

When Jim learned that the school had been allotted an entire section of land, he volunteered to break a quarter section for the students to use to learn agriculture. At times, he also helped them farm it in order to pay off some of the school's debts.

Throughout this time, the Gladstones watched with interest as the huge three-storey brick school arose on the bald prairie. At a distance it looked like a castle, or a prison, depending upon one's point of view. When it was finally finished in the spring of 1925, arrangements were made to move the students from the old school early in the new year.

"They travelled across the prairie in many wagons to their new home," said Nurse Jane Megarry. "They arrived the same evening; it was raining at times and they were all very tired and hungry and very much excited. In the old school they had been used to lamps and candles, and their rooms had been heated with wood and coal burned in stoves. Now everything was changed. There were bright electric lights in all the rooms, nice warm bathrooms with bathtubs and toilets. For the first few days the pupils kept running around the corridors and up and down the stairs. They were turning on water, drinking at the fountains, and flashing the electric lights on and off. After a few weeks, however, [they] all got settled down to the life and routine in the new school."[6]

With the school within view from their front door, the Gladstones hoped that they could bring their children home on weekends, but they soon discovered that Lucy and Fred were the property of the school throughout the year, with the exception of Christmas, Easter, and the summer holidays. Many times, a wistful Gladstone child looked out of the classroom window to see her home farm only a few miles away. Tears welled up in her eyes when she realized that her parents were there with the other children, their pet dog Kaiser Bill, and her favorite riding horses. Yet many months would pass before she would even be allowed to leave the school grounds.

To Nurse Megarry, the school was a happy place filled with bright-eyed children who were eager to learn. They arose at 6 A.M., with the senior girls going to the kitchen, bakery, dairy, and laundry, while the boys went to milk the cows and look after the horses. At 7:30 they had breakfast, the boys seated on one side of the dining hall and the girls on the other. After they said grace, they ploughed into their breakfast of oatmeal and milk. Prayers were recited again after the meal and at 9 o'clock everyone marched to the chapel for morning prayers.

The students were then divided, the senior boys doing farm work or going to classes, and the senior girls going to the laundry, dairy, or sewing room. The rest went to classes where the day was spent on regular instruction; the teacher punished anyone who spoke Blackfoot. Prayers were said again at lunch and supper, after which everyone went to the chapel for evening prayers.

There was time for recreation, as well as for the boys' cadet corps, the girl guides, walks on the prairie, and sports. And on weekends, parents could come to the school and visit their children in a special room which had been set aside for that purpose.

While Nurse Megarry may have seen this as a happy and fulfilling routine, an English woman who visited the school was not so sure. "What was there to say?" she asked. "Dormitories are dormitories. They are, as far as I can remember, always white, always bare, always there are many windows and a great glare. There were the usual rows of white beds, and not so much as a night table on which to place the childish treasures and reminders of home. A small square room like a well, with a top-light and some stiff chairs round a central table, was the meeting-place for parents and children. There was a playroom in the basement for bad weather, grim, severe, forbidding. In the kitchen, blank-faced girls were washing up. In the laundry, more blank-faced girls were ironing dresses for first Communion. There was no response to my smile, no smile in response to the Canon's genial greeting. Everything was just as I expected it to be, only infinitely more dreary. Ten years of life to be lived in this prison-reformatory."[7]

The year that the school opened also marked an upturn in the Gladstones' fortunes. For four years, Jim had struggled to establish his farm but was beset with depressed wheat prices and poor crops. Only his extra work at the pound and in selling prairie hay had enabled him to support his family during those difficult years. For him, the daily routine much of the year was to arise at dawn, check his growing cattle herd, and work all day in the fields. At times, particularly in the spring and autumn, he would not come in at all during the day, having his lunch and water brought out to him. If bad weather kept him at home, he was usually busy fixing machinery or going over his accounts. There seemed to be no end to the work that needed to be done, and no end to his willingness to do it.

By 1927, business had become so good that Jim was able to run the farm and support the family through custom work with his new Wallis gasoline tractor, as well as haying, and the sale of cattle. In that year, his cattle sales alone amounted to $320, which was almost enough to pay for seed, machinery repairs, hired help, and groceries. Much of his grain money was used to pay off his earlier Greater Production loan.

There was general prosperity among the 186 farmers on the Blood Reserve during that period. Some farmers had much larger acreages than the Gladstones and consequently produced more grain. Tom Three Persons harvested more than thirty-five hundred bushels of wheat, while not far behind him were Joe Bull Shield with twenty-eight hundred, Big Sorrel Horse with twenty-six hundred, and Charlie Davis with twenty-three hundred.

A journalist visiting the reserve in that year was impressed with what he saw. "Today," he wrote, "they drive automobiles and sell wheat to the wheat traders. And they're getting rich at it. Although the crop on the Blood reserve fared similarly to that on the farms of the white men, the Indian grain growers threshed 121,000 bushels, 45,000 bushels of which were taken from what is known as the Greater Production farm. In addition to the extensive fields of wheat, the native farmers are raising horses and cattle of excellent quality. Good breeding stock, purchased by the Indians, is raising the standard of the livestock and it is a rarity today to see the little ponies of other years with their coats of many colors, painted as it were by some devotee of the futurist school. The Indian horses now are heavy, well-bred agricultural animals and thoroughbreds.

"The Indian now enjoys his home comforts; he gets his orchestra concerts and market reports over the radio; he rides in his automobile; he houses his stock in good barns; he is a forceful, self-reliant thrifty member of society."[8]

While perhaps this was too rosy a description of the situation for everyone on the Blood Reserve, it did reflect the condition of many farmers who had suddenly prospered through the high prices of the late 1920s. It also gave rise to another source of animosity: rich versus poor. As long as he remained a poor farmer, living in a tent or granary, Gladstone experienced no hostility or criticism. But as soon as he obtained a new house, new tractor, and other amenities which money could bring, the antagonisms began to appear.

Gladstone was conscious of the danger and tried hard to avoid it. His greatest hope, next to providing a secure future for his children, was to be fully accepted by the Bloods, whom he considered his own people. When the wheat money started to roll in, he made loans to friends and relatives, drove people who needed a lift, hired men he really didn't need, and continued to support his church and the native ceremonies on the reserve. In 1927, for example, he teamed up with Fred Tail Feathers to run a store at the Sun Dance. Any money earned from the venture was used for sports activities for young Indians.

This was the only Sun Dance where he actually took part in the rituals, albeit reluctantly. Age old custom dictated that someone from a well-to-do family be "captured" during the ceremony and pay heavily for the privilege of cutting the hide used for tying the rails of the Sun Dance lodge. At this particular gathering, a young boy had already been chosen, so Jim thought it was safe for him to leave the store to visit the lodge. What he did not know was that the boy's parents refused to pay the fee, so when he arrived at the shelter, he met Heavy Shield and other members of the Horn Society just as they were leaving. Before he realized what was happening, Jim had been grabbed by the old medicine man and was being led to the main lodge.

Ernest Yellow Creek saw what happened but when he ran to the store to tell Janie, he used the Blackfoot word *Eyinakiks* to describe the captors. This could be translated either as "catchers" or the police. For a few minutes, Janie thought that her husband had been arrested, but when she learned the truth, she called upon her relatives to give gifts of horses and blankets. Jim and Janie put up four horses and a hundred dollars worth of goods from the store, as well as a bumble bee design tepee. These all went to Big Sorrel Horse, who had been caught at the previous Sun Dance.

"I was taken over to the lodge where Dog Child painted me," said Gladstone. "I hadn't shaved and I could see the red paint sticking out on the end of my bristles. Dog Child said I should have given him two horses, instead of one, for painting such a rough face."

A year later, the rights were transferred to a new victim, with Jim receiving the gifts that were proffered. But the new candidate was not wealthy and the presents which Jim got did not even come close to equalling what he had given. He did get four horses but three of them were walking skeletons. "One of these died as soon as I got it home," he said. "It just leaned up against the side of the fence and died."

Gladstone's support of the Anglican Church remained strong during this period and, beginning in 1927, he became a lay delegate to the synod in Calgary, continuing this responsibility for twenty years. During this time, he sometimes spoke on matters related to Indian education but usually he preferred to discuss problems privately with the bishop, rather than in the convention.

In spite of Jim's participation in tribal activities, he was still shown some hostility, and complete acceptance by the Bloods seemed to have been withheld. What pained Jim even more was the knowledge that his children also were experiencing the same situation at school, being called Crees or other equally distasteful names. But the pattern was always the same, whether at the farm or in school: when the people who had been deriding the family needed help, whether money, leadership, or guidance on how to deal with the Indian agent, they invariably turned to Jim. The Gladstones were the reliable ones, serving as secretaries on committees because they were literate, or as treasurers because they were honest.

Of course, other prosperous farmers also experienced discrimination at that time. Some were ridiculed and accused of being misers when they wouldn't loan money; others were said to be "acting like white men" when they bought cars and modern conveniences. The problem was a chronic one, but it was most pronounced in the late 1920s when the gulf between the car-driving farmer and the wagon-bound traditionalist was so vast. Abject poverty and relative affluence flourished side by side on a reserve that was going through the excruciating pains of transition.

Other problems occurred because of the almost limitless power of the Indian agent. This was demonstrated with tragic results in 1929, when the agent tried to play the role of grain speculator. That fall, the Bloods had taken off their fifth excellent crop in a row and were ready to take advantage of the high prices. However, under the Indian Act, none of the grain could be marketed without a permit and, believing he could get a better grade and price by handling the reserve's entire crop as a single unit, the agent required that all grain be deposited with the Alberta Pacific Grain Company Ltd., which had elevators adjacent to the reserve in Cardston, Hillspring, Glenwood, Raley, and Macleod.

Gladstone objected to the arrangement but as a treaty Indian there was nothing he could do. He harvested a bumper crop of thirty-five hundred bushels and then delivered it to Cardston, anticipating grossing at least $4,500 for the season's work.

There can be no doubt that Indian agent John E. Pugh had the best interests of the Blood farmers in mind when he decided not to sell their grain in October. Writing to the superintendent of the AP Grain Company in Calgary, he indicated that he had some 110,000 bushels in the company's elevators.

"In order that you may clearly understand the situation," he stated, "I want to place it this way. The wheat is grown by Indians and is marketed by myself, in trust you might say, hence I need to be extremely careful in the selling when holding for higher money."[9]

Wheat was selling at about $1.25 at that time, so Pugh accepted an advance of up to 82 cents a bushel for grade one wheat, which was in turn paid out to the farmers. The grain company, while unwilling to predict how prices would go, reported poor crops in Argentina and Australia but warned that "at the present time there are very large stocks of wheat in America and export demand is poor."[10]

As the days passed, the price of wheat slowly crept up to $1.30 and Gladstone, as well as other farmers, were into the office several times asking Pugh to sell. When it touched $1.34, Jim was back to the agency, but the agent said he would hold out and sell when the price reached $1.40.

Of course, it never made it. The Wall Street crash and the uncertainty of the entire market caused the price to plunge to $1.18. Then, just before Christmas it rallied to $1.30. Gladstone was haying down at Big Bend at the time and assumed that the wheat had been sold and that he could expect a handsome holiday cheque. However, when he got to the agency, he was appalled to discover that the agent was still holding fast, confident that prices would go up.

This was not a small business deal. Pugh had a huge quantity of wheat to sell, and even a one-cent variation in price was worth more than eleven hundred dollars. In the meantime, the Blood farmers were being charged for all storage costs while the wheat remained unsold. In January, as Canada slipped rapidly into the depths of the Great Depression, Pugh commented to his commissioner that "it is hoped that prices will be such towards the end of January that I may be able to sell satisfactorily. I would like to get around $1.30 net."[11]

What a hope!

Prices continued to slide during January and into February. Finally, a phone call was received from the AP Grain Company indicating that prices might fall below the 82 cents a bushel already advanced to the agency in the fall. If this happened, the company wanted to be assured that the government would absorb any losses. In the end, a directive from Ottawa guaranteed losses of up to fifteen thousand dollars if prices should continue to fall.

"No doubt I shall now be criticized," said Agent Pugh, "for my action in holding this wheat for higher prices. This action was, at the time of threshing, taken for the best."[12] And he was not alone, for the same problem was occurring all across the country. Even the prestigious Alberta Wheat Pool found itself facing bankruptcy when advances given to farmers surpassed the potential selling price. Only a guarantee from the Alberta government saved it from disaster. For his part, Agent Pugh was completely forthright and honest about the effects of his venture. As the reserve suffered through one of its worst winters in several years, he reported frankly in February, "The month has been a difficult one, in that the majority of the Indians have been hard up, due chiefly to my not disposing of the wheat."[13]

In fact, the whole winter was a disaster. The first snows fell late in October just after threshing was finished and the blizzards which followed shut down fall ploughing and haying much earlier than usual. Even the work in the sugar beet fields ended before all the crop was in, thus limiting the incomes of many Blood families. The haying was resumed in December but Indians who had no outfits were obliged to seek help from the agency or to go hunting in the foothills.

Then, just before Christmas, a savage storm swept across the prairies and for the next month the reserve was ravaged by one blizzard after another, with snow lying two feet deep on the prairie. By the end of January, temperatures dropped to forty-two below, Fahrenheit, after having been below the zero mark for several days. The supply of straw which was supposed to last the cattle herd all winter was almost gone and more than a dozen animals perished in the blizzards and extreme cold.

Then came a variety of chinooks and storms but March, instead of moderating, turned viciously cold, with a blizzard near the end of the month halting all movement on the reserve for several days. The result of the weeks of confinement was sickness and hardship. In February alone, more than a hundred Bloods were treated at the hospital while during the entire winter, fifteen died. "It is regretted," said the agent, "that the death rate was high."[14]

Gladstone was luckier than some. He had a warm house, a small herd of cattle, and Janie had put up preserves in the fall. But life was not easy for them as they broke ice in the trough to water the stock, doled out their dwindling supply of hay, and shared their food with relatives and neighbors.

During these months, Gladstone and the other Indian farmers watched the wheat prices slip lower and lower. Finally, early in March, the crop was sold. After the company had deducted $6,400 for storage charges and $2,900 interest on the money advanced in the fall, the total payment received by the tribe was less than $88,000, or about 77½ cents a bushel. However, the Bloods had already received more than $85,000 in advances, so when the grand tally was completed, Agent Pugh received a cheque from the grain company for $1,715.40. In some instances, farmers had been given advances which were in excess of the final amount received for their particular grade of wheat.

Gladstone was furious about the deal from beginning to end. Had the agent sold when he had been asked, Jim would have received $1,700 more for the wheat than the $2,800 he actually got. Not only that, but the original money was supposed to have been an advance and it was treated as such, being used to pay debts and covering expenses over Christmas and the winter. None had been set aside for 1930 as the remainder was expected later. Now, there was no remainder.

After he learned about the final sale, Gladstone stomped into the agency and loudly proclaimed to Pugh that he was giving up farming. As long as the decisions were in the hands of the Indian agent, he wanted no part of the business. When news got around about what he had done, several others also gave up in disgust. In fact, a combination of the aborted grain deal and the onset of the Depression resulted in mass disillusionment on the part of many farmers. By 1932, the number of acres under cultivation decreased by 50 percent while income from farming dropped from $97,000 for the 1929 crop to $24,000 by 1932.

As for Gladstone, he was true to his word.

"Tom Eagle Child heard that I wanted to move to Standoff," he recalled. "He wanted to live near Cardston, so we swapped. He had about a hundred acres broken, no crop, and lived in an old mission house. We made an even swap. I put my tractor in storage and took my cattle with me, about thirty-five head."

Janie was particularly anxious to make the move, as her mother had been ill and she wanted to be as close as possible. By this time, her own family was complete with the birth of her youngest daughter, Pauline Sylvia, on June 18, 1929. Her two girls, Lucy and Nora, were both in residential school, as were the boys, Fred and Horace. Only Doreen and the baby were at home, although Lucy was due to graduate in the following year.

Over the years Janie had also helped to raise other children, usually close relatives who sometimes stayed with them for four or five years. These included Janie's younger brother David, Ernest Iron Pipe, Harold Healy and, in later years, Clarence Melting Tallow. In addition, Janie's older brother Jim often camped at their place while her other brother, Joe, moved into the granary for a number of years after he married Philomene Hairy Bull.

When moving to Standoff, Jim's plans were to raise cattle and to make a living by haying and perhaps doing custom work. Accordingly, as soon as he arrived, he sowed the land to winter feed and welcomed Canada's Dirty Thirties.

CHAPTER SEVEN

THE DEPRESSION

The plunging grain prices were only one indication of an economy which had suddenly become deathly sick. As the stock market crashed, prices plummeted, and unemployment soared. People who were secure and happy in their jobs one week were out on the streets the next. Boys graduating from school could find no work so they jumped the first railroad train so as not to be a burden to their poverty-stricken families. Later, when forced to admit that there was nothing available, they swallowed their pride and went into one of the camps for the unemployed set up by the government.

At first, the farmers sat back and said, "At least I won't starve; I can live off the food I grow." But soon the mortgage companies were banging on the door, repossessing machinery which had been bought during the affluent twenties, or coming to take the farm itself. There was no money for gasoline, so the motors were taken out of cars, a tongue added, and the faithful horses pressed back into service. These vehicles were called Bennett buggies, named derisively after Canada's prime minister, who had the misfortune of being elected just as the Depression struck.

As if man's own folly in destroying his economy wasn't bad enough, Nature took a hand by turning off the water on the western Canadian prairies. For one year after another, many areas were so dry that the seed did not even germinate. Grasshoppers by the millions seemed to appear out of nowhere, devouring the little bits of green that had made it into the hot summer sun. And as the country shriveled up, each passing windstorm lifted clouds of black topsoil into blizzards of dust. At times, these great storms obscured the sun as they carried away a man's field and left only the clay and the rocks behind.

It was truly a Great Depression.

The Bloods fared as most westerners did, except that those who already were poverty-stricken did not notice the difference. In fact, some Bloods were to say in later years that they didn't even realize that there was a Depression outside the reserve. They were the ones whom a visitor in 1933 described as living in small log huts and tepees and could be seen "in all sorts of horse-drawn contraptions, sitting on the floor of the rig, riding over the rough prairie, or camped beside the highway. They are usually followed by numerous mongrel dogs."[1]

For Indian farmers, it was a tragedy which followed hard on the heels on their wheat fiasco. Many of them did not even have the money for seed in the spring of 1930 and the government, not willing to concede its mishandling of their grain sales, refused to issue free wheat. In the end, however, the grain was provided and the costs added against the farmers' individual debts. The disastrous droughts that followed caused many to become discouraged, particularly the Blackfoot-speaking old-timers, who found it easier to survive on the rations of beef, flour, and tea than to combat the vagaries of the weather and the white man's markets.

The cattlemen did not fare much better. The herds had never recovered from the mismanagement of 1919–20 and by 1930 the population totalled only thirteen hundred head. However, beef prices dropped with the rest of the economy and while the ranchers were at least better off than those on relief, they suffered with everyone else.

Yet, the disparity between the rich and the poor continued. Perhaps the margin was not so great, but those who had benefitted from high grain prices in the 1920s usually had good homes, a wardrobe of modern clothing, an automobile—even if they had no gas—and other luxuries which separated them from the indigent souls who still lived in tents and log houses.

For Gladstone, the anger and helplessness of being at the mercy of the Indian agent was soon replaced with a concern about his own future. The Eagle Child place at Standoff was large enough for him to make a meagre living with his cattle, a small crop, and haying, but not sufficient for him to support his family. Now, at the age of forty-three, he knew he would again be obliged to go off the reserve to work for wages. He had not done that since he had been admitted into treaty and had hoped that his labors could always be centered on the reserve. It was almost as though the little waif who had been brought to the reserve thirty-four years earlier was constantly being sent away, even though it was now his home.

As the father of a large family, Gladstone was happy, outgoing, and friendly with Indian and white alike. He was not prone to gossip, but more likely to see the good in people. Even after some questionable financial problems within the church, he chose to believe the matter resulted from an "inability to handle money matters" rather than any dishonesty.[2]

He enjoyed going to hockey games and listening to them over his radio whenever he could afford a battery, often with a number of friends and neighbors who dropped by for the occasion. When "Hockey Night in Canada" wasn't on, the whole family preferred old-time western music, with Jimmy Rodgers and Wilf Carter being among their favorites.

Like a convert to a new religion who was constantly trying to prove himself, Gladstone was always involved with projects which benefitted the reserve. He served as vestryman for his church, helped organize the reunions, gave money to the Sun Dance, and often discussed politics and Indian problems with friends of his who served on the tribal council. In daily life, Blackfoot was spoken more frequently than English, but he could slip easily from one language into the other.

In many ways, his father-in-law, Joe Healy, had taken the place of his old grandfather. The two men liked each other and often spent hours visiting and telling stories, particularly while Janie was with her mother. He found Joe to be a wise person and usually listened to his advice, especially when dealing with personality problems on the reserve. Stay out of needless conflicts, he was warned. Don't back down from a fight, but don't go looking for one either. And whatever else happens, don't worry about what other people say as long as you are sure in your own mind that you are right.

Healy knew what he was talking about. As the first English-speaking Indian on the reserve, he had been subjected to ridicule and scorn as a young man, but he had ignored it and risen above it. He had also followed the dictates of his conscience by becoming a Christian, yet he had not turned his back on his native religion. In fact, he had found that fine line between the comfortable life of a white man and the acceptance of his own people. His advice to Jim was to follow in his steps.

In the autumn of 1930, word came that Indians were being hired to work in the coal mines on the Blackfoot Reserve, so Fred Tail Feathers, Joe Bull Shield, and Jim Gladstone decided to apply. There was some opposition from the Blackfoot about hiring outsiders but the head chief, Running Rabbit, said that not enough men from his own reserve were willing to work and told his people to leave the Bloods alone.

Since the first coal mine opened on the Blackfoot Reserve in 1888, the Indians had worked spasmodically at the enterprise. Led by Calf Bull and Good Woman's Son, they had dug tiny rabbit holes into the cutbank of the Bow River, mining the coal in winter and dropping it onto the ice, where it was hauled away in sleighs. This was a small family operation which hired only a few local people as miners and teamsters.

In 1930, the Indian agent and tribal council decided to begin mining in a serious way. A Scottish miner was employed and by that fall he had a professional tunnel open and ready for business. With coal selling at five dollars a ton there were soon many orders on hand and as the winter progressed, sleighs were lined up at the mine. Even the neighboring municipalities co-operated, giving coal vouchers to debt-ridden farmers which were worked off in the following year.

By the time Jim and the other Bloods had arrived, long bunk houses, a cook house, and wash house had been erected, with the foreman having his office and living quarters in a twelve-by-fourteen-foot log cabin.

"Joe Bull Shield and I worked together in the mines," said Gladstone. "My job was to keep the clay cleared out of our room. There were two seams of coal with about two feet of clay between them. The room itself was about twenty-four feet wide and six feet high. There was about six feet of space between the props, and I dumped the clay there."

It was hard work with a pick and shovel. After enough coal had been taken from the face, it was piled in a bin and when that was full, it was loaded into a chute until it contained ten or fifteen tons. From there it was released directly into the wagons waiting below. Working sixteen to eighteen hours a day, the men sometimes hauled forty tons of coal from their room. At a salary of a dollar a ton, it was good wages for men during the Depression.

Jim, Joe, and Fred shared a cabin with Charlie Royal and his wife, who were from the reserve. Charlie's wife was also a cook for the camp. The village proved to be a lively place, with plenty of entertainment after work. There were card games, hand games, black-tailed deer dances, pow-wows, fiddle dances, and on Saturday night, someone was sure to show up with a few bottles of liquor.

During the winter, someone mentioned an old woman who could conjure up ghosts. They were told that among the spirits she could contact was Fred Tail Feathers' father, a noted Mounted Police scout who had been killed in 1907 in a gunfight with his chief. Tail Feathers had died instantly but the chief had lingered for several days. The Bloods believed that the scout's spirit had then drifted away, waiting for the chief to die, and had been wandering ever since. Because one of Tail Feathers' wives was a Blackfoot who had moved back to her reserve, stories were circulated that the spirit had gone to her reserve to be close to her.

Jim and his friend Ernest Brave Rock were fascinated with the story, so one day when they were bored they decided to see the old woman. She admitted that she could conjure up spirits but demanded fifty cents from each man before she would do anything. Then, money in hand, she sat in a darkened room with the two visitors and began to pray and call for Tail Feathers to appear. Suddenly there was a babble of unintelligible voices, startling the two men. When the woman came out of the trance, she informed them that she could not get in touch with Tail Feathers;

his spirit was down on the Blood Reserve, wandering through the Belly Buttes.

The two Bloods left quietly; what started out as a lark had ended up as a deeply moving and unsettling experience. Although both men were good Anglicans, they had seen enough of native religion to hold it in high regard. Gladstone never tried to rationalize between the two religions; he was a Christian but he respected the beliefs of his tribe.

At the coal mine, the Bloods paid only a dollar a week for their room and when payday arrived, people were around selling everything from vegetables to cream puffs and chocolate bars. Like the other Bloods, Jim saved most of his earnings and sent regular money orders down to Janie and the children.

In the spring of 1931, the three men returned to the Blood Reserve, where Jim found that the gophers had destroyed his crop of winter feed. He then went haying for the summer and kept busy until the mines re-opened that fall. The second season was a repetition of the first, but that year he had grown very lonely for his family. He made arrangements for Janie and the children who were at home to go with him for his third season, the winter of 1932–33. Janie's mother had died during the year and she was anxious to get away from the memories. At the mining camp they rented their own cabin and spent a pleasant winter, Jim mining and Janie looking after the children. She also helped Mary Royal in the restaurant.

In the spring of 1933, a chain of circumstances caused Gladstone to return to farming. For one thing, working on the end of a pick and shovel may have assured an income for his family, but at forty-six he felt he was getting too old for that kind of exertion. More important was the fact that Janie did not want to go back to Standoff; it was too close to the Healy home and all the painful memories that were associated with the death of her mother.

Also, Lucy had graduated from school and had promptly married Wilton Frank, the adopted son of Tom Three Persons. Jim liked his new son-in-law and when the young man announced that he could not get along with his step-father, it seemed like a good time to bring him into the family circle.

Jim was still angry about the mishandling of his grain sales and on the several occasions when M. Christianson, the inspector of Indian agencies for Alberta, asked him to go back to farming, he always brought up his grievance. Christianson said frankly that several other Indians had given up farming because of Gladstone's actions, and he hoped that if he went back to the land, others would follow suit. Now that Jim had a reason to go back, he sought out Christianson and laid the problem on the line. He knew more about farming than the farm instructor and more about selling grain than the Indian agent. He was not prepared to go back to the farm if others, less competent, were constantly telling him what to do.

"I'll go back," he said, "only if I can farm for Gladstone, and no one else."

The inspector agreed, but Agent Pugh wasn't so sure.

"If you do this, you'll have to pay your own debts."

"I always have," snapped Gladstone. "It's only your interference that's caused all the trouble."

When the word got around that Jim was going back to farming, Tom Eagle Child looked him up to see if he wanted to trade back for his old place. Until this time, Jim had been considering buying Owns Different Horses' land, adjacent to his former farm, but the idea of going back to his former place appealed to him. Before agreeing to an even swap, however, he went down to inspect the place. What he saw dismayed him. Fence posts, the outhouse, and a log corral had been torn down and used for firewood, the wire sold, the pump broken and the fields were overrun with wild oats. Not only that, Eagle Child had leased the land to a sheep herder and his flock was befouling the place. In the meantime, the Gladstones had made a number of major improvements to the Standoff location. After considerable negotiation, Jim finally agreed to the trade, with Eagle Child adding sixty-four dollars and a grey mare to boot.

Gladstone was happy to be back on the old place and when he planted his first seed in the spring of 1934, he had a reasonably good crop. By the time all his season's debts had been paid through the agency office, he was still $825 ahead. After harvest, he went down to the office to pick up the money, but the agent refused to give it to him. Gladstone reminded him of the deal he had made with the inspector and said if his money wasn't forthcoming, he would pull out again. Angrily the agent grabbed his book, wrote out a cheque for the required amount and literally threw it across the counter at Gladstone. But Jim didn't care; he had kept his part of the deal and expected the agent to do likewise.

Similarly, when the farm instructor came to his place and advised him when to plant or what fields to leave in summerfallow, Jim told him that he would make his own decisions. This time, Agent Pugh backed him up, and from then on, Gladstone farmed in his own way and prospered. Having shown others the way, men like Joe Bull Shield, Tom Three Persons, and Cecil Tallow also began to assume more and more of their own responsibilities, using the agency as a banking service and calling upon the farm instructor only when they wanted him. It was a subtle shift in government–Indian relations and, once started, it could never be reversed.

Since the Bloods had settled on their reserve in 1880, the Indian agent had been the ruler and custodian of their lives. An unco-operative man could have his rations cut off—all that stood between him and starvation.

If a family left the reserve without the permission of the Indian agent, he could send the Mounted Police to bring them back. And as they settled into farming and ranching, the Indians had to have permits to sell their products; their money was held for them in the agency office, and the agent decided how and when they should spend it.

The Bloods, although a proud and independent people, had accepted this way of life because, in the beginning, it was a means of survival. Since then, they had come to follow the rules out of habit, and no one had thought to question them.

Until Gladstone.

He had proven by his actions that he meant what he said; he had given up farming when he objected to interference and was prepared to do so again. Like many Indian farmers, he was perfectly capable of handling his own money and his own farming procedures. It took many years for the government to give up its permit system and rigid controls; the answer always was that the Indians "weren't ready yet." Many believed that officials were simply reluctant to change and feared giving up their undisputed power. In the years ahead, this would become the basis for battles which would carry Gladstone all the way to the nation's capital.

Interestingly, Jim had nothing against Agent Pugh. As a matter of fact, he admired the man for the task he was performing and disagreed only with the policy that placed power in his hands which Jim felt should belong to the Indians. After his own independence was resolved, Jim continued to have good relations with Pugh.

Because Gladstone now had his own working capital, he could bring in white farmers with their equipment to do his discing for him. Agent Pugh also had about a hundred acres that needed to be done but had neither the equipment nor the approval from Regina to hire someone. So when the outfit finished with Gladstone's land, Jim sent them over to the agency field and paid cash for the entire job. Later, the favor was repaid when the agency equipment was sent to Jim's place to do work of equal value. It was strange, Gladstone mused, but the agent was hampered by the same rules that held back the Indians.

During the early 1930s, three of Jim's good friends were elected to the tribal council. Shortly after Jim had moved back to his farm, they suggested to the head chief that there should be an advisory group of farmers and successful men on the reserve who could help the council and make recommendations. A total of fifteen was chosen, including Gladstone. While he was becoming involved in tribal matters, Gladstone's primary emphasis still was on his farm work. In later years his sister-in-law summed it up when she said: "Jim was always a hard worker. That's what I remember the most about him; he was always working."[3]

Drinking never became a major problem with him. Sometimes he drank too much and a few times he landed in jail, but most of the time he was perfectly sober and made no regular attempt to patronize the many bootleggers in Cardston and other towns surrounding the reserve. Part of the reason, perhaps, was his pride in himself and his family. He was always worried about someone bringing shame to the Gladstone name; he did not want to be responsible for it. He also realized that excessive drinking could affect the positive and stable relationship which he had created for himself on the reserve. He felt that most people accepted him as one of the tribe, yet if his actions ever became embarrassing or objectionable, it would not take long for attitudes to change.

By the 1930s, a definite social hierarchy had appeared on the reserve, based mostly upon the affluence of certain families and their willingness to sponsor dances, support their churches and the Sun Dance, and to display the obvious symbols of wealth, such as automobiles and modern homes. As an anthropologist noted at the time: "Among the Blood, more and more, wealth has become the determining factor in status, and increasingly it is wealth divorced from the old horse economy. . . . It is with the successful man, be he herder or farmer, full-blood or half-breed, that the young men wish to identify."[4]

The cattle owners, once the privileged class on the reserve, had never recovered from the winter of 1919–20 and their social status had declined in ratio to their herds. Similarly, the old-time full-blood who still measured his wealth in horses was given homage for retaining the customs of the tribe, but had no real influence in the community. If any group had a measurable standing, it was the holders of medicine pipes and the members of the secret societies. Their status was one based upon generations of respect tinged slightly with fear. In the religious activities of the reserve, such as the Sun Dance, they ruled supreme, but in secular matters they were merely individuals who were judged on their economic well-being.

This movement towards an affluent elite caused a humorist on the reserve to take a page from American society and coin the term the "Upper Ten." These consisted of the families of Percy Creighton, Tom Three Persons, Fred Tail Feathers, Joe Bull Shield, Dick Soup, Charlie Davis, Cecil Tallow, Chris Shade, Morris Many Fingers, and John Healy. Gladstone was just as glad not to be on the list, as continuing economic and social advancement were possible sources of antagonism. Besides, he was not concerned about social elitism. However, another wag from the reserve was not to be outdone and indicated if there was an Upper Ten there should also be a second group known as the "Lower Seven." This consisted of the families of Gladstone, Mike Mountain Horse, Henry Standing Alone, Billy Wadsworth, Harry Mills, Night Gun, and Ben Strangling Wolf. It was all in fun, but beneath the surface was a recognition that this indeed was the social structure of the reserve.

The country was still in the depths of the Depression when Gladstone's eldest son Fred was released from school. Realizing that the boy needed an occupation if he was going to be able to support himself, Jim saved the $825 that Agent Pugh had thrown at him and used it to buy a one-and-a-half-ton Ford truck. As soon as his boy was out of school, the firm of Gladstone and Sons, General Truckers, was organized. If successful, Jim anticipated that Horace would also join them upon coming home.

This was the first trucking outfit on the reserve and they were prepared to haul anything. In the autumn and early winter the firm usually carried wheat to the elevators, painstakingly loaded and unloaded by hand. In the winter they freighted coal from the mines near Lethbridge, and took loads of cattle to market.

A year later, they got contracts from the Indian Department to haul coal for the agency and then took similar contracts from St. Paul's, the hospital, and the Anglican residential school at Brocket. Most of the work was done for people on the reserve; because they did not have a commercial license, they made no attempt to get off-reserve contracts.

The business went so well that they got a two-ton truck and later added a grain loader. After three or four years, Jim dropped out of the active work and left it to the boys to run.

As the children were now growing older, Jim began to give more thought to their future. At the time when Lucy graduated in 1931, there were no real opportunities beyond the residential school. A girl tried to have a good marriage and a boy looked to farming or ranching for his livelihood. The venture into trucking had been the first attempt to help his children to break away from the limited opportunities that society had set for them. But the next to graduate would be his daughter Nora; if he could set precedents by becoming independent of the Indian agent and then setting up his own trucking business, perhaps he could do something for his girls as well.

William S. Gladstone, the man who raised his grandson Jim and was an inspiration to him, is seen here at the turn of the century. Gladstone was a boat builder and carpenter for the Hudson's Bay Company. He is shown with a great-granddaughter. (Gladstone Papers)

The cabin where Jim Gladstone was born is seen nestled in the valley of Mill Creek in the 1880s. (Glenbow Archives, NA-1162-1)

This is how St. Paul's Anglican mission looked when Jim Gladstone arrived there in 1894. At extreme right are the church and boys' dormitory. (Glenbow Archives, NA-1811-49)

In 1911 Jim Gladstone, upper left, was photographed with relatives at Pincher Creek. The others are Mrs. Elmire Gladstone and Jim's sister Lucy, in front, and his brother-in-law William Tourand, rear right. (Glenbow Archives, NA-8-1)

An avid football player, Jim Gladstone joined the St. Paul's team after he graduated. At Calgary Indian Industrial School, he also played on the football and soccer teams. He is seen here in the middle of the center row as they posed with the Calgary Caledonians (wearing striped uniforms) in 1905. (Glenbow Archives NA-3-1)

When Jim Gladstone married Janie Healy, he became part of a large Blood family. The adults in the back row, left to right, are Jim's father-in-law Joe Healy; Jim White Bull, who married Janie's sister; Jim Gladstone; Jack Hind Bull; John Healy; Mrs. Joe Healy, in blanket; Janie Gladstone; Mrs. Louise Healy; Janie's sister Suzette Eagle Ribs; sister Mrs. Rosie Davis, with baby; sister Amy Healy; and Jim Healy. The photo was taken in front of the Healy home in 1916. (Glenbow Archives, PA-604-5)

Joe Healy, or Flying Chief, was one of the first members of the Blood tribe to become fluent in English. As Jim Gladstone's father-in-law, he was Jim's friend and teacher. (Courtesy Canadian National Railways)

The Gladstone family posed for this studio picture about 1927. Left to right, front row: Jim Gladstone, Nora, Horace, Janie, and Doreen. Back row: Bella Healy, Fred, and Lucy. (Gladstone Papers)

Jim and Janie's first real house is seen here in 1927, soon after it was built. Their old granary-house is in the background. At the time, this was one of the most modern homes on the reserve. (Gladstone Papers)

Jim Gladstone purchased the first privately owned tractor on the Blood Reserve. A few months after this picture was taken in 1929, the bottom fell out of the grain market and he went coal mining. (Glenbow Archives, NA-8-2)

Gladstone worked on the Blackfoot Reserve for three years as a coal miner at the beginning of the Depression. Seen here at the mines in 1933, left to right, are Jim Gladstone, Mr. and Mrs. Charlie Royal, Fred Tailfeathers, Dorothy and Joe Bull Shield, Percy Creighton, Clarence McHugh, and Napoleon Pelletier. (Glenbow Archives, NA-190-1)

Jim Gladstone and Joe Bull Shield were friends from their school days. They are seen here after church services in 1931. (Gladstone Papers)

The Gladstones and their daughters were photographed at the farm in 1936. Left to right, back row, Lucy, Janie, Jim, and Nora. Front row, Pauline and Doreen. (Gladstone Papers)

CHAPTER EIGHT

THE CORONATION

Before any plans could be made for Nora's education, a series of incidents occurred which affected the future of the entire family. It began when the National Council of Education for Canada decided to sponsor two Indian girls and two boys to attend the coronation of King George the Sixth in June of 1937. An appeal was sent out through the Anglican residential school system and Principal Middleton was among the first to respond. When it appeared as though one of the female candidates would come from his school, various ways were devised to pick the lucky girl. These included high scholastic standing, the ability to be a good representative of the Indian people, and traits that best symbolized the kind of students that the residential schools were producing.

The news that Nora Gladstone was the final choice came as a pleasant surprise to her father. He had always taken a lively interest in the activities of his children and had fond, if not unrealistic, hopes for their future. Nora's selection seemed to be an opportunity of a lifetime. Quickly a white buckskin costume was borrowed from her sister Lucy, a suitcase purchased in Lethbridge, and by the end of April the sixteen-year-old girl was on her way. En route, she met a Cree from Saskatchewan, Ida Vandal, who was the other western candidate, while the two boys were from Ontario.

A tremendous responsibility was placed on these four youngsters to be the representatives of their people at the coronation of the king and queen. The Indians were avowed royalists, believing that because their treaties were signed with Queen Victoria there was a hallowed pact between the Indians and the Crown. As for Jim, he was so proud he didn't know which way to turn. His blue eyes twinkled with pleasure when he heard the news and every time someone congratulated him he burst out in a broad grin. To think, he had started out as almost a homeless urchin and now his daughter was going to see the king! And his enthusiasm was shared by most people on the reserve, so great was their feeling for the Crown.

The excitement heightened as Nora travelled by train to the east and by boat to England. Suddenly the Gladstones were thrust into the limelight, both at home and farther afield. Articles and pictures of the winsome Indian girl began to appear in newspapers all across Canada and the United States and radio stations carried regular news on the progress of the two representatives.

"The radio went dead on us after we got home," wrote Jim excitedly after seeing Nora off, "and after a couple of days while in Cardston, I heard that CJOC was talking about you leaving Calgary, so I just went to the Cardston Motors and got new batteries. Two girls from New York wrote you a letter, asking you to send them an autograph."[1] A few days later, he added: "I saw your picture in the Great Falls paper today and also in a group of your friends from Alberta before you got on the boat, so you are getting real famous."[2] Soon, friends and church members from all across Canada were sending clippings from newspapers in Toronto, Winnipeg, and other centers. Each time a letter was received from Nora, it was taken to the school where it was read aloud to the students.

Then came the Coronation. Heedless of the rain, the girls sat on the bleachers set aside for them opposite Buckingham Palace; from there they saw the royal procession and the appearance of the king, the queen, and the little princesses on the balcony of the palace. Later, they were presented to Queen Mary, the queen mother, at a formal reception. It was a never-to-be-forgotten experience.

Arrangements also had been made for the Indian students to attend school in northern England for three weeks. They were treated kindly by their curious fellow classmates but usually the visitors were off touring the area and even travelling into Scotland. A short time later, they were on the *Empress of Australia* bound for Canada and home.

During all the excitement, Jim saw the event as a possible doorway to Nora's future. "My earnest wish is for you to continue your studies," he wrote to her. "Canon and Nurse both would like you to take up some sort of profession, to continue with your studies and go to Normal School and take up teaching or something like Nursing."[3]

Upon Nora's return several weeks later, there was a gala reception and dance at St. Paul's. She was the first person from the school to gain national acclaim and, with the tour geared so closely to the work of the Anglican church, it was considered to be a personal credit to St. Paul's. But the whole reserve was honored and excited by the trip. Accordingly, Gladstone decided to sponsor an honoring dance in the old round hall; this was the first time his family had put on such an event.

On the appointed day, wagons, buggies, saddle horses, and a few automobiles followed the trail to the hall. Among the crowd were visitors and old friends from the Peigan and Blackfoot reserves, together with a few people from Montana who had come to celebrate Nora's return. The occasion was best described by the English visitor.

"It was nearly ten o'clock when the signal was given to 'drum' them in!" she recorded. "The procession was preceded by the two daughters of the Bishop of Gloucester. Chief Shot-on-Both-Sides, dressed in his Mercantile Marine coat, occupied the throne on the dais that was especially prepared for him. He was conforming in his official capacity to the official presence of Mr. Pugh, but ten minutes later he reappeared in all his regalia.

"After supper there were speeches. The Canon presented oratorical bouquets to Norah [sic], and Mr. Pugh contributed his quota. Norah had to respond, and Norah's father had to express his appreciation. The wall behind us and the bandstand in front of us were richly decorated with Union Jacks and Coronation flags."[4]

Gladstone announced that the chair on the dais, used by the head chief, was his gift to Shot Both Sides in recognition of the event. He said his daughter had seen the king placed on the throne and he wanted the head chief of the Blood tribe to have a throne as well.

After the officials had departed, the dance began in earnest and continued all night, including a giveaway where the Gladstones presented blankets, money and gifts to those from other reserves. By 6:30 next morning, while babies slept and women busied themselves with their shawls and blankets, the dance ended. "The hall began to empty rapidly. The reason for this sudden exodus was daybreak. In the dark no one could have found his horses or harnessed them, or showed the family and their equipment in the carts. That's why the dance was an all-night affair, they had to wait for day in which to get away."[5]

During the months after Nora returned, she was constantly on tour, telling of her experiences at the coronation, reciting poetry, and acting as a goodwill ambassador for her people. In recognition of her contribution to the tribe, she was given the new name of Ninaki, or Princess. These events placed a great responsibility on the young girl but they were sources of wonderment for her proud father.

As the time for the 1938 school year approached, Jim tried to make arrangements for Nora to complete her high school. When he heard that Fred Tail Feathers had rented a house in Cardston so that his children would qualify for school in the town, Jim followed suit and bought a town lot for two hundred dollars. However, the local school board ruled that they would not permit any Indian children to attend school in their town. Taken aback by the outright discrimination of the decision, Gladstone contacted Anglican church officials and, at the last minute, made arrangements for his daughter to complete her schooling at Bedford College in Saskatoon.

Gladstone had hoped that his youngest son, Horace, could also continue his studies in Cardston, but when that door was closed, he tried to find other means of providing him with an education.

Gladstone unsuccessfully proposed that Horace be permitted to take his senior high school subjects at St. Paul's and to come home every evening. He would not be part of the regular student body, but would receive classroom guidance for correspondence subjects received from the Alberta Department of Education. "There was no reason why Horace could not be attending High School studies," he complained, "and still come home at night and I feel grieved about him not being able to do so. But still I don't feel any disloyalty to Canon or St. Paul's as it is not his fault, but Mr. Pugh's or the Department."[6]

As a matter of fact, the discouragement of Horace's education was based upon federal policy. A few months later, the Indian agent showed Principal Middleton a directive he had received stating: "The Department doubts the advisability of encouraging the older pupils to proceed along academic lines. It is felt that when pupils reach the age of thirteen or fourteen years, the school management should emphasize vocational rather than academic training."[7]

Gladstone contacted Janie's sister Mary, who had married a white man and was living in Lethbridge, hoping that she could board the boy while he went to school in that city. However, she had no room at her place. Through a friend, Fred Botsford, he tried to rent a house in Lethbridge, but that plan also fell through. In the end, Horace stayed at home and, being more interested in farming than trucking, usually worked in the fields. Not until many years later did he get the coveted chance to finish his education. By then he was a grown man, but two successful years in business administration at Lethbridge Junior College showed that his father's faith in him had not been unfounded.

By the end of the decade, the Gladstone family had settled into a typical farming life, with the exception that they lived on an Indian reserve and were constantly shifting between the two cultures. With the Depression still upon them, money was always a problem and every opportunity was taken to add to the family income. For example, while Nora was in England, the town of Cardston had a coronation day celebration. Instead of basking in the limelight of his daughter's adventure, Gladstone took a job issuing Indian rations on behalf of the town for those people who pitched tepees and participated in the parade.

Lucy and her husband Wilton Frank were always on the move between the Gladstones, Tom Three Persons', and jobs on nearby ranches and sheep camps. Fred spent most of his time trucking and rodeoing, while Horace usually worked on the farm with his father. The other children were in school.

Taking 1939 as a typical year during the period, the family welcomed the New Year by attending Watchnight services at the church. With the weather being good, Fred spent most of the winter hauling coal, except for times when the snow had drifted into the mines and closed the roads. Horace helped his father with the cattle and to build a garage for the family's two cars.

The school was quarantined because of a typhoid epidemic for part of the winter, so Doreen and Pauline could not come home weekends, and Sunday services were cancelled. By the time the epidemic had run its course, four children and one adult had died.

They always had at least one car working all winter, so they were called upon to drive their neighbors when the need arose. On one occasion Nelson Rabbit and his wife were driven to Browning, while on another, Percy Creighton was taken across the line for three days. The Gladstones attended two dances during the winter, one at Pete Black Rabbit's, and the other at the old hall. "They had a good [honoring] dance," said Janie. "The Weasel Fat boys put it up for their mother; she's been dead for about five years now. They payed a lot of stuff to the visitors & we were eating all night."[8]

When the mission's quarantine was lifted in February, the family resumed its regular church services and had a chance to visit with their neighbors. Sometimes they went to the Tail Feathers' and when the Bull Shields came back from a trip to the Crow Reservation, they stopped by to give Janie a quilt. Harry Mills also came regularly from his farm across the road to visit or play cards.

On a couple of occasions, the family went to Lethbridge to see a hockey game, Janie taking this opportunity to visit her sister and other members of the family. On weekends, whenever possible, they took the girls into Cardston to see the matinee at the movie house. They were particularly interested in the Lone Ranger serial, which had started that year.

As Easter approached, all dancing stopped for Lent, while Jim and Janie went to church to practise in the choir for the Easter services. About the only break in their winter routine occurred when Pauline ran away from residential school on a dare, but was caught when she got to Henry Standing Alone's place. When her mother saw her "the poor child had bruised her nose & pretty near broke her ankle, besides being all bruised up from her whipping [by one of the teachers]. Poor Pauline was feeling very sore."[9] Yet she received no pity from her father. As far as he was concerned, she shouldn't have run away.

Everyone knew that spring had come when twenty-seven new wagons were issued to families who were just starting to farm. After the Easter services (the choir did very well) the Gladstones went for a brief holiday

to Browning, Montana, getting back just in time for the spring planting. For the next several weeks, the only break in their schedule happened on two succeeding weekends. On the first, the bishop came down
from Calgary and among the girls he confirmed at school was the second
youngest Gladstone daughter, Doreen. On the following weekend,
the twenty-seventh annual reunion of St. Paul's ex-pupils was held, Mike
Eagle Speaker acting as president of the group and Jim Gladstone
as secretary. During the banquet, Chief Shot Both Sides gave the toast
to the king; Teddy Yellow Fly from the Blackfoot Reserve toasted the
ex-pupils, responded to by Mike Eagle Speaker and Ethel Tail Feathers;
and Percy Creighton gave the toast to the Indian Department, which
was answered by Agent Pugh. Then followed a toast to the diocese by
Principal Middleton, answered by Joe Bull Shield and Fred Gladstone.
The speeches concluded with a toast to the guests by Mike Mountain
Horse.

After the banquet there was a dance, featuring fox trots, waltzes, and
two steps. "We had a long session of dancing," said Gladstone, "even
the Lambeth Waltz. You should have seen Mother at it."[10]

Once the crops and garden were in, the family had a little time to
relax as they waited for rain. Treaty payments were made, with everyone
going down to the agency to get his five dollars. It was earlier than usual
that year, as the king and queen were just starting their royal visit to
Canada, and the money issued was to help any Indians who wanted to
go to Calgary to see them. Some tepees were going to be set up, and
selected members from each tribe were to take part in a welcoming committee. Among them were the Gladstones.

Once in Calgary, the family went to the campsite near Mewata
Armories and found that the chiefs and their wives had come up in a
special railroad car with their tepees and furnishings. The Gladstones
helped erect the lodges, got hay for the beds, and water from the armories.

"My! it was exciting," wrote Janie. "We camped in with Ethel [Tail
Feathers]. She had her tepee & we were lucky to have had a place to
stop in. I took Lucy's outfit with me; Ethel & Dorothy [Bull Shield]
each had a buckskin outfit they borrowed from different ones, & what
do you know, Yellow Fly chose us to meet their Majesties if they
stopped."[11]

Until the last minute, there was no assurance that the royal couple
would even see them. The encampment had been erected to provide color
along the tour route, but it was left to the discretion of the king and queen
if they actually wished to leave their car. Of course, they were attracted
to the sight and, much to the delight of the Indians, the procession did
come to a halt. As it did so, the Indians put their buffalo hides down
for the royal couple to walk on.

Janie thought the queen was lovely. "She gave us such a sweet smile when we shook hands with her," Janie wrote. "I just kept my eyes on every move she made. We made a curtsy to them & the King looked kind & handsome too. They shook hands with [us] . . . . Then old Spear Chief took it upon himself to walk up & shake hands with the Queen & I guess he didn't know which was the King; he was dressed in plain clothes, but I guess he was glad he shook hands with one of them."[12]

During the summer, Jim and the boys were kept busy haying, hauling, branding, and doing other farm work. There was time to drop in on the Sun Dance and to go berry picking near the old mission school. As soon as fall came, Fred was back to hauling grain while the others worked from morning until night on the harvest, hoping that the weather would hold. Then the storm clouds gathered and work came to a standstill. "It's raining and raining," Jim observed glumly, "and the threshing isn't finished yet. Only 3 or 4 more nice days would have seen all the work done. My crop isn't much this year and I'm afraid after paying for all my debts we won't have much left. I had great hopes of building a new home here . . . . I guess I'll have to wait till another harvest rolls around."[13]

Janie agreed, adding that "I believe it's going to be a hard winter for some of the poor Indians on the reserve, especially the lazy ones. We try to help all we can; we couldn't help all winter. As it is, we will find it hard too."[14]

A social event of the autumn took place when the school principal's daughter married a wealthy writer from the eastern United States. Everyone was excited about the big reception, which was to be held at the school, but Jim's enthusiasm was cooled by the way the Indians were treated.[15] "We were all asked to go of course," he said, "but not to any Wedding feast. Not one of us even saw the Wedding Cake. All of us were directed down stairs to the dining room and only a small number were able to sit at a table. The rest had to be contented with the forms we were sitting on. Oh well, we are all so used to the Canon's ways, but others noticed the gulf that was placed between the Indians and the Palefaces."

That fall, war was declared with Germany and immediately Gordon Small Eye, George Good Dagger, and Long Jim went to Lethbridge to see if they could enlist while the women of the reserve were asked to volunteer for Red Cross work. Before the year was out, Janie and other members of the women's auxiliary were busy rolling bandages.

As the farm work ended for the season, Fred switched to hauling coal while Horace pitched in and helped his father build the rock dams. A few dances were planned but the family had no time for them, at least not until after Christmas. About the only distractions were the occasional movie in Cardston, plenty of visitors, and a trip to Browning to take

Eagle Ribs and Jack Hind Bull and their wives across the line. The Gladstones prepared for Christmas, both the religious observances and the family festivities.

As Canada became more and more involved with the war, there were numerous enlistments from the reserve and girls found for the first time they could earn good wages in the towns and cities. A number of Blood girls went to work in hospitals in Calgary while others benefitted from the shortage of labor by finding work as babysitters or nannies to people who had been accustomed to bringing their help out from Britain.

As Nora finished her high school classes in Saskatoon, her father could not help but express his pride. "One thing, I will be proud that one member of my family will have a finer education than the rest have ever attained and you will never regret it. In spite of the hard path, I think it's worth the try and pray you will succeed."[16]

Yet this was just the beginning of his family's education. Jim may not have realized it, but his determination to get an education for Nora had opened the doors for other members of the family and acted as an inspiration to many other young people on the reserve. As had happened when he exerted his independence from the Indian agent and when he started the trucking business, Gladstone was showing the way for others. Already he was belying Canon Middleton's earlier statement that he was "by no means a leader." All he had needed was the chance. And now, comfortable in his role as a member of the Blood tribe, and feeling accepted by all of those who were important to him, he was intent in devoting his leadership qualities in the direction that was most important to him: his family.

His close association with the English church affected his attitude towards the war in Europe. In his eyes, and of many other Indians, England was threatened with invasion and their king was in danger. On the morning of the fall of Paris, Gladstone was on his way to Stephen Fox's house to get some deer hides tanned when he stopped at the Indian agency. There he found everyone depressed by the war news.

"Why don't we do something about it?" Gladstone challenged the Indian agent.

"What can we do?"

"We could all chip in and buy some bullets."

"That's easy to say," responded Agent Pugh, "but no one on the reserve would be interested."

Unconvinced, Gladstone spoke to a number of friends and when his suspicions were confirmed that the Bloods would be more than ready to help, he suggested that a meeting be called. The obvious person to chair it was Shot Both Sides, the head chief, so Jim went to his farm and found him resting in his tent.

"Oki!" said Gladstone. "Let's go to war."

He explained to the head chief about buying bullets to kill their enemies across the water. Shot Both Sides, who had been a warrior in his younger days, immediately gave his support to the idea but because he was ill, he made Frank Red Crow his representative. At the meeting, a number of men told the Indian agent to sell some of their cattle and to donate the money to the war effort. Cecil Tallow said that his entire herd could be sold if it would help to beat the Germans. The chiefs also agreed to donate two thousand dollars from tribal funds for the fight.

Later, when the Indian agent tried to conclude the donation, he discovered that the government had no mechanism for accepting outright gifts to help the war effort. In the end, the money was used to buy war bonds. In fact, the whole idea of war bonds caught on quickly on the Blood Reserve and the drives were well supported. Right from the time the first colorful certificates were issued indicating support of Canada's Victory Bond drives, Gladstone and other Indians proudly displayed them in their homes.

As the war continued, the Bloods saw more and more of their boys joining the forces, while girls went away for war work. Fred and Horace both registered for the draft but initially were given deferments because farming was considered to be an essential service. Later, Horace served briefly in the Canadian Army.

Late in 1940, Gladstone learned that milk was becoming in short supply in the Cardston area because so many ranchers had joined up. One of the first places to suffer was the Indian hospital which, because of the slowness of the government in paying its accounts, was not an attractive contract. Convinced that it was necessary for the hospital to have a plentiful supply of milk at all times, Gladstone bought nine dairy cattle and, after complying with all the wartime requirements, he took the contract to keep the hospital supplied.

It was not an easy task, particularly when added to the other farm work. The cattle had to be milked and the cans taken to the hospital every day. This was not much of a problem in the summer, but during the winter months it sometimes became a battle with nature. On days when they would normally have stayed on the farm doing basic chores, Gladstone or the boys had to take the milk to town, sometimes spending two hours on the road digging through snowdrifts. Yet the work was carried out regularly until the end of the war.

Gladstone had one major fault which became more of a problem as the family grew older. He was always so sure that his own ideas were the best that he seldom bothered to discuss them, even with those affected. On the matter of education, he constantly pressed his children to get the kind of training he wanted for them, not always what they preferred at the time. Even Janie was not consulted. One time, while in a reflective mood about Nora's education, he wrote: "Sometimes I feel whether it was the right thing for you to do, to leave home and go on this great adventure, especially as your mother seems to not understand what it really means. And the answer that my conscience tells me is that it was the only thing to do, and I pray you will succeed. Every night I always ask our Maker to be with you."[17]

Fred, the oldest son, was another matter. As strong-willed and determined as his father, he left school even though he was pressed to remain and more and more he turned from farming and trucking to follow his first love, rodeo. His father at first thought it was a waste of time, but when the honors and trophies began to come Fred's way, Jim became a strong supporter of his son's activities. On weekends, the whole family packed off to Pincher Creek, or Coleman, or Macleod to see Fred perform in the calf roping and wild-cow-milking events.

But Jim did have his way with the new house. In 1939 he had delayed construction because of a poor crop but finally, two years later, the harvest was good enough to justify starting the project. In his own mind he knew what he wanted, so without any family discussion or consultation with Janie he began a large two-storey house. He got only the basement poured and the flooring in place in 1942; with a shortage of building materials during wartime, the house was not finished for another two years. During much of that period, the family lived in the basement.

When completed, it was one of the finest homes on the reserve. It was the first to be wired for electricity and even had space for a bathroom in case good water could be found on the land. From the front porch, one could get a magnificent view of the Rockies, with Chief Mountain standing out like a lonely guardian on the southwestern horizon. Located just a few yards from their former place, the new house was the pride of the family, but always clouded by the fact that Gladstone had done it the way he wanted to, right or wrong.

But that was his way.

As the war was drawing to a close, Gladstone could look with some satisfaction upon what he had accomplished in his family. Nora had gone from high school in Saskatoon to a Mothercraft house in Toronto and now was studying for her R.N. at the Royal Jubilee Hospital in Victoria. Doreen had worked in Vancouver and Claresholm for a while, then she too planned to go to Toronto for the Mothercraft course and for training in midwifery. Pauline was just about ready to leave St. Paul's, and when she did so, her father intended sending her to Prince Albert Collegiate to finish her high school. She had already shown an interest in secretarial work so her program would be geared in that direction.

As for the others, Lucy, Fred, and Horace stayed on the reserve, each following his or her own vocation. Fred was winning more and more rodeo events while Horace revealed a growing interest in farming, not just as a manual task, but as a science.

Jim Gladstone was fifty-eight years old and a successful farmer and rancher. He was also a Blood Indian . . . and proud of it.

CHAPTER NINE

INDIAN ASSOCIATION OF ALBERTA

By 1945, with his children moving away, Gladstone's focus on his family had altered as he saw them enter adult life. He was still concerned, but his driving ambition to have them educated was either being realized or was too late. Now, at middle age, he relaxed, letting the boys do more of the labor around the farm. He was still a hard worker for that had been implanted in him since his childhood, but he no longer lived under a dawn-to-dark regime that demanded his every waking moment.

His old friends also were beginning to enjoy themselves. Joe Bull Shield was around quite frequently, particularly as their wives were such good friends. Joe, now a big heavy-set man, still retained his dark handsome features which were in marked contrast to Jim's fair skin and angular frame. But together, they looked like a couple of farmers and when they talked, it was usually about crops, cattle, and the children.

Joe had successfully trod that fine line between the Indian and white societies. He was a firm adherent to the Anglican church and was a favorite of Canon Middleton. At the same time, he actively supported the Sun Dance and loved to dress in his buckskin costume and eagle feather headdress for the pow-wows. In many ways, he did not have the keen analytical mind of his old friend from school days, so he tended to look to Jim for leadership. But the relationship was warm, comfortable, and relaxed.

Cecil Tallow was another friend from St. Paul's who continued to visit him regularly. As with Joe, his wife and Janie were close and the activities at the Anglican school often brought them together on social occasions. In many ways, Cecil was the most outgoing of the three. He liked to joke and was even good-natured when people pointed to his middle-aged spread which was starting to fold over his belt. Smaller than his two friends, Cecil was a keen businessman and operated one of the most successful farms on the reserve. His children, like Jim's, were being well educated and mixed easily both on and off the reserve.

Together, Jim, Joe, and Cecil made quite a trio. When liquor was around they liked to drink, but more important was the conviviality of their friendship. While the women sat in the kitchen and drank tea, the men listened to the hockey game on the radio, talked Indian politics, or planned picnics, berry picking, or church outings.

One of their trips, however, changed the whole course of Jim's life. In the spring of 1945, the trio had gone to Calgary to attend the annual meeting of the Anglican synod when they met a group of Crees from Hobbema. These men said that they were going to a meeting of the Indian Association of Alberta near the Stoney Reserve and that it was open to everyone. The three Bloods decided to attend.

Driving in Jim's car, they followed the trans-Canada highway to the shadow of the Rockies and there, in a Boy Scout camp, they found a large gathering of Indians from the north, as well as representatives from the Blackfoot, Sarcee, and Stoney tribes. There were no other Bloods.

During the two-day session, the three Bloods were just observers but the more he saw, the more Gladstone became excited. Hearing Indians from the north discuss the same kind of problems as the Bloods were having, and listening to their possible solutions was like a revelation to him. By this time he was already starting to dabble in Blood politics and realized the significance of a series of events which had started two years earlier. At that time, the local member of parliament, John Blackmore, had written to the Blood tribal council enquiring about the general conditions and welfare of the Indians. In order to draft an appropriate reply, two of the chiefs had been authorized to call a general meeting to talk about the question. The first session was at Joe Eagle Ribs' house in January of 1944 and was attended by most of the chiefs, as well as Gladstone, Cecil Tallow, and several others.

Many meetings had been held in the past to deal with specific grievances but this was the first in response to a general enquiry from a member of parliament. The Bloods soon found that they had much more to talk about than could be covered in one meeting, so Jim invited everyone to continue their deliberations at his place. Over the next few weeks, a series of three more meetings were held at his farm, with Gladstone acting as secretary and taking a leading role. Another old friend, Chris Shade, had missed the first sessions but took part in the final summations.

The letter which Gladstone finally drafted dealt with five main topics: the need for community wells, eliminating hay permits, assistance for young men to go into ranching, the problems with hunting at their timber limit and, most important, "the great need today for our children who are growing up and many are already young men [to be] educated or trained enough to overcome the difficulties of going off and getting jobs as mechanics or any trade or office work."[1] The latter point had considerable personal significance for Gladstone, as his daughter Doreen had left for Mothercraft training in Toronto while the sessions were in progress. Like others in the family, she had been denied the chance to go to school in Cardston.

As a result of Blackmore's letter, the Bloods saw real advantages in bypassing the Indian agent and Ottawa officials in protesting the inequities which existed on their reserve. But Jim also realized that a united voice from several reserves could be even more advantageous. Therefore, he told the member of parliament that "we are considering getting all the tribes in Alberta to join in a joint effort to get all our problems together and send a letter from all of the tribes, or a delegation from that body should be got organized."

Now, sitting with Joe and Cecil amid strange but friendly company at the Indian association meeting, Gladstone found that the movement he had envisioned was already alive and active. "My first impression," he recalled, "was that this association would make us more united to present our views with one voice. I also met John Laurie for the first time. He seemed to spend most of his time writing and I was impressed with the interest he took in our affairs."

Laurie, a white school teacher from Calgary, had become the organizing force behind the association. His presence was the culmination of almost a quarter century of work by Indian leaders.

Gladstone learned that the first Indian movement in western Canada had started in 1920 when a Mohawk Indian named Fred O. Loft had come west to organize the League of Indians of Western Canada. Once he heard this, Gladstone remembered that Chief Shot Both Sides had received a letter from Loft about this time and had asked Jim to translate it for him. It was an appeal for Bloods to join the new organization but the chief was unimpressed. Jim was instructed to reply, saying that "the chief had made his treaty with the Queen and would remain faithful to it. He did not know what kind of treaties the eastern Indians had and he had no interest in Indian matters outside his own treaty area."

However, the league had gone ahead and had been formed without active support from the Blackfoot-speaking reserves. In fact, it was dominated almost entirely by Crees and Stoneys. From it, the League of Indians of Alberta had been formed in 1933 and four years later, an Indian farmer near Edmonton, John Callihoo, agreed to become its president. Under his strong leadership, a tremendous jealousy had developed with the League of Indians of Western Canada, which now was primarily Saskatchewan-based under John B. Tootoosis. The problem was that the Saddle Lake area of northeastern Alberta had its Indian agency offices in Onion Lake, Saskatchewan. Both leagues claimed the disputed area and in 1937 a head-to-head confrontation between Callihoo and Tootoosis caused a permanent rift. Two years later, with the help of a Metis organizer named Malcolm Norris, Callihoo had changed his organization to the Indian Association of Alberta.

Then, strangely enough, the Bloods became indirectly responsible for the association becoming a successful political movement. Late in 1943, Norris was stationed at an air force base in Calgary where he was introduced to John Laurie. He also met a Blood art student named Gerald Tailfeathers, who was boarding with the teacher, and through him met Chris Shade. Like Gladstone, Shade realized the value of organization, so when he went back to his reserve, he got Jim, Joe, Cecil, and a few others to form the Blood Indian Local Association. It is unlikely that any of the others realized that this was intended to be part of a provincial organization and not until Gladstone visited the meeting at the Boy Scout camp did he realize what Shade had been trying to do.

However, Norris saw his meeting with Shade as a way to draw the southern Alberta tribes into the almost moribund association, so he wrote to Callihoo, telling him about the interest of the Bloods and also recommending that John Laurie be invited to help in the organizing work. The result was that in 1944 the Indian association was reactivated, with Laurie elected secretary and Norris as organizer. Interestingly, the Bloods who had been the catalysts in the situation had no representatives at the meeting. However, in order to draw the Bloods into the fold, Norris made arrangements for Callihoo to visit the reserve and to meet with the organizers. This proved to be a disastrous mistake and one which was to plague the association for many years.

When Shade knew that Callihoo was coming, he called a small meeting which was attended by most of those who had been at the earlier session. Callihoo spoke earnestly to the group, explaining how the association would help them all. He pointed out that two resolutions of the association had been similar to ones which the Bloods had sent to Blackmore, i.e. the elimination of the permit system, and provisions for higher education. His message was well received, but when the meeting was over, Shade neglected to take Callihoo to pay a courtesy call on Shot Both Sides, his head chief.

As soon as members of the tribal council heard that a Cree had been on the reserve trying to organize the Bloods and had done so without discussing the matter with the chief, they immediately concluded that the group was being organized to oppose the council. At this time, there was some controversy over the system of electing chiefs for life and members of council were sensitive about any move which might restrict their authority or introduce an elective system. The Indian association was immediately dubbed the "Cree Association" by the outraged chiefs, while its supporters on the reserve were considered almost traitors to their tribe. Under these pressures, Shade stopped all organizing work and the abortive effort to establish a local branch was abandoned.

That was the last Gladstone heard about the association until he went to the meeting at Seebe a year later. Returning to his reserve, he immediately contacted Chris Shade and together they made plans to organize local chapters. In taking this action, Gladstone realized the sacrifice he was making. Already, the association was looked upon as anticouncil and Cree-dominated. By becoming involved with this movement, he knew he would be re-opening all the old wounds which had taken so long to heal. There was the obvious association of his own Cree background with the Cree association. There was the suspicion that, never having been a chief, he was trying to get control of the reserve by other means. And there was a fear that he would try to undermine the tribal council. His involvement would set him apart and make him different from the traditional members of the tribe. Ever since his daughter had gone to the Coronation, the acceptance of the Gladstones had been almost universal; now he was knowingly taking steps that would destroy the favorable relationship that he had worked so hard to establish. His reasons were deeply rooted.

Far more important than his own comfort was a commitment he had made to himself as a young man, and to the Bloods in 1920 when he promised that he would work on their behalf. He always remembered the words of Heavy Shield: "When you grow older, be sure you help us and not the white people." In his mind and heart he knew that the association was good for his people, even if tribal jealousies made it anathema to the Bloods. He had been to the meeting at Seebe and realized that many reserves had common problems which could best be solved through unified action. If to take this course he was to revive old antagonisms, well, so be it.

Once the decision was made, Gladstone did not shy away from controversy. In the summer of 1945, for example, he learned Ottawa officials were encouraging the cancellation of Blood grazing leases so that the land could be used for farming purposes. The theory was that the land could be worked by young Indian farmers but upon investigation, Gladstone determined that neither the tribal council nor the Indian Department had any money available to get them started.

When a meeting was called at the Black Hall to discuss the matter, Cecil Tallow and Jim were there but, apart from the tribal council, the session was not well attended. A number of federal officials waited outside until the question was resolved. It was apparent to Gladstone that the councillors were indifferent to the matter, that they had already made up their minds to do what Ottawa was asking.

Tallow observed that they would never get anywhere with the attitude of the councillors. But Jim suggested that someone ask the officials waiting outside in the car if the councillors had the power to grant a lease without the consent of the band.

When Charlie Good Rider put the question to C. P. Schmidt, the inspector for Alberta, he gave a negative answer. Gladstone then argued that the council could neither approve nor reject a lease without the consent of the band. Later, he arranged for the officials to come inside the hall where they repeated the information and added that there were not enough present to vote on the question. Later, the leases were renewed for five years with provision for an increase in the acreage fee.

The action did not endear Jim to some members of the council, although he did receive constant support from Joe Bull Shield, John Cotton, and Fred Tail Feathers, who were lifetime councillors. However, even his old friend Percy Creighton was angry with him for disputing the chiefs.

Later, one of the government officials spoke privately to Jim, asking why he had opposed cancelling the leases; Gladstone responded by questioning how young farmers could start to work without financial help. When no answer was forthcoming, Jim made an alternative suggestion that the horse range at the north end of the reserve be leased for farming purposes and that the income from it be used to launch new farmers. He later expressed this idea to members of council and to the new superintendent, Ralph Ragan, and was gratified a few years later when the lease was made. According to one journalist, "The new era for the Bloods began breaking during the winter of 1947–48 when Jim Gladstone, a successful farmer and cattle rancher on the reserve, came to Superintendent Ragan with the proposal that some of the band's surplus land be leased to white farmers for agricultural purposes."[2] The funds, while not being used to start young farmers as Gladstone hoped, did become the first step in breaking the chronic economic malaise which had gripped the reserve for so many years.

The first meeting on the Blood Reserve in an attempt to form a local of the IAA occurred on February 13, 1946, with interested persons gathering to choose an executive. Because of their large population, the Bloods decided to form two locals, one at Standoff and the other at the Old Agency. At the Standoff meeting, Chris Shade was chosen president, with Gladstone as secretary and Percy Creighton as director. Those attending were largely the old crowd—Joe Bull Shield, Charlie Davis, Emile Small Face, Cecil Tallow, Tom Eagle Child, John Cotton, Dick Soup, and a number of their children. Both Lucy and Horace Gladstone were there with their mother. The other local elected Fred Weasel Fat as president, Steve Wadsworth, secretary, and Ben Strangling Wolf as director.

Among the matters discussed that winter by the two locals were school holidays, high school education, the permit system, a new community hall, farm loans, old age pensions, mineral rights, no land surrender or enforced enfranchisement, no allotments of land, Indian veterans' grants, the status of an irrigation canal which might cross the reserve, cattle for young ranchers, the need for revision of the Indian Act, and for a royal commission to enquire into Indian problems. In the spring, the two groups met jointly, approving eight resolutions and eight delegates to go to the annual conference at Hobbema. They were allowed to send one registered delegate for every ten paid-up members.

When they went to the conference, Gladstone was the unofficial leader of the delegation. Friendly and outgoing, he soon made friends with other members from the north and was admired for his knowledge of Indian matters and for his ability to listen to the problems of others. When the Bloods were welcomed to the opening session, he was asked to respond, and when the resolutions were submitted from his local, he was the only one from his group to speak. The others, inhibited by the meeting, chose to remain silent and to leave the discussions to their more voluble spokesman.

Of the eight Blood resolutions, three dealt with hay permits, land surrender, and cattle for young ranchers, and were restatements of the information given to John Blackmore two years earlier. Another asked that children in residential schools be permitted to go home once a month, while a fifth opposed the legal allotment of land to individual Indians. The remainder involved changes to the Indian Act.

"I am keenly interested in education," Gladstone told the meeting as he spoke on the school resolution. "We find that when our children leave school they have become so accustomed to the institutional form of life that they have to be broken into family life as a new experience. Much of the influence of the home is gone."[3]

As for hay permits, he explained there were some families who had no cattle, but they made money by putting up hay for sale. However, the Indian agent wanted to be sure there would be enough hay to feed the band herd all winter, so he would not give permits to sell hay until the needs of the reserve herd were assured. Sometimes this meant that hay makers had to wait until mid-winter before they could sell; in the meantime, they had no other source of income. "The Blood Reserve is one of the best hay-making centres in the province," said Gladstone. "Surely the hay industry should be encouraged and a man should be able to sell his hay just as a grain farmer can sell his grain at harvest time." [4]

Besides speaking on his local's own resolutions, Gladstone joined freely in the remainder of the discussions. He spoke out against the oppressive powers that the Indian Act gave the superintendent-general of Indian

Affairs, asking the meeting, "Who is the better protector of the people, the House of Commons or one man, the Superintendent-General?" He advocated a system of rotating loans, so that young farmers could get started and repay their loans directly into the fund as their crops were harvested. It was similar to the idea expressed to Ottawa officials in making the lease on the Blood Reserve.

The whole conference was an exhilarating experience for Gladstone and when the Blood delegation was preparing to leave, he said, "We, of the Bloods, sincerely hope that the Indian Association of Alberta will continue the good work it has been doing and we assure the delegates of our continued support."[5] There was no concern at the meeting about Gladstone's status, racial origin, or position in the community; he was accepted as a treaty Indian, the delegate from the Blood Reserve. He felt a kinship for people like Peter Burnstick, Mark Steinhauer, Dan Minde, and Johnny Crier. They were progressive men from other reserves who saw things the way he did and they respected his opinions. In fact, his impact upon the meeting had been quite significant; not only was the association pleased that the Bloods were finally with them, but Gladstone proved to be a man with the kind of leadership capabilities that could unite the north and south. The hostility between the Cree and Blackfoot-speaking tribes was well known, but he appeared to be a catalyst that could turn them into a single united voice. Accordingly, although it was his first meeting, Gladstone was chosen to be one of the directors to serve on the executive of the association.

There was no doubt that the organization already was becoming effective on a national scale. Together with the Native Brotherhood of British Columbia it was a major political force, largely through the efforts of John Laurie and Malcolm Norris, in carrying out an incessant letter-writing campaign to members of parliament, newspapers, and other supporters. Such organizations as the Alberta Federation of Home and School Associations, Women's University Club, Alberta Council on Child and Family Welfare, and the B.C. Society for Indian Arts and Crafts all had pledged their support. Also, where the Indian Department had once ignored the association, it now sent its top officials to attend their annual meetings and to meet with them.

When Douglas Harkness was elected as Conservative member for Calgary East in 1945, he became the unofficial Indian Affairs critic for his party. Much of his material was provided by Laurie, which meant that the Liberal party in power could not afford to ignore the association's resolutions or requests for information. However, support was not limited to one political party, for both the Social Credit and Co-operative Commonwealth Federation received data as well. John Blackmore of Cardston (SC) and G. H. Castleden of Yorkton (CCF) both became useful allies in the struggle for native rights.

Within a relatively short time, a number of improvements occurred in the condition of Canada's Indians and in most cases the association could claim at least partial credit. These included the extension of widows' allowances, blind pensions, and family allowances for Indians. In Edmonton, an old army hospital was converted into the Charles Camsell Indian Hospital to serve tubercular patients.

Then, in 1946, the government announced that it would establish a special joint committee of the Senate and the House of Commons to "examine and consider the Indian Act . . . and to suggest such amendments as they may deem advisable, with authority to investigate and report upon Indian administration in general . . ."[6]

One of the first actions of the committee was to have its liaison officer, Norman E. Lickers, send an enquiry to all bands and organizations in Canada, asking them to submit their comments on several specific topics. The Blood locals of the IAA immediately drafted their replies, which were submitted through the association. About two weeks later, the chiefs announced that Lickers' letter would be discussed by them at an open meeting to be held at the Sun Dance. They had no intention of letting the Blood locals usurp their role as spokesmen for the reserve.

"Aloyisius Crop Eared Wolf was reading Lickers' letter," recalled Gladstone, who attended the meeting, "but wasn't translating it properly. He was trying to put in his own opinions, so Tom Eagle Child walked up and tore the paper right out of his hands and said, 'Why don't you read it properly?' Aloyisius had been against our association from the start; he was one of those who called us the Cree Association. So Tom took the paper and read it properly. Each point was discussed and the answers put down for each point."

Gladstone took the minutes of the meeting and then prepared the document, which was signed by the chiefs. Their answers to the specific questions were short and to the point. Treaty rights: "To be kept according to Treaty No. 7." Band membership: "Not to be changed as [now] written in the Indian Act." Taxation: "Not acceded to by the tribe." Enfranchisement: "We are not in favor of enfranchisement, either voluntary or involuntary." Right to vote: "We are not in favor of voting in Dominion Elections until further consideration." Trespassing: "We do not want white persons to be encroaching our Reserve." Education: "We do not want day schools. We are in favor of Residential or semi-Residential Schools, and these schools provided with qualified teachers at all times. And that any student of these schools who desires or attains the educational standing for higher education be permitted to go at the expense . . . of the Government, and more grants provided for each pupil attending these schools." Social and economic conditions: "Yes, we have other matters and suggestions to make . . . pertaining to our advancement and welfare, such as Education, Health, Housing, Agriculture,

Finances, and other needs . . . . The band fully agrees to have delegates attend before the Committee and will take up other matters such as to amend and revise the Indian Act . . ."[7]

After the letter had been submitted, the chiefs gave the matter further consideration and decided to hold another meeting among themselves. They also asked Jim to attend.

"This meeting was called by Shot Both Sides in Jim White Bull's tent beside his house at Standoff," said Gladstone. "I went in and sat down. They could not get a chairman for their meeting, so John Cotton nominated me to do it. I said I would not accept unless every councillor present agreed to it. I did this because the first two questions affected my position on the reserve [i.e. treaty rights and band membership]. They all agreed so I acted as chairman and secretary. I took the Indian Act and read them the sections relating to each question. I translated everything into Blackfoot and they answered each of the questions, which I wrote down. In the end, they answered the first six questions the same way as our brief to Ottawa. The last two, dealing with education and welfare, they deferred until another time."

When the Indian Association of Alberta had collected comments from all its locals, its letter of submission was not much different from the one that had come from the Bloods. Because of Laurie's literary talents, the presentation was more verbose, but the essential thrust was the same. The major difference was that the association probed more deeply into the social and economic sphere, seeking better housing, improved health care, development of resources on reserves, and training of Indians to work for the Indian Department.

When word came that the Alberta delegation would testify before the joint committee in Ottawa late in April, 1947, the government agreed to pay the expenses of three Albertans—two being official representatives and one unaffiliated—but others could come as observers if the IAA wished to incur the expense. The spokesmen were John Callihoo and John Laurie, while other delegates were Bob Crow Eagle, Frank Cardinal, Albert Lightning, Mark Steinhauer, Dave Crowchild, and Ed Hunter. Teddy Yellowfly from the Blackfoot Reserve was invited as the unaffiliated representative. The executive then decided that a delegate also should come from the Bloods, so the local was notified to select someone.

"St. Paul's school was having its annual reunion at this time," said Gladstone. "I knew there was going to be an association meeting and on Monday I was going to drive there in the pickup truck. There were two gas drums on it and the boys were busy so I just rolled them off onto the ground. When the second one fell, it hit a pickaxe which flew up in the air and hit me on the forehead. The boys saw the accident and took me to the hospital where I had four or five stitches put in."

He was resting at home when Joe Bull Shield and John Cotton came to take him to the IAA meeting. Joe would not believe that he was hurt, so Jim took three aspirins to relieve the pain and went to the school. A number of people had already gathered in preparation for the ex-pupils' reunion so, in order to clarify the purpose of the session Gladstone told them that this was an association meeting and anyone who wanted to vote on the choice of a person to go to Ottawa would have to buy a membership card.

"Some of them got up and said it was just a trap to get them to join the Cree association," said Gladstone, "but quite a number of them bought cards. Five were nominated, Joe Bull Shield, Frank Red Crow, Chris Shade, Albert Many Fingers, and myself. I won on a secret ballot. I then got up and said I wouldn't go alone, as I wanted everyone to believe me when I got back. Mrs. Rosie Davis got up and Mrs. Dick Soup after her to say that the only person who could represent our tribe in Ottawa was the head chief. I said I would be proud if the chief could go and I offered to put up fifty dollars to help pay his fare. Chris Shade offered fifty, which would have paid for his fare both ways. But nobody else would chip in — not even those who had wanted the chief to go. He didn't have any money, so we had to take another vote to see who would accompany me. In that vote, Joe Bull Shield beat Frank Red Crow by one vote."

On the following day, with his head still bandaged, Jim left with Joe to catch the train in Calgary. Once there, they were surprised to meet Cecil Tallow, who decided at the last minute that he would like to come along at his own expense. Besides, his daughter Jennie was in Sault Ste. Marie, Ontario, and he could visit her. So the journey was a pleasant one, and while John Laurie nervously checked and rechecked his papers, Jim and the others sat back and enjoyed themselves. This was the first time that Gladstone had ever been to eastern Canada, but as he was going only as an observer and was not expected to speak, he had no real worries. Because the addition of Joe and Cecil was unexpected, no rooms had been set aside for them in Ottawa and, with racial discrimination being a reality, nothing was available at any of the nearby hotels. At last, with Jim along, they got rooms at the YMCA and from there they walked to the immigration committee room where the joint committee was meeting.

Although Gladstone was there only as an observer, he could not resist rising to speak when the regional supervisor's report made reference to the importance of farming and ranching. Checking himself, he was just sitting down when the chairman noticed him and requested that Jim stand up and speak.

Suddenly overcome with nervousness, Jim stammered out his concern about haymakers on his reserve. He complained that those without farms were not permitted to sell their hay until mid-winter, as the government wanted feed available for the band herd in case they had bad weather. He believed this to be unfair and wanted to see the permit system abandoned. However, as he was not an official delegate, his comments went unrecorded.

The trip had its amusing sidelights. On their way back, Joe, Cecil, and Jim stopped at Sudbury after having visited Jennie at Sault Ste. Marie. It was evening and they had four hours to wait for the train, so they decided to go to a beer parlor. Both Jim and Cecil were of fair complexion and Joe was dark, with the typical features of a Plains Indian. When they sat down, the waiter asked Joe if he had a blue ticket.

"What's that?"

"If you can't show a blue ticket I can't serve you."

"Well," responded Joe, looking at his two friends, "if I can't drink then neither can these two guys here as they don't have blue tickets either."

After the waiter had kicked out all three of them, both Jim and Cecil scolded their comrade, saying that if he had kept quiet they would have brought some beer out to him. Just then, Joe noticed another hotel in the distance and suggested that the boys go and buy a case of beer. But they both laughed and said he'd already had his chance.

During this period, Gladstone still devoted much of his attention to farming. Association work was important but occupied only a fraction of his time. As a director, he had no responsibilities other than attending executive and general meetings and encouraging the active support of the association on his own reserve.

At the end of the war, he had found it hard to get help on the farm, particularly in the fall, as the Indians in the area had discovered that good wages could be made picking fruit or hops in the state of Washington. In fact, Jim's daughter Lucy moved down there for a number of years, while for two summers, Gladstone himself went down to pick apples and hops.

To overcome the labor problems, Jim bought a big International Harvester threshing machine, the first privately owned one on the reserve. At the same time, Chris Shade bought a heavy-duty tractor, so the two of them teamed up to do custom work. In the meantime, Fred mixed calf roping with his trucking business, while Horace concentrated on the farm.

By 1947, Gladstone's children were scattered. Nora was employed as a nurse in Victoria, B.C., and Doreen had gone to New Zealand to practise midwifery. The youngest, Pauline, was at Alberta College in Edmonton taking secretarial training, while Lucy lived in Tieton, Washington. Only Janie and the boys were at home, Fred being married with a family of his own. He still considered rodeo to be his first love and in 1948 he brought honor to himself and his family when he became the calf roping champion of Canada. In rodeo circles, he was liked and respected as much as his father was in the Indian political sphere.

Jim Gladstone was always protective of his family and that, combined with alcohol, provided an unusual sequence of events in 1946 that saw him end up in jail. Nora was home on holidays and had gone with her parents to visit relatives in Pincher Creek. While at the home of Helen Tourond, Jim's sister, they started to drink beer and when they were ready to leave, Gladstone realized that he was in no condition to drive. Nora had been taking driving lessons although she did not yet have her license, but as she had not been imbibing, she volunteered to get them home. However, she had driven for only a few miles when she lost control at a curve, hit the guard rail and overturned in the ditch.

When the police came to investigate, Jim claimed that he had been the driver; he did not want Nora to get into trouble. Accordingly, he was arrested for driving while intoxicated and sentenced to seven days in Lethbridge jail. Later, when he told a policeman what had really happened, he was informed that if he had been truthful, his daughter would have gotten off with a warning. He was so determined to help his children that he would go to any length to protect them. The accident also had long-term effects, for Gladstone suffered a minor spinal injury and, while it did not bother him at the time, it became a source of pain in later years.

In 1948, the joint committee concluded its hearings and after due consideration, it made a number of recommendations to the House of Commons. The IAA agreed with many of the points, such as the establishment of a treaty claims commission, giving women the right to vote in tribal elections, improving welfare assistance, and appointing an Indian as assistant deputy minister. However, it objected to the recommendations that Indians be given liquor privileges off their reserves and that they receive the federal vote.

The liquor suggestion was rejected by one Alberta faction because it went too far and by another because it did not go far enough. The Methodist-based Stoneys said, "Liquor is entirely harmful and contrary to the laws of Christianity,"[8] while Joe Bull Shield said, "If we could have beer in the beer parlour why cannot we have it at home? If a man takes a drink in a beer parlour and drives home, he may break a law and have a charge of drunken driving."[9]

Gladstone was politically neutral on the issue, clearly favoring more relaxed liquor laws but preferring to see a concensus from IAA members, not just from the executive. "The majority of opinion on our reserve," he said, "would prefer to be allowed to do their drinking in their homes and not in the beer parlours. We must consider this problem from all angles."[10] In the end, the recommendation was rejected by the executive, but not before Gladstone had gained the ill will of both Callihoo and John Laurie for his proliquor comments. Laurie in particular was vehement on the subject, insisting that the matter of liquor not even be discussed at association meetings. While Gladstone saw liquor rights as a step towards equality which was fraught with potential dangers, Laurie saw it as a means towards destroying the Indian race.

Similarly, Laurie believed that the suggestion of Indians obtaining the federal vote was simply a way to introduce taxation, which would ultimately lead to the dissolution of reserves and the end of any special status for native people. Certainly the undertone of the joint committee's recommendations supported this concern. It spoke of reserves becoming municipalities in their respective provinces, and that "all officials dealing with Indians [should] assist them to attain the full rights and to assume the responsibilities of Canadian citizenship."[11]

The 1949 general meeting of the IAA was held at Cold Lake, in the far northeast part of the province and, because of the distance, no Bloods or Blackfoot were present. A handful of Stoneys and one Sarcee, David Crowchild, were there, the latter being a personal friend of John Laurie, who had driven up with him. The only representative from the Blackfoot nation was Bob Crow Eagle from the Peigan Reserve. "I attended the General meeting," he later reported to the Bloods. "It is a long way north east of Edmonton but the invitation was so sincere that I went feeling that we would be welcome and it so happened we were very pleased with the way we were treated."[12]

The association had already protested to Ottawa about some of the recommendations made by the joint committee but now the whole matter was in the hands of the Department of Justice which, in collaboration with the Indian Affairs Branch, was drafting a new Indian Act.

The Bloods sent only one resolution to the 1948 IAA meeting: this reinforced a previous association stand and reflected the adamant position of the tribe. It asked that the "Association again go on record as being completely opposed to any form of voting in federal elections, provincial elections, or municipal elections on any basis whatsoever."[13] It was carried unanimously.

In spite of his failure to attend the conference, Gladstone was re-elected as a director. Bob Crow Eagle believed it was time for a meeting to be held in the south, so he offered to host the next annual conference on the Peigan Reserve. Until that time, no such meeting had ever been held on a reserve in the Treaty Seven area. When the offer was accepted, the Blood local met jointly with the Peigans, at which time Gladstone and four others donated five dollars each to help with expenses while all agreed to take extra tents and bedding for visitors. In order to raise more money, the Blood local sponsored an Owl Dance and basket social.

The southern Alberta tribes were well represented at the 1949 Brocket meeting, and they saw Gladstone at his best. From the outset, he was speaking to motions, recommending amendments, and even acting as prime mover of resolutions where the sponsoring local was not present. His own local submitted five resolutions, including two which were intended to transfer authority for estates and divorces from the government to the tribal council.

Early on the second day, the election of officers was held by secret ballot. When the results were counted, James Gladstone had defeated Callihoo and had become the new president of the association.

Callihoo had led the organization since it had been formed in 1939. Highly respected in the north, he had welded the Cree reserves together in a unity which previously had been unknown. In particular, he had been able to overcome the differences between the reserves in the Edmonton area and those at Saddle Lake, and laid the foundation for a powerful organization. He worked well with John Laurie, leaving all aspects of lobbying, publicity, and political strategy to the Calgary school teacher while he visited reserves and urged people to support the association.

However, since the strain of making the 1947 presentation in Ottawa, Callihoo's strength had begun to ebb. Laurie observed, "I really believe that he was, in the most un-Indianlike fashion, relieved to hand over his duties to Mr. James Gladstone."[14] He was, at the same time, unanimously elected as honorary president of the organization with Gladstone being among those who arose to pay tribute to his many years of service.

As Jim took the gavel and chaired the remainder of the general meeting, it became apparent that Callihoo's feelings were not entirely those of relief. Rather, he considered the action in part to be a rejection of his leadership and he was particularly unhappy with Gladstone for having ousted him. He believed it was more than a coincidence that he should be defeated the first time a general meeting was held outside his own treaty area.

Gladstone and Callihoo always got along well, but both were leaders and under no circumstances could Callihoo relegate himself to become a follower. Rather than contest the issue, he was more inclined to limit his active participation in association business to its periodic meetings. In fact, the role of honorary president rested well upon his shoulders. "He never lost his interest," commented Laurie, "but was quite content to relinquish the responsibilities of office but remained always the senior statesman and advisor."[15]

If John Laurie was sad to see Callihoo depart, he was more than apprehensive about Gladstone's election. The two men got along together and there was no question of open discord, but there were a number of basic differences. Gladstone was an open, outgoing, friendly man who often won people over by the force of his own personality. He got along equally well with Cree or Stoney, Blackfoot or Sarcee. He was not intimidated by officials and had a friendly personal relationship with many of the government people in Alberta. He was able to separate government policy from the men in the field who had to enforce it and saw no reason to exclude them from his circle of friends. He was comfortable with the press, able to express himself well, and tended to accept people at face value until proven wrong. He also enjoyed drinking and, while it was not a serious problem, every time he took a sip of whiskey or a bottle of beer, he was breaking the law.

Laurie, on the other hand, was a Calvinistic bachelor whose daily life was governed by hard work and a strict code of ethics. He was honest to a fault, completely dedicated to his work with the association, yet always conscious that it was an Indian organization which should reflect the wishes of the Indians. He seldom took part in discussions, but was busily engaged in writing minutes, guiding the executive on rules of procedure, and helping locals to properly phrase their resolutions. If he did have a strong personal opinion on a matter under discussion, he was likely to let his feelings be known to friends Dave Crowchild or Ed Hunter; if either agreed with him, that person was capable of carrying on the public arguments. In this way, Laurie seldom appeared to be taking an active part in the deliberations.

His role was largely one of organization. There can be no question that the association would have failed had it not been for Laurie. People like Callihoo and Norris had been excellent in unifying the native people, but Laurie's genius and persistence turned a well-meaning group of Indians into a viable political force. His use of the press, members of parliament, and sympathetic white organizations gave the group a level of influence that often far outweighed the number of its paid-up members.

He and Gladstone were both dedicated to the same cause, but Laurie tended to be suspicious of any government action and of its men in the field. They were The Enemy. Sometimes reflective and sombre, he was less open than Gladstone and limited his close friends to an intimate few, like Gerald Tail Feathers, Dave Crowchild, and Ed Hunter. He was also jealous of his standing with the press, and as long as Callihoo was president, there was no question as to who was the public spokesman. With Gladstone, however, he was not so sure.

There was also another area of concern on the part of Laurie, one that is difficult to pinpoint. Laurie was a romantic—that is what drew him to the Indians in the first place. In his writings, he glorified the symbolism of the tall warrior clad in buckskin, or the Mountain Stoney living in harmony with nature. Callihoo, although a mixture of Cree, Iroquois, and French, was typically Woodland Cree in appearance and possessed many of the characteristics which at that time were associated with Indianness: his English was limited and was delivered with a Cree accent; he was dark-complexioned, and spoke with an oratory which was simple yet expressive. He was the kind of person that Laurie could introduce to the press without a second thought. Gladstone, on the other hand, spoke perfect English, was fair-skinned and blue-eyed — nothing like Laurie's image of an Indian. It was almost as though he admired Gladstone but was embarrassed by his presence. Just as some of the Bloods were wary of Gladstone because he was too Cree, so did Laurie have private misgivings because he was too fair. It was not, of course, a conscious resentment but showed itself in subtle ways as the two men set out to work together for the betterment of the association.

CHAPTER TEN

PRESIDENT GLADSTONE

The first time I met James Gladstone was when he chaired a meeting of the Indian association executive in Edmonton early in 1950. I was a junior reporter who knew nothing about Indians and considered the assignment to be just another story. I had to do some checking around to find out where the association was meeting and finally located them in a church hall in a seedy part of Edmonton's Ninety-sixth Street.

There were only a few people in the room. My first impression of Gladstone was of a kindly looking old farmer who seemed to be running the meeting. Beside him was a white man who was busy taking notes, while sitting around were a few Indians in overalls or jeans. To one side were some women, mostly wearing dark clothes, kerchiefs covering their braids, and rubber overshoes pulled over their moccasins. Among them was a strikingly attractive girl who was obviously from the city. Only later did I learn that she was the president's youngest daughter Pauline.

As a neophyte, I was tremendously impressed with the way these seemingly uneducated Indians were conducting their meeting. This was my first lesson in understanding that wisdom should not be confused with education, nor knowledge with literacy. Over the years, I found this small group of native leaders to be among the most wise, sincere, and dedicated people I have ever met.

At the meeting, everyone was waiting for the new Indian Act. Already, unofficial word had filtered through that the Indians were not going to be consulted before it was tabled, so the association remained vigilant and ready for action.

"We can see the goal we want to reach," I heard Gladstone tell the members. "Co-operation will get us there. Let us not be jealous of each other, but all work for the welfare of all our people. We have done wonderful work in the past and we believe in the success of the Indian Association." He then suggested a motto: "Hold together, pull together, work together."[1]

By the time the meeting was over, I had become a convert. I had heard first-hand the problems the Indians were facing and the efforts they were making to redress them. As a reporter, I thought that my access to the news pages might help, so I offered my services. Both Gladstone and Laurie, aware of the need for press co-operation when the new Indian Act was introduced, readily accepted.

That was the beginning of a long and happy relationship with the Indian Association of Alberta — and the Gladstone family. On my trip to cover the annual meeting of the association, held on the Blood Reserve several weeks later, I was invited to stay at the Gladstone farm and, before the year was out, I was involved with the association and courting the youngest Gladstone daughter.

After the death of John Laurie, I had the privilege of acting as secretary of the Indian Association of Alberta for about six years. By this time, non-Indians were not allowed full membership so my participation was listed as unofficial and I was accorded the role of honorary secretary.

Meanwhile, Gladstone's supporters were enthusiastic about his election to the presidency. When they arranged for the 1950 annual conference to be held on the Blood Reserve, they were pleased to learn that even some of the chiefs were beginning to rally behind the new president of the association. Foremost among them were Percy Creighton, Albert Many Fingers, Frank Red Crow, and John Cotton. When the association announced it was "making strong representation asking the Government at Ottawa to give the Indian Chiefs and Head men of Alberta the right to review the new Indian Act before it was made Law,"[2] the chiefs applauded the move.

Yet there were others who saw Gladstone's leadership of the IAA as another indication of his Cree background and a reminder that he had not been born on the reserve. Already there were rumors that the new Indian Act would allow for the expulsion of certain people from the band rolls and in anticipation of this happening, three members of the anti-Gladstone faction from Standoff prepared a petition to have him kicked out.

As Arthur Healy explained to members of his local: "I attended a meeting of Local No. 1 on 29th March at their Community hall as I heard that there was a movement going to ridicule the I.A.A. and make it disband. I know there were three non-members present at that meeting who were gunning at our Secretary, Jas. Gladstone, and trying to get signers to petition to have him expelled off the Reserve. Now I call this persecution. When these three persons found that they could not succeed, they left the meeting."[3]

Joe Bull Shield was equally angry at this attack on his old friend and "cautioned those who are going around with a petition about having a member of the Band expelled off the Reserve without any reason. It looked like defamation of this person's character. He told them to do these things openly and not behind a man's back."[4]

So now it was out in the open. Ever since his grandfather had brought him to the reserve to give him a chance to get an education, Jim had been an outsider to some. His legal status as an Indian and his tireless work on their behalf made little impression on his detractors. In their eyes, he was someone who had become rich on their land, while they were still poor. As long as he had stayed poor and quiet, his past was ignored, but his involvement with the Indian association had placed him in the spotlight and the ugliness began to surface.

For example, Jim's daughter Lucy had overheard a neighbor, to whom her father had given food and shelter, accusing Gladstone of getting rich at the expense of the Bloods. The neighbor added that Gladstone was a trespasser and should be kicked off the reserve. Lucy was quick to defend her father and sharply reminded the man that he had not hesitated to ask for Jim's help when he needed it and that he had never been refused. The other children experienced similar problems, often at school, but they loved their father and admired him for ignoring his detractors.

But now Jim was worried and upset. He knew he had treaty status but he also was aware that the government had ejected some Indians from their reserve farther north because of questions regarding the status of their ancestors. His home was the Blood Reserve, his children were there, and it was the only life he knew. After all those years of drifting, he thought that the problem had been resolved once and for all in 1920. Now his opponents believed they had found a legal way of getting rid of him.

Gladstone put up a good front, telling Laurie, "I am not at all alarmed about it. I am carrying on as usual as I know the chiefs are satisfied with me."[5] That was true but he was still worried. What more did he have to do to prove himself? The chiefs and most of the people had accepted him, so why wouldn't the others leave him alone?

Over the next few weeks, more and more friends dropped around to say they were behind him. Among them were a number of chiefs who told him he had nothing to worry about. Then he began to hear stories that no one would sign the petition and that his three detractors had abandoned the attack, at least until the new Indian Act had been passed. So Jim breathed a sigh of relief, but he knew the matter was not over.

The long-expected Indian Act was finally tabled in the House of Commons on June 7, 1950, during the dying days of the session. Entitled "Bill 267, An Act Respecting Indians," it was quickly fired across the country by friendly members of parliament, who were appalled by its contents. Obviously, the government hoped to push it through before the House recessed for the summer.

Members of the IAA executive were equally shocked. In the bill, every decision of importance had been left to the discretion of the minister of Citizenship and Immigration or the governor in council. As Gladstone feared, the minister had the power to expel people from their reserves if their status was in doubt. Also he could dispose of a band's capital or revenue funds without the consent of the Indians; enfranchise and dispose of entire Indian bands; and arrest persons engaged to press claims against the government on behalf of the Indians. "You should see the terms of the proposed new Act," Laurie wrote. "Its only equal is the miscegenation laws of the deepest South."[6]

The bill failed to provide for the gradual extension of self-government to Indians; failed to guarantee the continued recognition of Indians as Indians; failed to ensure Indian hunting and fishing rights; and failed to honor the intent of the treaties.

When Laurie received his copies of the bill, there was no time to call a general meeting or even to consider the matter at a local level. As soon as the document's contents had been analyzed, he phoned Gladstone and David Crowchild to plan a course of action. Within hours, the association had telephoned, wired, or personally contacted about fifty non-Indian groups and individuals, urging them to telegraph or airmail their protests to Ottawa. The press immediately responded to word of the demonstration and soon news was coming from other parts of Canada that groups like the Native Brotherhood of British Columbia were equally dissatisfied. In the House of Commons, such men as Douglas Harkness, John Blackmore, John Diefenbaker, M. J. Coldwell, H. W. Herridge, and J. A. Charlton arose to point out the native protests and to add their own opposition as well.

During this period of feverish activity, Gladstone took home a copy of the bill and called an emergency meeting of the two Blood locals. The members on the reserve were upset by the powers that the proposed act was placing in the hands of the minister, and wired their protest directly to Ottawa. Similarly, Crowchild called a meeting of the Sarcees so that they could register their dissatisfaction.

As a result of the swift and organized action, Bill 267 was hastily withdrawn after its first reading. The minister then announced that time would be given for Indian groups to study it and to recommend revisions before it was presented at the next session of the House of Commons. The Indians were jubilant over the victory. They hoped that never again would the government try to ramrod through the House something dealing with Indians without consulting the people themselves; they had become a powerful political force.

Laurie was still fearful that the government would re-introduce the same bill at the fall session, so each local and each tribal council was urged to consider the document during the summer. Early in August, the Blood council asked Gladstone to attend a meeting with them to review the bill and to select three chiefs who would accompany him to a special conference which the IAA had called. At this time of crisis, all differences between the association and the chiefs were set aside. Acting as interpreter and spokesman, Jim led the chiefs through Bill 267 step by step, explaining the legal clauses and reducing them to basic language.

The part that personally concerned Gladstone was a provision for a new band list to be implemented as soon as the legislation was passed. For six months after that date, any ten members had the right to protest the inclusion of a name on the list if that person, or an ancestor, had accepted half-breed scrip or had become enfranchised. Jim had never received scrip and the application of his mother on behalf of his brother or him had been rejected. However, his mother had taken scrip herself, so his status under the proposed legislation was unclear. However, the Blood chiefs rejected the whole idea of a new band list, thus knowingly or unknowingly supporting their recalcitrant interpreter.

On many of the other clauses, the chiefs also agreed with the association, except that they wished to have the minister's discretionary powers placed in their hands, while the IAA wanted to eliminate the clauses entirely. The Bloods and Gladstone had a harmonious meeting, with Joe Bull Shield, Albert Many Fingers, and Mike Eagle Speaker being chosen to represent the tribe at the later conference.

During August, Gladstone called three general meetings of the association to consider the proposed Indian Act. The first was held in Calgary on August 10, and included representatives from the Blood, Sarcee, and Stoney tribes. A week later he held another session in Calgary with a large representation from Cree reserves as far north as Goodfish Lake, Chipewyans from Cold Lake, and local leaders from the Blackfoot, Peigan, Blood, Sarcee, and Stoney tribes. Then, in the following week, he chaired another session at Hobbema with a good turnout of Crees from all over the province, as well as some Chipewyans, Sarcees, Stoneys, and Bloods. By the time the marathon sessions were over, the IAA had heard the opinions of more than fifty chiefs and councillors from across the province, as well as from numerous members of the association.

Most of the delegates were happy with the decisions made at the meetings. The only word of protest came from John Callihoo who accused Laurie of deliberately neglecting his reserve's wish to retain a clause in the bill which permitted an entire reserve to enfranchise if it wished. Laurie replied that Callihoo's band would have its minority opinion registered and told the honorary president, "We have gone too far to forget that brothers often disagree. Such a disagreement does not need to last forever. I hope you do not think that I influenced opinion in this matter."[7]

As a result of the sessions, the association compiled a list of all the revisions that it wished to see and, in a covering letter, explained why Bill 267 was unacceptable. When the House of Commons reassembled in September, a copy of this letter and the revisions were placed on the desk of every member of parliament. Shortly afterwards, the minister, Walter E. Harris, announced that Bill 267 would not be re-introduced but that he and his associates would travel across Canada to hear evidence from the various Indian bands and organizations.

There could be no question that a decisive battle had been won with the Ottawa bureaucracy, but not the war, for it was far from being over. And in many ways, the fight was not with the politicians as much as it was with the entrenched civil servants who had, for so many years, carried out programs with callous disregard for Indians as people. Even though they often denied it, Indian Affairs officials still considered Indians to be their wards who were "not ready" for responsibility. In individual instances where a person was progressive and responsible, then clearly he should be removed from treaty status to take his place in Canadian society.

During the late fall of 1950, Harris wrote to Indian councils and organizations all across Canada, visited reserves, and tried to obtain some concensus about proposed legislation. Realizing that the most organized opposition came from the prairies, he arranged for a meeting to be held in Winnipeg in late January to personally meet with some of the leaders. For the IAA, President Gladstone, Dave Crowchild, and John Laurie were invited to attend.

Following his usual practice of having a Blood Indian—preferably a chief—accompany him to any official meeting with Ottawa officials, Jim called for a meeting on his own reserve. His purpose was twofold. On one hand, having a member of the tribal council with him would avoid the gossip that he had done anything which would adversely affect the tribe, while on the other, it enabled him to maintain the delicate balance between his own leadership of the association and the local authority of the chiefs. He knew his opponents would enjoy blaming him if parts of the Indian Act proved to be repressive or if the authority of the chiefs was in any way diminished. His detractors were a small vocal minority, but they could always gain a sympathetic ear if their gossip was exciting enough or if there was any suggestion that Gladstone's actions were more beneficial to the Crees in the north than to the Bloods.

The meeting called to choose Jim's travelling companion was held in Cardston where it was presided over by Frank Red Crow, a chief and an association supporter. Several other chiefs and a large turnout of members were on hand to hear Gladstone explain the significance of the Winnipeg trip and of picking a delegate they could rely upon. Albert Many Fingers, a chief who had been to the earlier discussions, was elected by a large majority. At the same meeting, fifty-eight dollars was raised to help pay his expenses and a resolution was passed objecting to the expulsion of women from treaty status when they married non-Indians.

When they arrived in Winnipeg, Gladstone and the Alberta party had a long session with Harris and members of his staff. The minister indicated that a new Indian Act would be submitted during the winter and while he could not reveal its contents, he told Laurie, "The Indians of Alberta will not have the vote forced upon them against their will, and there does not need to be any change in the liquor laws for the Alberta Indians."

The minister also said that the IAA would have a chance to comment on the new bill before it was passed through the House of Commons. True to his promise, Harris invited nineteen representatives of Canadian Indian associations and councils to Ottawa on February 28, 1951, so that they would be there the day after the bill received first reading. Among them were the elite of Indian organizations across Canada: William Scow and Peter Kelly from the Native Brotherhood of B.C., Andy Paull from the North American Indian Brotherhood, James Gladstone and John Laurie from the Indian Association of Alberta, John Tootoosis from the Union of Saskatchewan Indians, and John Thompson from the Indian Association of Manitoba. Others represented individual bands, mostly from the Maritimes, Ontario, and Quebec. The IAA also had two observers—Crowchild and Many Fingers.

When Gladstone and Laurie received their copies of Bill 79, they compared it clause by clause with the discredited Bill 267. They were elated to discover that many of the more abhorrent sections had either been removed or rewritten but were chagrined to learn that the other sections remained unchanged. During the next four days, they participated actively in the meetings as Indians from each area of Canada brought forth their particular concerns.

The IAA was the best prepared and presented the greatest number of objections to the new bill. In some they were supported by other areas but for many they stood alone. The entire conference agreed to oppose provisions relating to income tax and the necessity of waiving exemption in order to gain the federal vote. The majority also disagreed with Section 112, which had existed in Bill 267 and provided for involuntary enfranchisement. The IAA won limited support for other questionable clauses, such as opposition to certificates of possession whereby an Indian could have legal title to a portion of the reserve, and to the surveying of reserves without band council approval. However, they did not receive a majority.

By the time the conference had finished, the Ottawa officials had been able to obtain unanimous approval for 103 sections of the bill, while only 6 sections – mostly dealing with liquor – were rejected by a majority vote, and two were unanimously condemned. More important, however, was the fact that fully three quarters of the objections registered by the IAA to Bill 267 had been remedied in the new bill.

Later, John Blackmore read Gladstone's comments to the House of Commons, including the statement that "the Indian has to be educated before Bill 79 can be applied in its entirety. . . . It may take a generation. We want to be Indians, always Indians, even though we gradually take full responsibility as Canadian citizens."[8]

From a personal standpoint, Gladstone was disturbed that the clause providing for expulsion of Indians from treaty lists had stayed in the new act and his opinion was strongly supported by other members of the association. They were not concerned for Gladstone alone, but were afraid that the clause would encourage a witch hunt. Any ten members of a band who disliked someone could sign a petition and cause a hearing to be held, even if they had no concrete evidence.

When the bill went to committee, the minister refused to acknowledge that the association's concerns were real. "There is one further objection made by the Indian Association of Alberta," he told the committee. "It was stated that this section would lead to a great many petty complaints by one Indian against the other and there would be efforts made by Indians to remove other Indians from the present band list and that therefore in order to avoid that unpleasantness we should freeze the lists which are now in operation and say that everyone who is on the list, on the 1st of April, 1950, should automatically remain on not subject to appeal as provided for in the section."[9] Harris went on to state his rebuttal, commenting that "while we were not going to engage in any kind of witch hunt we should not close the door so that anybody who is not properly on the list today should be able to remain . . ."[10]

The day would come when the Liberals would rue that decision.

However, when the new Indian Act was passed, President Gladstone and the association had good reason to be proud. As Jim told a meeting of Indians shortly after his return, the IAA had been largely responsible for the Ottawa conference and for bringing about several changes in the proposed Indian Act. Their nation-wide publicity campaign, the support of white organizations, and the influence of members of parliament all combined to give it a power base which previously had been unavailable. It proved to be the most notable achievement of the decade and would remain for many years as the organization's finest hour.

At the 1951 general meeting of the IAA at Goodfish Lake, President Gladstone reported that Ottawa now considered the association to be the spokesman for all Alberta Indians. While British Columbia and Saskatchewan had been represented at the Ottawa conference by more than one organization, Alberta had come to the meeting united. In order to live up to the responsibility, the president continued to concentrate on organizational work, leaving the lobbying to the competent Laurie.

Although the Blackfoot had been involved with the IAA during its early years, the local had fallen apart. However, Gladstone's old friend from coal-mining days, Clarence McHugh, managed to reactivate the group and went with delegates to the Goodfish Lake meeting. That left only the far northern part of the province without representation; but opportunities of organizing in those remote communities were limited because of lack of funds and contacts in the region.

The situation changed dramatically during the summer of 1951 when the association received a letter from a fur dealer at Little Red River, complaining about the way Indians were being treated and offering to pay the air fare for someone to come north. After some investigation to make sure that the dealer was of good character, the visit was endorsed by the local priest at Fort Vermilion and by the Indian superintendent. The latter, who was the subject of the complaints, commented that "The people of this Agency need leadership and strength in the worst sort of way. They are divided to the extent that they have no strength and it is earnestly hoped that your visit may give the Chiefs and the Band some of the strength which will go a long way in helping them to adjust themselves to the rapidly changing conditions of this country."[11]

Gladstone was enthusiastic about organizing the north, so his leather suitcase—which was receiving frequent use these days—was again packed by Janie and he was soon off to the land of bush and muskeg. Arriving at Fort Vermilion in mid-August, he was met by J. P. Sewepagaham, chief of the Little Red River band, and one of the most respected leaders in the district. From the airport they went to a meeting which had been called to form a local of the IAA. Acting as chairman during nominations, Gladstone explained the system of voting and choosing delegates, then saw George Cortorielle elected as local president.

One of Gladstone's greatest gifts was his adaptability. As soon as he reached the northern community, he settled in and felt at home, even though the land was entirely strange to him. Miles of unbroken forests and muskegs offered only a few isolated patches where farming was possible. Log houses along the shores of the mighty Peace River marked communities from which the men spent much of their time on their traplines. Moose meat and bannock were standard fare, while in the nearby trees the huge Arctic ravens let the prairie visitor know that he was far away from home.

But to Gladstone, being comfortable meant being with people he knew and liked. He quickly made a number of friends in the Fort Vermilion region, both Indian and white. He took what accommodation and food were offered and settled easily into sleeping in log cabins and going to the mission house to hear the grievances of the association's newest local.

He determined that there were three main problems in the district. The first had been a misunderstanding of the Indian superintendent's directive regarding debts. Because trapping had been good that year, the superintendent was afraid that some of the Indians would splurge their earnings and forget the debts they had incurred with local traders. However, the message was misinterpreted, leaving many Indians believing that they did not have to pay their debts. Confusion continued even when the superintendent posted a notice that "an Indian is a bad Indian if he does not make an effort to pay his debt."[12]

The second problem related to the inadequacy of schools in the district. The Fort Vermilion school was overcrowded, so the Little Red River group wanted one on their own reserve. They also objected to any of their children being sent "outside" to Grouard to attend residential school. The third problem revolved around the hospital at Fort Vermilion and conflicts with the superintendent. Accordingly, the local passed a resolution "that our present Doctors are giving perfect satisfaction to us and on no account should the Doctors be interfered with by anybody and that the Indian Agent should not obstruct them in their duties at any time."[13] They asked that an airplane be furnished immediately in cases of medical emergency "and not in two or three days time."[14]

Gladstone called for an open meeting at the mission hall to explain the purposes of the association. Besides the Crees from Little Red River, there were Beavers from Eleski, and visitors from Fort Vermilion in attendance. After the discussion, the Beavers invited Gladstone to the north side of the river where they showed him an area they wanted to develop for farming, but complained they could get no help from the government.

The president heard numerous personal complaints: a man who had been denied a trapline, a woman who wanted her child back from residential school, and the problem of the Indian superintendent making promises which he could not keep.

The problems were quite different from those experienced by the prairie-dwelling Indians, who were concerned with farming leases and cattle herds, but during Gladstone's years with the association he had become familiar with the northern concerns for traplines, hunting, and game regulations. The difficulties with Indian agents and residential schools were matters that he had coped with in his own life, so he could easily identify with the complaints.

After visiting the superintendent, the local priest, and some of the traders, Gladstone returned south to see what he could do about their problems. The first person he saw was George Gooderham, who was in charge of all Indian agencies for Alberta. Formerly the Indian agent on the Blackfoot Reserve, Gooderham was known to be a fair man who sometimes got into trouble with Ottawa because of his obvious sympathies for the Indians. Gladstone had always gotten along well with the man and was able to gain a sympathetic ear on the problems of the Fort Vermilion people. After hearing about the complaints, Gooderham promised to send an investigating team north to get at the root of the matter. While the difficulties were not solved through the one trip, the Little Red River group now had a voice through the IAA which it used regularly over the next few years. Not only that, but the association could truthfully say that its influence extended from the extreme south to the far north and was completely provincial in scope.

CHAPTER ELEVEN

ACTIVE YEARS

The new Indian Act had not yet been proclaimed when Gladstone's troubles surfaced. As he feared, the men who had tried to expel him a year earlier had seen a copy of the act and decided to press their complaint. This time, instead of circulating a petition, they sought the services of a Lethbridge lawyer, M. E. Moskovitch. Not only was he to look into the expulsion of Gladstone, but they wanted to press charges against the superintendent and the whole tribal council for letting certain clauses appear in the new act. They were particularly opposed to certificates of possession, which entitled a man to have individual title to a portion of the reserve. These Bloods had seen how a similar policy of allotment in the United States had resulted in the breaking up of their reservations.

The lawyer took a $200 deposit from the three disaffected Bloods and then called a meeting on the reserve to discuss their grievances. Gladstone, who had heard about the troubles, was present with the head chief, the Indian superintendent, and a number of councillors. Moskovitch opened the meeting by explaining the clauses of the new Indian Act and then asking Chief Shot Both Sides if the terms were acceptable to him and his council. The chief nodded. Later in the meeting, evidence was provided which showed that Gladstone and the IAA had been unalterably opposed to the certificates of possession and had carried their fight all the way to Ottawa. Gladstone's status was never mentioned.

"After the meeting," said Gladstone, "Mr. Moskovitch asked me what I thought of the gathering. I replied that what he had done had vindicated the work of the Indian association in their endeavor to have their way of life continued, even though we realize that, at some long further date, we shall eventually be forced to accept the white man's. I thanked Mr. Moskovitch for his advice to his clients."[1]

The meeting so discredited the protestors that they abandoned all efforts to press their case against Gladstone. In fact, the whole confrontation became a comic opera. After the meeting, the lawyer told the protestors that the chief and Indian superintendent had nothing to do with the drafting of the Indian Act and there was no way they could press charges against them. Angered and humiliated, the trio demanded their $200 back, but Moskovitch said that the money was for services already rendered. Had he continued to pursue the case and worked on the Gladstone matter, it would have cost them another $800.

At that point, the Bloods looked around to see who could help them get their money back. Who else? Gladstone. One of the trio went to the man they had so recently attacked and asked him if he could write a letter to Ottawa, forcing the lawyer to refund their money. Patiently, and not without amusement, Gladstone explained there was nothing the government could do; if they really thought they had a case, they should hire another lawyer to sue Moskovitch.

Under the circumstances, there was little likelihood that the men would press their case against Gladstone personally, but just to be on the safe side, he wrote to the minister of Indian Affairs in Ottawa, telling him about the incident. "All my life I have striven to be an asset to my reserve rather than a burden," he said. "I have always tried to use my influence to lead my fellow tribesmen to make their own living and to get a better education for their children."[2] Privately, he wrote Laurie that "I am the one they are after but I am proud of the fact that insofar as they are concerned it is all jealousy and the support I have from the intelligent ones gives me the determination to carry on."[3]

During the six months after the act was proclaimed, Gladstone was on tenterhooks in fear that his status on the reserve might still be protested, but the petition was never prepared. When the deadline passed, he knew that he would never again have to worry about his legal status as a Blood Indian. Perhaps he would still be criticized and villified by his opponents, but he had a tough skin and could withstand their jabs. Over the years, he had become more and more positive of his role as a Blood and felt less need to defend himself. If people wanted to criticize him for working with the Crees, or being a prosperous farmer, or raising a successful family, he would not worry about it.

As the Indian association had predicted, however, the expulsion clause became a perfect weapon for Indians to re-open old arguments or to resolve intraband quarrels. On the Blackfoot reserve, a petition was signed against the Solway and Cayenne families, one of those facing expulsion being an organizer of the IAA. Before the matter could even go to a hearing, eight of the ten protestors asked to have their names removed from the petition, claiming that they did not understand what they had signed.

At Hobbema, the situation was more serious. The first information about the problem came in a telegram to Gladstone just as he was leaving to visit his daughter in Victoria. "The band has on the Samson Reserve," wired Dan Johnson, "started to expel Indians from the reserve."[4] Not only was Johnson an active member of the IAA, but he was one of the men being protested. Gladstone contacted Laurie in Calgary and advised Johnson to organize a protest against the expulsion.

According to information that later came to light, the protest had been filed because of a two-family feud. As one reporter observed: "The Hobbema reservation had divided into factions when two Indians, Antoine Saddleback and Billy Samson, had quarrelled over a horse. An Indian RCMP scout, Dan Johnson, was sent out to investigate the original quarrel. No sooner was the new legislation in force than ten Indians, led by Saddleback, asked that 103 other members of the band be driven from the reserve where they had lived all their lives."[5]

The petition claimed that two families, the Johnsons and Lightnings, were descendants of three common ancestors who had taken half-breed scrip and had been admitted into treaty in 1901. As such, said the petition, none of these men's descendants had any right to have his name included in the membership lists. Although only three men were affected in 1901, their descendants numbered 103 and would increase to 118 before the case was finished.

The Indian association supported the persons being protested and contacted Calgary lawyer Ruth Gorman, who had previously done work for the association. She agreed to take the case and began to gather information for a hearing which would be scheduled as soon as a registrar had been appointed and material prepared by the government for the defense. This did not happen until the spring of 1954, by which time considerable support had been gained for the Hobbema cause. The hearing itself proved to be extremely informal. The ten men who had signed the protest admitted they had no evidence to support their petition; in fact, one of the signers later learned that he was protesting the inclusion of his own mother and, incidentally, himself.

With no firm conflicting evidence at hand, the registrar halted the action and informed the Indians they could remain on their reserve. This was taken to mean that the case was over, but it proved to be only a postponement. When it resumed it became the source of considerable embarrassment to the Liberal government which had introduced the clause into the 1951 Indian Act.

But that was in the future.

During the period while the new Indian Act was coming into force, Gladstone devoted almost all of his time to organizational work. He turned his share of the trucking business over to his son Fred, who also did most of the farming between engagements in his rodeo career. The rest of the children were pretty well on their own. The youngest, Pauline, who had graduated from Alberta College after being featured as the year-book "cover girl," was a secretary for Indian Affairs in Edmonton. She and I were dating regularly after our first casual meeting and it had developed into a full-blown romance. Doreen had married a New Zealander and after an extended visit home, she was on her way back to her husband's homeland. Her departure was most keenly felt, as the distance made visiting virtually impossible. Nora, on the other hand, continued nursing in Victoria from where she made regular trips back and forth to Alberta. Similarly, Lucy was living in the orchard country near Tieton, Washington, where she was within easy reach of the family.

Of the boys, Horace had built a house across the road from the family home and was farming on his own. He had married a girl from the Blackfoot Reserve and was beginning to raise a family. Fred lived in the old house next door to the main residence; he had married a non-Indian girl some years earlier and had a growing family of two girls and one boy. Fred's son, first born in that generation of the reserve clan, was named James, after his grandfather.

At fifty-five years of age, Gladstone was contented with his life. His emphasis on education for his family had paid dividends, even though he was sad that his daughters had been forced to find their livelihood away from the reserve. Yet there was little opportunity for them if they had stayed at home. Nor did he wish them to experience the problems faced by their schoolmates who had stayed on the reserve, or to face uncertain futures as day laborers or welfare recipients.

His was a sacrifice which he felt was necessary for the future of his children; he wished that Janie had understood, but she could never accept the fact that most of her children had chosen to marry off the reserve. Yet the bond within the family remained strong, and there was seldom a day when there was not a letter, if not a visit, from one of the children. And at Christmas, most of them managed to come for the holiday.

The Christmas season was usually a happy one for the family. The first time I was down to the reserve for the yuletide holiday, Pauline and I were already thinking seriously about marriage. Her circle of friends had become mine, with Irene and Gerald Tail Feathers being among our closest companions. In addition, our Sundays were spent visiting Indian tubercular patients at the Charles Camsell Hospital and my interest in native history was beginning to flower. People like Jack Black Horses and Albert Wells spent many hours telling the legends and traditions of the Blackfoot nation.

So it was only natural that I should be invited to the Blood Reserve to celebrate the holidays with the Gladstones. Pauline and I left Edmonton after work on Christmas Eve and drove my old 1941 Ford on the seven-hour journey to Cardston. On approaching the farm, the whole place was ablaze with lights, and from a mile away we could see the reflection from the windows as they shimmered across the frozen snow. Coming closer, we passed some of the Gladstone cattle huddled together near the shelterbelt, their backs encrusted with snow.

When we pulled up to the back door, there were a half dozen cars and pickup trucks already there. As we pounded the snow off our feet in the porch, Pauline's folks came out to give us a hearty greeting. Everybody had been drinking but no one was drunk; they were just boisterous and happy. Fred and Edith were visiting from their little house next door, while Doreen and her New Zealander husband were among the well-wishers.

It was well after midnight when we went into the living room where people were already opening their presents. As someone who always had had to wait until Christmas morning, the idea of opening gifts at midnight was something new for me. But it was all part of the gaiety that rang through the house.

I was taken upstairs and given a comfortable room under the eaves; it used to belong to Pauline. Other people were scattered throughout the remaining four bedrooms in Jim's house and the two at Fred's. Next morning the women were up early, getting the turkey ready. Fred had already been out looking after the cattle and was now doing the chores. I was awakened by the radio which was turned on about 7 A.M. and blared throughout the house. I was a city boy and when I got up, I found that everyone else had eaten hours ago. Only Pauline had waited so that I wouldn't have to eat breakfast alone. Then her dad and I sat in the front room, listening to the radio and visiting. Over all our years together, we never had any problem in finding something to talk about. We took to each other right away and in many ways he seemed like a father to me. We could discuss with equal ease Indian problems, history, current politics, or even make small talk about the weather. I enjoyed listening to him and soon came to admire the range of his knowledge and his down-to-earth philosophies.

By suppertime the house was crowded with kids and adults. Most of the Gladstones were there with their spouses and children, and there were a few other guests as well. There was Janie's sister Suzette Eagle Ribs and her brother David with his family, while later in the evening there were visits from neighbor Harry Mills and his son Buster, who sometimes worked at the farm.

The meal itself was a grand spread—turkey, dressing, potatoes, giblet gravy, vegetables, pickles, and all kinds of pies and cakes. The children ate in the kitchen but even then the dining room table was crowded with food and people. As master of the house, Pauline's dad said grace and carved the turkey, everyone passing their plates to him. He remarked how Janie's father used to serve flaming plum pudding on such occasions but nowadays people preferred to drink the brandy rather than burn it.

After supper, we piled into two or three cars and went to the dance at the Bullhorn Hall. The shortest route was down the old highway but as this was often drifted in during the winter, we took the long way around. As we approached Bullhorn Coulee, we saw pickup trucks, cars, and even a few sleighs and saddle horses heading in the same direction.

Two big dances were held during the holidays. The one on Christmas night was sponsored by the Magpie Society—a group of young men in their twenties—while the New Year's Eve dance was put on by the Horn Society, the secret religious organization on the reserve. Both were pow-wows, featuring prairie chicken dancing, owl dancing, and the various kinds of round dances, chiefs' dances, and honoring dances, all to the beat of several drumming groups which were at the hall.

It was a strange sight for me, but a familiar one for the Gladstones. There were almost fifteen hundred Bloods jammed into the converted air force building, most people having brought their own folding chairs. We found a place with the Bull Shields and Tail Feathers, and soon Jim was busy talking politics with his old pals. In the meantime, the women greeted each other while Pauline and I got together with Gerald Tail Feathers and Irene.

Most of the dances, such as the prairie chicken, are done by individuals, but periodically the drum beat changed and the owl dance was featured. For this, people danced as couples, with the women asking the men to dance. A man wasn't supposed to dance with his wife so Pauline's dad was usually seen with Dorothy Bull Shield or one of his other "near relatives." About midnight, the Magpies started bringing out the food—bologna sandwiches, pop, cookies—and to give away gifts to visitors. Some received blankets while others got dollar bills. I noticed that Pauline's dad gave the announcer a fistful of bills, designating the visitors from the Blackfoot Reserve that he wanted to honor.

Somewhere about 2 A.M., when the dance was still going strong, we pulled out for home. We knew the drumming would continue until sunrise but we were all tired. We hadn't seen a drunk all evening and must have shaken hands with two or three dozen people. During the whole time when he wasn't dancing, Pauline's dad was visiting, talking politics, and listening to people and their problems.

During this Christmas visit, I also learned something about the mother-in-law taboo. I was not yet a member of the family, but saw how Janie tried to avoid her New Zealand son-in-law. I was told that custom forbade a mother-in-law from speaking to her son-in-law. The practice was no longer strictly enforced but Janie still felt uncomfortable with Max. For the same reason, I found her friendly but hard to talk to; she would chatter away to her daughters-in-law but there was always that cultural barrier between us. It was the first of many lessons on how the Gladstones had successfully found that fine balance between Indian and white.

During my visit with the Gladstones, I learned that Jim was pleased with the way the Blood Reserve was progressing. His suggestion during the winter of 1947–48 that the north end be leased for farming had received the enthusiastic endorsement of the tribal council and had resulted in 36,000 acres being made available in 1949. Within three years, annual production from the lease—described as the largest grain field within a single fence in the British Commonwealth—was valued at more than one million dollars, with one third going to the Bloods' revenue fund.

Encouraged by the income from these leases, the council had made a further lease in 1952 of 7,300 acres near St. Mary's River, where white farmers agreed to break the land and farm it for three to five years. After that time it would be turned back to the tribe so that individual Indian farmers could settle on it. During the period of the lease, the tribe was receiving payments of more than $50,000 a year.

These funds were being put to good use. Interest-free loans were being made available to farmers and ranchers; a seed-cleaning plant was built on the reserve; interest-free houses were being constructed; and water wells were being drilled at strategic locations throughout the reserve. For the first time in many years, the Bloods had money to improve their own lot. And it had all started with Gladstone's idea for the big lease.

It was apparent to me that the IAA and the welfare of his tribe were his life. By the time Pauline and I left the farm and turned north again to Edmonton, I had come to understand more fully both the man and his goals. At sixty-five, his zeal was so contagious that I offered to do whatever I could to help. I learned that he had a good working relationship with secretary John Laurie, although at times he found the man to be exceedingly suspicious in his dealing with governments. For example, early in 1952 the federal Old Age Pension scheme had been extended to include Indians over seventy years old, but old age assistance for the sixty-five to sixty-nine year age group was a responsibility of the provinces. Enquiries from the IAA indicated that a cost-sharing arrangement with the federal government had not yet been worked out but an announcement would be made as soon as a decision had been taken.

Suspiciously, Laurie pressed the minister of Public Welfare for an immediate answer and when one was not forthcoming, he wrote directly to Premier E. C. Manning. As it happened, the delays were occurring because of a dispute over the wording of the agreement, but on the instructions of the premier, top priority was being given by his officials to resolve the matter as quickly as possible.

When the IAA general meeting assembled on the Blackfoot Reserve in mid-June, Laurie assumed that the provincial government was being obstructive and so he announced to the gathering and the press that "the Province of Alberta has so far refused to grant old age assistance."[6] He also drafted a resolution which Dave Crowchild presented, attacking the government for its "punitive laws and all restrictive regulations."[7] On the second day of the conference, Laurie phoned Edmonton to see if there were any new developments and learned that Old Age Assistance would be given to Indians retroactive to January 1. When he made the announcement at the meeting, there was jubilation among the members, and reporters rushed forward to interview the elated secretary.

When the press reports appeared in the Calgary newspapers, Laurie was given credit for getting Old Age Assistance for the Indians of Alberta. The implication was that the Alberta government had been a reluctant participant in the federal-provincial scheme, but Laurie had won them over.

The premier was furious about the press reports. By this time, I was a publicity writer for the Alberta government and worked closely with people in the premier's office. When I heard what had happened, I wrote to Gladstone: "The Indians almost didn't get the old age assistance. Apparently an Order-in-Council was ready to go before the Executive Council at least three days before the IAA meeting, and Mr. Laurie's remarks at the convention almost made the premier tear up the bill."[8]

There was no question that Laurie was a devoted man. In ill health for several years, he had suffered a number of heart attacks and was constantly being warned by his doctor to slow down. Yet every minute that was not taken up with school work was involved with the IAA. He was indefatigable in writing letters to officials, executive members, and politicians. He kept up steady correspondence with Calgary MP Douglas Harkness and had a stream of Indian and white visitors to his Calgary bachelor suite. He did not try to impose his own ideas on the association—with the possible exceptions of liquor and voting rights. Normally he preferred to stay in the background, listening, advising, and handling the secretarial chores. The ideas, innovations, and decisions he left to the president and members of the association.

As for Gladstone, I soon discovered how much he respected Laurie and admired him for the work he was doing. As president, Gladstone knew how demanding the association could be, for he personally found time for little else. If he was not attending an executive meeting, he was being invited out to a reserve to a pow-wow, a sports event, or some other activity where he could promote the work of the IAA.

Mind you, he loved it. His job called for him to be with people and to speak about something he believed in. Quiet and soft spoken, there was often a twinkle in his eye as he told a funny story, or a hardening of the mouth when he discussed a particularly serious problem. While no longer dressing like a farmer, he still had a distinctly rural appearance, his three-piece suit unable to hide the windblown hair which was rapidly turning white, the leathery face with the lines becoming more deeply etched, and the powerful hands which were evidence of a lifetime of hard work.

As he sat talking politics, a cigarette was constantly in his mouth or between his fingers. He had a habit of stroking his ear while he talked, making one lobe longer than the other, and because the hand usually had a cigarette in it, his hat had little scorch marks around its brim.

He walked slower now, but he still had a distinctive Gladstone gait, observed among other members of the family. He walked firmly but with a slight roll, his head cocked to one side as though he was listening to someone. And usually he was, for he seldom had to walk alone. If it wasn't Janie or one of the association people beside him, it was probably one of the children. He was warm and friendly with everyone but he reserved a particular place for his sons and daughters, whether they were talking politics, farming, fashions, or sports.

Meanwhile, my own relationship with Pauline blossomed and I proposed marriage. We were greeted with general jubilation on both sides of the family when she said yes. There were some questions as to whether the ceremony should take place on the Blood Reserve or in Edmonton, but we finally compromised with a wedding in the capital and the reception at St. Paul's School, August 31, 1953.

Along with my own family, the whole Gladstone clan was at the ceremony—even Fred who arrived late because of a rodeo. We then travelled south, where dozens of southern Alberta well-wishers turned out for a reception and dance. Many were from my father-in-law's past, others were Pauline's schoolmates, while a few were elders I had come to know through my studies in native history. It did not take me long to realize that I had become part of a close-knit extended family of brothers, sisters, aunts, uncles, cousins, and people whose exact relationship was uncertain. That is a wonderful thing about Indian families— blood lines are less important than a mutual acceptance of someone as "family."

For example, Charlie Reevis and his wife were introduced to me as relatives from the Blackfeet Reservation in Montana. When I tried to pinpoint the exact relationship, no one was quite sure, but Charlie was said to be definitely closer than a distant cousin. When I asked Charlie, he said that Jim Gladstone was his son. This confused me completely.

In later years the story gradually became clear to me.

Shortly after the Gladstones had started farming, an Indian named Bobtail Chief had been injured when he was dragged by his horse. He could not work, but Gladstone hired him for the winter and looked after him while his body mended. In the spring, Bobtail Chief was visited by his brother, Charlie Reevis, and when he learned what Gladstone had done, he adopted him as his son. He was only about fifteen years older, but the relationship was taken seriously by both parties and persisted over the years.

Barely a month after Pauline and I were married, tragedy came to Gladstone when his old friend Joe Bull Shield died suddenly of a heart attack. Joe and Jim had been inseparable since Joey had been brought to St. Paul's school as a frightened child. Jim had protected him at first and then in turn had been befriended by old Bull Shield, Joe's father. For Gladstone, the little waif from outside, the Bull Shield family gave him his first real sense of belonging to the reserve. And over the years Joe had never questioned Jim's right to be there; rather, he vigorously defended his friend whenever there were questions about his status.

Gladstone had loved Joe like a brother and, together with Cecil Tallow, they had been through many hard times and adventures. Now, he and Cecil had the painful experience of being pallbearers and saying farewell to a man who had been a friend, chief, fellow Anglican, and firm supporter of the association. It would never be the same without Joe.

Back in 1951 during the Ottawa conference, the minister had promised there would be a review of the Indian Act in about two years. Nothing more was heard about the matter until just after Joe's funeral when Gladstone received a telegram saying that the session was scheduled for later in October. Many of the people who had attended the earlier meeting were now asked to re-assemble to determine how the act was working. Laurie was the other approved delegate from Alberta.

Within a matter of days, Gladstone had called a meeting on the Blood Reserve and, as in 1951, the tribe chose Albert Many Fingers to accompany him. This time, no collection was required, as the council agreed to pay all the expenses. Times were changing.

The short notice caused most Indian organizations to go to Ottawa unprepared; only the IAA had had a series of meetings earlier in the year in anticipation of such a conference. In particular, the association wanted the involuntary enfranchisement clause removed from the act, certificates of possession abandoned, any offer of a federal vote withdrawn, mandatory land surveys left to the discretion of tribal councils, and a return to the definition of an Indian as provided in the old act. In almost every case, the unprepared delegates could not come to a consensus. The only matters that gained unanimous support were the questions of income tax and enfranchisement. At the 1951 meeting they had asked to have these two offending passages removed from the Indian Act, but nothing had been done.

"It was very clear from the beginning," said Laurie, "that the people of eastern Canada and of British Columbia had strong and different opinions from the opinions of the prairie provinces. We found that the representatives of the other provinces had three big points of difference from us: they want surveys and allotments; they want to vote in federal elections; and all, except one Ontario band, favoured that part of the Act dealing with Indian status. Your delegates put up your arguments to you. When the minister called for a vote of the delegates, we were defeated."[9]

The failure of the delegates to bring about any changes, particularly in the certificates of possession clause, was a setback for Gladstone as president. The organization had never suffered a major defeat in its various campaigns and although its resolutions sometimes had been ignored or its recommendations unheeded, its success rate was impressively high. Perhaps that is why so many locals were sure that the certificates of possession would be cancelled.

These certificates were a form of land deed, acknowledging the legal right of an Indian to possess specified properties within a reserve. In Alberta, most band councils had recognized an informal right of occupancy as long as an Indian was utilizing the land, but the entire reserve was considered to belong to the band as a whole. Aware of the precedents in the United States, where land allotments eventually led to clear title and the breakup of reserves, the Indians of Alberta were opposed to any move which appeared to be heading in that direction. They also were against surveying the reserves into quarter sections as they feared that the government might peremptorily order that the surveyed land be allocated to individuals and the reserves thus destroyed.

In the spring of 1954, when Gladstone began preparing for the annual meeting of the association, he heard persistent rumblings of dissatisfaction about the way matters had gone with Ottawa officials. Members were saying it was time for a change. Even internal matters seemed to be going sour as the association's entire funds, some $870, mysteriously disappeared and the treasurer was too sick to make an accounting. The money was all the association had to work with and as a result, expenses such as the printing of membership cards and other routine work were incurred only as new membership fees were paid.

The 1954 meeting was held on the Sarcee Reserve and was heavily attended by members from the southern reserves. One of the first resolutions was an angry one dealing with certificates of possession, requesting that "all such certificates be cancelled so that the lands of the Reserve may be held in common as previously."[10] As the conference continued, more and more resolutions were tabled, seeking changes in the Indian Act that the delegates had been unable to achieve during their Ottawa session.

When the election of officers was held, the dissatisfaction became open as Gladstone was challenged by his old friend Clarence McHugh from the Blackfoot Reserve. Clarence had served the previous term as southern vice-president and when the ballots were counted, McHugh had been elected as the new president. At the same time, his wife became the treasurer.

After five years, three national conferences and thousands of miles of travelling, Jim Gladstone was out of a job.

OUT AND IN AGAIN

As a seasoned politician, Gladstone took his defeat gracefully. He urged everyone, including his closest supporters, to continue working for the association, as he intended to do. He liked and respected McHugh, so he believed that the leadership was in good hands.

He put his defeat down to a number of factors. These included the failure of the Ottawa meeting, a lack of support from friends of the old treasurer who were embarrassed by the shortage of funds, and by a large turnout from the Blackfoot Reserve, who came to the meeting to elect one of their band.

But while Gladstone could easily accept the change of leadership, Laurie could not. The secretary had had disagreements with McHugh in the past and expected more difficulties in the future.

He did not have long to wait.

Before the meeting was finished, a number of Indians showed evidence of drinking. Although none of them came into the hall, Laurie heard about it and commented that he thought the Blackfoot were to blame. Later, when a Sarcee and two Blackfoot were arrested, he further complained that the Blackfoot were getting the Sarcee boys into trouble. When a number of delegates from the Blackfoot Reserve heard about the comments, they indignantly walked out of the sessions. McHugh was angry, but stayed in the chair until the meeting was over.

The real break between the two men occurred about two months after McHugh was in office. Laurie learned that Callihoo's reserve north of Edmonton was contemplating enfranchising all of its members and selling the land. Appalled, he sent an appeal to McHugh to go there to discuss the matter, but the trip was a failure and in Laurie's opinion, "McHugh made a mess of it."[1] Relations between the two men further deteriorated during the winter when Laurie claimed the president had used his position to bring about the transfer of the superintendent on the Blackfoot Reserve—a friend of Laurie's.

Then, near the end of April, 1955, McHugh received another call from Laurie to make a quick trip to a northern reserve. "When I got there," recalled McHugh, "I found it was a wild goose chase and on my return I found that Hon. J. W. Pickersgill, minister of Citizenship and Immigration, had been to Calgary and an IAA delegation consisting of John Laurie and Dave Crowchild had seen him. I'm convinced that John got me out of the area because he did not want me to see Pickersgill."[2]

With this type of bickering and in-fighting going on between the two senior leaders of the association, not much was accomplished. As the 1955 general meeting approached, Laurie bewailed the fact that "so pitifully few resolutions concern the good of the people as a whole in the province. . . . It is so discouraging. We always represented a minority, it is true, but in the last year or two, we seem, in my personal opinion, to have got the wrong few."[3]

During the year-long feud, Gladstone still supported the association but had time to turn his attentions elsewhere. No longer on the executive of either the provincial body or his own local, he had few meetings to attend; consequently he had more time with his family.

Gladstone spent many hours driving me around the Blood Reserve so we could visit the old patriarchs he had known for years. Jack Low Horn spent a whole evening telling of the reincarnation of his father; Bobtail Chief related his experiences as a young man; and even the head chief, Shot Both Sides, was willing to tell the white stranger about his war experiences as a youth.

It was obvious that Gladstone was a highly respected man. Everyone knew who he was, whether among the Bloods or on one of the other reserves in southern Alberta. And while we may have gone seeking historical information, the informants soon had Gladstone aside to talk about their problems and to see if he could help them.

By this time, Doreen had returned from New Zealand and was working in Vancouver, while Horace had become a farm instructor on the Blood Reserve. While he still carried on with some of his own farm work, he was beginning a long career in the public service.

By the time the 1955 general meeting came around, McHugh and Laurie had become completely alienated. The session was scheduled to be held on the northern reserve at Driftpile, bordering on the shores of Lesser Slave Lake. According to McHugh, northern vice-president Albert Lightning announced his intention of running for the top post and went through the camp campaigning on the night before the meeting started.

Normally, the first day of the two-day session was occupied with speeches and resolutions, with the election taking place on the second day. However, according to McHugh, Laurie called for the election on the first day and Lightning was victorious. "A lot of the southern delegates had not yet arrived," complained McHugh, "and in the voting everyone participated whether or not they were delegates. It was the votes of the non-delegates from Driftpile that gave Albert Lightning the majority."[4]

Gladstone attended the meeting, but with only a few southern delegates on hand, he decided to refuse nomination, rather than split McHugh's vote. In the end it would have made little difference as Lightning had a resounding majority. McHugh was angry at the "railroading job" and decided to pull out. Not only did he take the Blackfoot delegation with him, but the entire local was dissolved and remained inactive for the next six years.

The new president, Albert Lightning, was a long-time faithful supporter of the association. A member of Samson's band at Hobbema, he had served in various posts on the IAA executive and often acted as interpreter. He was intelligent, respected, and had the full support of Laurie. He also was a good friend of Gladstone's and although not as outgoing or friendly to the press as either of the two former presidents, he was dedicated to the Indian movement.

During McHugh's tenure, Laurie came to realize just how much he had depended upon Gladstone in the daily functions of the IAA. At times exasperated by late meetings, ineffectual leadership at the local level, and non-responses to their resolutions, Laurie tended to turn to Gladstone for constant advice and reassurance. Even after Lightning had been in office for almost six months, Laurie wrote to Gladstone: "In my opinion, only two men in Alberta fully understand the province-wide problems enough to represent anyone at an Ottawa conference—yourself and Mr. Callihoo."[5]

Gladstone's second year out of office was offset by his increasing activity at the local level. At his suggestion, the invitation was extended to hold the 1956 meeting on the Blood Reserve, which meant several weeks of feverish activity to prepare for the event. With Howard Beebe as local president and Gladstone now serving as local secretary, donations of ten dollars each were sought from all Blood members to defer the costs of the meeting. In addition, invitations were sent to the Peigans to bring extra tents and tepees and to act as co-hosts. As the convention date approached, the council agreed to donate a beef while potatoes were bought from St. Paul's at a reduced rate. Gladstone and Emile Small Face were delegated to pick up supplies for the meeting while others arranged for drinking water, tents, and other necessities.

At the general meeting, it was apparent that a new pattern of voting was beginning to emerge. Although McHugh had complained that Lightning gained office because of an early election, the fact was that Lightning was a Cree in an area where he was well known. Even without any manipulation, he probably would have received the presidency.

Similarly, when the 1956 meeting was held on the Blood Reserve, Lightning was a Cree now running for office in Blackfoot country. As a result, when Gladstone let his name stand for president, he had an easy victory over his opponent. Although the IAA constantly spoke of unity, tribalism was still strong; Blackfoot against Cree; Stoney against Blackfoot; and north versus south. It was a strange anomaly that some Bloods should refer to Gladstone derisively as *Sai-apikwan,* the Cree, but would solidly support him when faced by a real Cree.

A number of important changes had taken place on the national political scene while Gladstone was out of office. Walter Harris, the popular minister responsible for Indian Affairs, had been replaced by J. W. Pickersgill and, as Laurie commented, "He is not the man Harris is. We knew right away where Mr. Harris stood on any matter."[6]

One of Pickersgill's actions late in 1955 was to call a third conference to discuss the Indian Act. This time, however, he did not turn to the politically wise Indian organizations, but made the choice through various band councils. None of the three delegates from Alberta was actively involved in the province-wide movement and, like other delegates from across Canada, they endorsed most of the recommendations which were persuasively presented by Ottawa officials.

The revision that most disturbed Laurie dealt with the use of liquor. More liberal than the 1951 version, it made it possible for the provincial government to give Indians virtually unrestricted access to alcohol. As usual, Laurie and Gladstone were at opposite ends of the spectrum on the matter. Laurie believed that liquor privileges were a plot to destroy the Indian reserves, that they would be followed by the vote, allotment of lands, and the eventual thrusting of Indians into the mainstream of Canadian society.

Gladstone, on the other hand, saw the movement of Indians into Canadian society as a positive force, as long as it was at a pace set by the Indians themselves and permitted them to retain their distinctive identity. As part of this transition, he believed that the Indians should accept, or demand, those privileges enjoyed by other Canadians even if some, like liquor, appeared to be a questionable asset. As he told his vice-president, "I have been listening to the different conversations of Indians at different places, and the answer is usually in favor of accepting the law as it is amended. Sometime in the near future we will have to meet this problem."[7]

Gladstone was glad to be back in the presidential saddle, particularly after two years during which the association had gone through a period of malaise. He was in office for only two weeks when he got an urgent telegram to attend a meeting on the Saddle Lake Reserve. Happily he was off, driving first to Calgary to see Pauline and me. I had just accepted the position of archivist with the newly formed Glenbow Foundation and we were starting to get settled in our new home. After a brief visit, he went on to Hobbema where he stayed with John Samson for the night; next day the two of them proceeded north through Edmonton to Saddle Lake. The purpose of the meeting had not been explained in the wire, but when he got there, Gladstone discovered that he was the central attraction. In the preceding months, interest in the association had fallen off badly, so Mark and Ralph Steinhauer decided to have a meeting in an effort to encourage young people to support them. They chose that particular time as there was a stampede going on, and a large number of Indians from the Cold Lake and Kehiwin reserves were on hand. "The result," wrote Gladstone, "was that quite a few of the younger men & women . . . decided to join."[8]

By this time, Gladstone was the most famous Indian leader in Alberta and one who was well known in native circles across Canada. He was less familiar to the non-Indian population, as most of the publicizing work was handled by Laurie.

During Gladstone's absence from the presidency, the ugly situation at Hobbema had resurfaced. When insufficient evidence had been found in 1954 to expel 103 members of Samson's band whose common ancestors had purportedly accepted half-breed scrip, everyone believed that the issue had been resolved. However, the government persisted in its research into old records until it believed it had the evidence it needed. This consisted of documents supposedly signed by the men in question when they took scrip. The original ten protestors were no longer involved in the issue; the government itself was carrying on the vendetta launched by the petition.

The Indian association again rushed to the defense of the Hobbema victims and, through the efforts of Ruth Gorman, the IAA legal adviser, a case for the defense was prepared. However, late in 1956, the government-appointed registrar heard the case and found in favor of the protestors, ordering the expulsion of the Hobbema group, now risen to 118 through additional births. All but two of these people lived at Hobbema; all had been born there, and had received an average grade five education at the local residential school. The two absentees were a young man and woman, both in the Canadian armed forces in Germany.

Among those caught up in this net of bureaucratic intrigue was Albert Lightning, the immediate past president of the IAA. Like the others, he faced the threat of having his Indian status stripped away, his home taken from him, and his right to live on the reserve denied. His only hope, like that of the others, was to file an appeal within ninety days, at which time the matter would be referred to a judge of the court.

A number of developments had taken place on the national scene which ultimately were to become entangled in the Hobbema question. For one, the Liberal party had been in power for more than twenty years. Earlier in 1956, the great pipeline debate had occurred, during which the Liberals had invoked closure for the first time since 1913 in an effort to get the massive project started that year. During the debate, C. D. Howe became a perfect target for the Conservative opposition and when the bill was finally rammed through the House, the Liberals had gained the image of being arrogant, dictatorial, too long in power, and out of touch with the people. Later in the year, when Great Britain bombed Egypt, Canada's prime minister, Louis St. Laurent, was clearly on Egypt's side and was particularly angry because he had no prior knowledge that the attack would take place. However, he managed to keep his personal feelings to himself because of the strong British sentiment in Canada. Finally, when he was pressed by a Conservative to explain why Canada had interfered in the matter at the United Nations he could restrain himself no longer. "Because," he snapped, "the era when the supermen of Europe could govern the whole world has and is coming pretty close to an end."[9]

With its large majority, the Liberals sat back to weather the storm, confident that when the election came in the following year, its indiscretions would be forgotten and it would be returned to power. However, it failed to measure the mood of the country, which had been shocked by the callousness and insensitivity of the Liberal politicians.

The Conservatives, on the other hand, sensed the turning tide of public opinion and went for the Liberals like a pack of hungry dogs with a stag at bay. The selection of John Diefenbaker as leader of the Conservatives during this crucial time gave added fuel to the ambition and enthusiasm of a party which had been out of office for more years than most of the members could recall.

The Hobbema case, a perfect example of Liberal insensitivity and callousness, was tailor-made for the Conservative cause. Douglas Harkness, the Indian Affairs expert in the Conservative ranks, led a long and spirited attack, which was soon joined by the NDP and Social Credit members. On the receiving end was J. W. Pickersgill, the minister responsible for Indian Affairs.

Gorman obligingly delayed any action in filing an appeal, as the matter could not be reported in the press once it was before the courts. Soon there were headline stories across the country, questions in the House of Commons, and numerous letters and petitions from Indian and non-Indian groups protesting the actions of the government.

Albert Lightning travelled to many points in Alberta, telling women's organizations and farm groups why he was being expelled from his home. The *Calgary Herald,* a Conservative newspaper, carried front page stories day after day in January, 1957, recounting the latest developments, and then attacking the Liberals on its editorial pages. Even *The Albertan,* a Liberal supporter, found it necessary to question the expulsion.

The IAA gave its full support to the campaign, circulating petitions, raising money for the Hobbema Defense Fund, and speaking to the media. In mid-January, while the campaign was at its height, Gladstone called a meeting of the IAA executive which publicly condemned the government and explained that it had pointed out the dangers of the expulsion clauses even before the Indian Act was passed. At the end of the meeting, the association decided to send a petition to the prime minister, asking that the band membership clause be removed from the act.

Harkness's well-prepared attacks in the House of Commons were contrasted by Pickersgill's apparent obstinacy, which many people took to be arrogance. As the pressures mounted, the minister pondered aloud, "I have found it somewhat difficult to understand why this appeal was not entered immediately,"[10] while privately, efforts were made to press Gorman and her clients to launch their action. When they refused, the questions in the Commons and the newspaper headlines continued. Harkness accused the minister of "evading the question and evading the responsibility of the government" by continually falling back on the argument that that matter would be decided by the courts once an appeal was launched.[11]

The *Calgary Herald* used the debates to attack the Liberal party as a whole. "The present Liberal government," it said in an editorial, "apparently considered that a promise is only made to be broken at some future date providing it has a sufficiently large majority in Parliament to railroad it through, over the protests of the opposition."[12]

As the deadline for the appeal neared, another ploy was devised to keep the issue alive. At an IAA meeting, Howard Beebe made a motion, seconded by Walking Buffalo, that the queen be asked to intercede in the case. When the legal adviser dispatched a document to the governor general, asking that it be forwarded to the queen, it was sent instead to Pickersgill. When news of the action reached the House of Commons, there was an uproar. "Does the Minister of Citizenship and Immigration believe he is holding a pretty hot potato when he delays for 24 hours a message sent to Her Majesty the Queen by her subjects?"[13] asked a Conservative critic.

The *Herald* joined the outcry, claiming that the Liberal government acted as if "such words as principle, honor, decency and the sanctity of contracts and solemn treaties were no more than pawns to be moved willy-nilly over the chess-board of politics."[14] In demanding that the petition be sent to the queen it added that "somewhere, this basic right is being denied to the Indians and someone must be held responsible."[15]

It was, of course, all political rhetoric, but letters to the editor in both Conservative and Liberal newspapers indicated a strong public feeling of sympathy for the Indians. The expulsion itself gave the Conservatives almost a month to harass the government about its callous action, while the denial of the queen's petition seemed to strike at the heart of British justice. In the end, the petition to the queen was determined by the clerk of the House of Commons to be "irregular" as it was not addressed properly, bore no signature, and did not include a prayer—all required under the rules of order.

When the appeal for the expulsion case was filed by Gorman and a team of lawyers on February 5, 1957, two days before the deadline, the debate ended in the House of Commons. It was almost an anticlimax a month later when an Edmonton judge overruled the expulsion order and informed the Indians that they could remain as members of the Samson band. His decision was based upon a technicality dealing with the way the protest had originally been filed. To the 118 Hobbema people, however, the result was a relief and a victory, whatever the reason.

During the whole campaign, Gladstone had kept in close touch with the Hobbema people. Through his efforts the Bloods raised $100 for the defense fund—the most from any reserve in Alberta. "It's going to take a lot of money to hire an outside lawyer," John Samson told him. "If we lose this case here, the other reserves will be affected."[16]

One can speculate what impact the Hobbema question had on the Conservatives' surprising victory at the polls four months later, on June 10, 1957. Certainly it was a minor clash as far as national politics were concerned, yet it served as an example of Liberal arrogance and, when added to the other incidents of that period, helped to create the image of a tired and unfeeling government that had been in power too long. People could see the contrast with Diefenbaker's charismatic and personalized message to Canadians as he created his own visions for the country's future.

By itself the Hobbema debate had not accomplished victory for the Conservatives. But it had helped.

The Gladstone family leaving for town about 1937. In the wagon are Jim and Nora; standing in front are Horace, Pauline, Doreen, and Jim's brother Steve. (Gladstone Papers)

Season's Greetings
from Nin-aki.
1938-1939.

After her return from the Coronation in 1937, Nora Gladstone was photographed for this school Christmas card. (Gladstone Papers)

After Nora's visit to the Coronation, the Gladstones received a call from Ida Vandal, who also had made the trip. They are seen in front of the Gladstone house in about 1940. (Gladstone Papers)

Jim Gladstone and friends in front of the St. Paul's school. Left to right, front, Jim and Janie Gladstone and Joe Bull Shield. Back, Mr. and Mrs. Cecil Tallow and Dorothy Bull Shield. This was in the late 1940s. (Glenbow Archives, NA-3910-22)

Janie and James Gladstone, about 1941. (Gladstone Papers)

In 1946, the Gladstones gathered for a family portrait. Left to right, front, are Doreen, Jim, Janie, and Nora. Back, Lucy, Fred, Horace, and Pauline. (Gladstone Papers)

Joe Healy and his wife, Topitkini. (Gladstone Papers)

Fear and resentment spread through the Blood Reserve in 1917 when the government attempted to force the Indians to surrender part of their reserve. Here, an official reads the surrender proposals outside the Indian agency. Not trusting the government's interpretation, some leaders turned to Gladstone to translate the document. (Glenbow Archives, NA-1400-35)

Most of the early leaders of the Indian movement in Alberta were with this delegation which went to Ottawa in 1948. Standing, left to right, are Eddie Hunter, Frank Cardinal, Albert Lightning, Jim Gladstone, John Callihoo, Peter Burnstick, and Mark Steinhauer. In back are Dave Crowchild, Joe Bull Shield, and John Laurie. (Photo by Lorne Burkell, The Calgary Albertan*)*

Jim Gladstone presides as president of the Indian Association of Alberta executive meeting in Edmonton in 1950. Flanking him are Joe Bull Shield and Philip Soosay; immediately behind him is John Laurie. Former president John Callihoo is at the rear, second left. (Glenbow Archives, NA-179-2)

Gladstone addresses an evening meeting of the Indian Association of Alberta in 1955. Standing beside him is Albert Lightning. (Gladstone Papers)

TO THE SENATE

In late June, 1957, when Gladstone learned that the new prime minister, John Diefenbaker, would be attending the Calgary Stampede, he suggested that the IAA honor the political leader for the work he had done on behalf of the Indians.

Earlier, when John Diefenbaker was still a Conservative opposition member, he had spoken out on behalf of the Indians and had raised the suggestion of appointing an Indian to the Senate of Canada. The Indians did not have the federal vote, he said in 1955, and "They have no members in the House to speak for them. There are 160,000 of these first citizens in Canada, and I have often thought that one of the finest gestures this government could make would be to appoint a full-blooded Indian to the Senate of Canada in order that the views of the Indians might be expressed and Indians in general would have an opportunity of having a spokesman in the parliament of this country."[1]

The matter was mentioned again during Diefenbaker's election campaign, so when the Conservatives formed a minority government the question was soon raised in the press. Within a month of the victory, both Laurie and Harkness had written to the prime minister, recommending Gladstone for the appointment. At the same time, more names were being put forward from other parts of Canada.

Gladstone had no knowledge of these proceedings.

In the meantime, the on-again-off-again presidency of the IAA had taken another turn. Just a week after Diefenbaker's victory, the general meeting was held at Hobbema, where a Cree majority had triumphantly brought Albert Lightning back into the chair. Being honest, Gladstone was somewhat miffed by the results, as he had always counted on Hobbema's support in the past. Tribalism seemed to be becoming more and more of a divisive factor and he even wondered aloud whether the southern tribes should have their own organization. However, he quickly rejected the idea, for he was the first to realize that there was political strength in unity. One of the reasons that the IAA had been so strong was that it spoke for the province with a single voice. Saskatchewan, on the other hand, was divided into three warring factions, while British Columbia had one organization for the coast and another for the interior. So, in the end, Gladstone accepted his defeat gracefully and was mollified later in the conference when he was named as honorary president.

In this capacity, he had suggested the tribute to Diefenbaker and was pleased when arrangements were approved for a ceremony in the Indian village at the stampede. A scroll and painting were commissioned from Gerald Tail Feathers, a Blood artist, and Jim was asked to make the presentation. This raised an unusual problem, as protocol required that all ceremonies in the stampede village be done by Indians in full buckskin regalia. Being blue-eyed with grey hair that once had been brown and curly, Gladstone had always avoided Indian costumes, preferring to wear a business suit or work clothes. He did not even own an outfit, although his wife and daughters had costumes and participated regularly in pow-wows and native dances. Although he felt uncomfortable about it, Jim borrowed a beaded buckskin shirt, leggings, moccasins, and an eagle-feather headdress so that he could make the presentation properly attired.

He did not know it at the time, but the meeting clinched his appointment to the Senate. Diefenbaker told him in later years that as soon as he saw him and spoke to him, he knew he was the man for the job.

Three days later, the news was leaked from Ottawa that the selection of an Indian senator had narrowed down to three people. One was Gilbert C. Monture, a brilliant Mohawk Indian who had recently retired as chief of the mineral resources division of the federal Department of Mines and Surveys. He was strongly backed by a number of influential Conservatives in Ontario. The second was Andy Paull, for many years leader of the North American Indian Brotherhood. Hailing from Vancouver, he was a self-taught lawyer who had gained a nation-wide reputation for his defense of Indian rights. And the third was James Gladstone, Blood Indian rancher and farmer.

From the first, it was obvious that the Ottawa mandarins preferred Monture. As a career civil servant he had gained a world-wide status for his work in engineering and would be a distinguished candidate for the Senate. And, more important to senior officials, he had no direct involvement with Indian movements and had taken no active role in the long battle against the Ottawa bureaucracy.

Gladstone was surprised and delighted when reporters phoned to tell him that his name had been put forward. As he wrote to Andy Paull a few days later, "The very fact of being mentioned as a possible choice is a great tribute to the work of our Indian Association of Alberta."[2] In an editorial, the *Calgary Herald* voiced the same opinion; after praising Gladstone's leadership it pointed out, "It is in Alberta where the most recent and victorious battles on behalf of Canada's treaty Indians have been fought. The eyes of the whole nation were focused on Alberta earlier this year during the notorious Hobbema case. . . . It seems to us that Alberta's Indians have won, literally in battle, the right to this honor."[3]

During the interim before the appointment, and almost as though he was being groomed for a diplomatic role, Gladstone was one of ten Canadian Indians who received an invitation from the prime minister to meet Queen Elizabeth and Prince Philip during their visit to Ottawa in October of 1957. There was only one person from each province and when Jim reached Ottawa he learned that most of them had had no experience with city life, one representative being unable to speak English. Gladstone, with his relaxed style and friendliness, soon became the unofficial leader of the group. By signs, he communicated adequately with the non-English-speaking northerner and successfully led him through the maze of protocol.

Their schedule had called for the Indians to have a roadside seat where they would be able to see the queen during her parade through the city. However, after sitting in their places for a few minutes, Gladstone announced that if they stayed where they were, they would see Her Majesty for only a fraction of a minute; he intended, instead, to go back to his hotel room and watch the proceedings on television! Several other representatives thought it was a good idea, so they gave up their reserved places, pushed through the curious crowds, and made their way back to the Chez Henri, in Hull, where they saw the entire parade in the relaxed atmosphere of their own quarters. Later, they all attended an official reception at the Chateau Laurier where they were presented to the queen.

A staunch royalist, Jim loved every minute of it. He recalled to the press how his daughter Nora had witnessed the coronation of the queen's parents and how his wife had met the royal couple in Calgary. This, however, was the first time that he had ever been in the presence of royalty.

Rumors continued to fly during the winter about the Senate appointment, but whenever the matter was brought up in the House of Commons, Diefenbaker would give no direct answer. "I want to see an appointment made at the earliest possible date," was all that he would reveal when asked by Frank Howard, the NDP authority on Indian Affairs.[4]

Early in January, 1958, while attending an IAA executive meeting in Calgary, Gladstone, Pauline, and I visited John Laurie, whose deteriorating health had prevented him from participating in the gathering. All evening, Laurie seemed to have his own private joke; his eyes twinkled, he seemed to be on the point of saying something but would

then restrain himself, and smile again. It was an unusual performance
by a man who was normally restrained and somewhat reserved.

Four days later, Gladstone was still at our house when he received
a telephone call from the prime minister, asking him if he would accept
an appointment to the Senate. There was only one problem; the rules
of parliament required that a senator, upon appointment, must have real
property free of all encumbrances valued at $4,000. The status of land
on a reserve was unclear, so Gladstone was asked if he could buy property off the reserve. Excitedly, Gladstone agreed.

The next day was spent in Cardston, house hunting. At last Jim and
Janie found a little cottage at the east end of town which was available
for $6,700. Arrangements were swiftly processed at the bank for a loan
to pay off the entire amount, with some of the Gladstone cattle to be
sold to cover the down payment. However, the cattle were jointly owned
by Gladstone and his son Fred, so the other party was needed before
the animals could be marketed and the title issued.

But where was Fred?

The last time anyone had seen him, he had gone to a party with a
bunch of his cowboy friends. As the day wore on, his trail was followed
into the United States and finally ended up at the Galbraith ranch on
the American Blackfeet Reservation. Hurriedly, Fred was shepherded
back to Cardston where the cattle deal finally went through.

Sighing with relief, Gladstone and Janie went to Calgary to phone
the prime minister from our house. That way, no one would be listening
in on the rural party line. Diefenbaker said he would take the matter
to cabinet as soon as possible, and for Jim to have his Indian costume
ready for the photographers.

His Indian costume! He didn't have one; the outfit he had borrowed
for the Calgary Stampede had long since been returned and, with the
announcement in the offing, he didn't want to go back to the Blood
Reserve. His old friends in Calgary finally came to his rescue. John Laurie
loaned him a shirt, leggings, and moccasins, while George Gooderham,
the retired Blackfoot Indian agent, let him use his feather headdress.

The official appointment was approved by the cabinet on the last day
of January, 1958, but not until the following day did we get the news.
The message came from a *Calgary Herald* reporter who said the publisher
had received a personal phone call from the prime minister about the
selection.

Talk about excitement! For the rest of the day, our phone was ringing,
friends and media came calling, and telegrams started arriving at our
door. The first people on the scene were the *Herald's* reporter and
photographer. In the turmoil, the family had forgotten to get a costume
for Janie, but resourcefully she grabbed an Indian blanket that was used
as a covering on our chesterfield and draped it around her in Indian

fashion. The photograph, showing a proud new senator in a feathered headdress accompanied by an equally happy wife, was transmitted all across Canada and appeared in many daily newspapers. And so it went all day. "We were all excited," said Janie in her diary. "We had to take a nip to ease our nerves."[5]

Gladstone had come so far. The little waif in his grandfather's cabin at Mountain Mill had attained one of the highest pinnacles of the land. His long upward climb had not been spurred on by personal ambition, but through an unending desire to prove to the Blood Indians that he was worthy to be called one of their own. From the time he was a boy, he had suffered the indignities of being different, yet his goal had been to make the Bloods proud of him and to accept him.

Now almost seventy, Jim had been to see his doctor a few months before the appointment and had been told to slow down, to leave the active work to his sons. Now that he was no longer president of the association, he took the news as a sign that he was washed up, both at home and in politics. Just about this time, someone bought him a lazy-boy chair and for a while it looked as though he would become permanently implanted in it. Discouraged by the enforced inactivity, he slumped into the chair, turned on the radio, and listened. He heard the soap operas, hockey games, western music — anything that was on the air. He had seemed disinterested when people came around, and began to talk about being "old" — something he had never done before. In his own mind, he had outlived his usefulness.

Then came the Senate appointment. "They need me!" was one of the first comments he made after the announcement. Like a war horse called back into battle he discarded the lazy-boy and with a renewed twinkle in his blue eyes, set out to conquer new fields.

Janie and the family were just as pleased and proud. Within minutes of the announcement, Janie was on the phone to her daughters, telling them the wonderful news. As for Pauline and me, we had been holding our breath for the past four days, praying that nothing would go wrong.

By now the entire nation had accepted him as the most prominent Indian in Canada. And, over the next few months, even the Bloods showed that they cared. Upon the recommendation of the tribal council, the new community center was named the Senator Gladstone Hall; both the Anglican and Catholic schools put on banquets in his honor; and the IAA local made a special presentation to him. Of course, his old enemies from Standoff were not won over by the acclaim. One of them, indignant over the publicity, wanted to know why the Senate appointment had not been put to a vote of the Blood tribe.

Just as Gladstone's involvement with the Indian association had taken him out of the realm of reserve politics and into the provincial scene, so did this appointment elevate him to a national level. Instinctively, or perhaps consciously, he realized that each step gave him an added responsibility to adequately reflect the wishes of the people he represented. When he had been involved in tribal politics, he had been concerned with such matters as water wells and the sale of hay. When he joined the executive of the IAA, his perspective broadened to encompass hunting and fishing rights and improvement of the school system. Now, he would need to find out what the Indians across Canada wanted, for although he had been appointed the senator for Lethbridge, the prime minister had made it clear that he was the Indian voice in parliament.

As each step was made, Gladstone knew that some of his decisions would not be popular. Just as he opposed the Bloods on the elective system when he reached the provincial level, he now expected to take stands which would run counter to IAA policy—liquor laws and the federal vote, for example. But he had to grow with the job and, as he told the press, "I'll never be too old to learn."[6]

Another decision he had to make early in his new career was the political role he would play. Although he stated in the *Canadian Parliamentary Guide* that he had no political affiliation as "Treaty Indians do not have the Franchise," he was, in fact, a lifelong Conservative.[7] Before he received treaty status he had consistently voted for that party, just as his grandfather had done. In addition, the problems the Indians had suffered under the Liberal regime seemed to create an image of John Diefenbaker as a knight in shining armor coming to the rescue with his party stalwarts. As a result, Gladstone had an almost blind loyalty, both to the party and to the leader who had appointed him.

Opposition politicians, particularly in the NDP ranks, applauded Gladstone's original statements that he would be independent, as they wanted him to speak for all Indians, not, as they expressed it, just the Conservative Indians.

Yet Canada's political situation and Gladstone's loyalty to Diefenbaker made independence almost impossible. At the time of his appointment, the Conservatives had a minority government with a new election scheduled for only two months away. So when the prime minister's office asked him to hit the campaign trail, he threw caution to the winds and set out. Before the election was held, he had visited Saskatchewan, Manitoba, the Yukon, and various points in Alberta. He also appeared on the platform with Diefenbaker during his campaign stops in Edmonton and Calgary.

In Jim's mind, he was not openly campaigning for the Conservative party, but he was always accompanied by the local candidate and was paraded as a living example of what the Conservative government already had accomplished. Gladstone didn't mind, for in his view it gave him a good opportunity to visit Indians across Canada and to see their problems first hand. If this also benefitted the Conservatives, then he was doubly pleased. Of course, the Indians still were not able to vote federally, but there was a large supportive community, particularly in the northern areas, which was sensitive to native problems.

After the Conservatives' sweeping victory in March which gave them a majority government, Gladstone continued to travel whenever anyone invited him. He appeared on the Toronto television show "Front Page Challenge," where he weathered an attack from Gordon Sinclair, who doubted that he had ever lived on a reserve. Later, however, Sinclair changed his opinion, praising the man for doing more to brighten the Senate than any other ten senators could. "What this country needs," said Sinclair, "is more senators on the Indian list!"[8]

Gladstone officially opened a farm machinery plant, presented certificates to graduating Eskimo cooks and spoke to innumerable clubs and organizations. He also was invited to the Blackfoot Reserve where the Sun Dance was in progress. After the dancing circle had been erected, the senator was asked to talk to the assembled crowd, the majority of whom were Indians. Speaking entirely in the Blackfoot tongue, he described the work he was doing for the Indian people, and his hopes for the future. It was an impressive, eloquent address and when he was finished there was thunderous applause and the beating of drums. Afterwards, a white visitor came up to him.

"Senator," he complained, "why didn't you speak in English? I couldn't understand a thing you said."

"I wasn't speaking to you," he smiled. "I was talking to the Indians."[9]

Instead of being tired by the new responsibility, Gladstone was exhilarated by it. He liked people, and the constant travelling gave him the opportunity to see old friends and make new ones. And it was not all milk and honey on the tours. For example, when he was in Edmonton to join Diefenbaker he stayed in a suite at the finest hotel in town. When he took the train south, he made arrangements for it to stop at Hobbema, a whistlestop, and walked from there to the log house of a friend, where he spent the night on a mattress on the floor. He was just as happy in the cabin as he had been in the hotel suite.

After the federal election, he was invited back to Manitoba where a provincial campaign was taking place, and where the Indians were voting for the first time. Although his earlier travels had been almost diplomatic tours, this one was crassly political, with the Conservatives out to get the Indian vote. A journalist described Gladstone's method of campaigning.

"In the early afternoon he arrived at Koostatak, end of the road leading north from Winnipeg through the centre of the Interlake country. The chief and councillors of the Fisher River band of Cree Indians were sitting on the steps of the post office waiting for him. While candidate Olsen waited in the car, Sen. Gladstone shook hands with the Indians, sat on the steps with them and lit a cigarette. For about five minutes, nobody said anything. Then the conversation started, so quietly it was inaudible several feet away from the group. They talked about trapping rights, the young people marrying outside the reservation and the way Indian children were forgetting their own language."[10]

Gladstone told them about the need for organizing and how they should look to the future. Not once did he mention politics or the forthcoming election; he didn't have to, for they all knew why he was there.

Now that he was part of the political scene, Gladstone expected to be criticized, and he did not have long to wait. The first blow was struck by the Liberal *Lethbridge Herald,* which stated that his participation in the Manitoba campaign meant that "he has weakened himself as an independent spokesman for his race."[11]

In addition, he got an immediate response when he made the statement that residential schools should be abandoned and that children who were sent to integrated schools were four or five grades ahead. For this, he was soundly attacked by the Catholic clergy and teachers. On his own reserve, a priest insisted that his students had academic levels which were equal to white schools. At Hobbema, a teacher challenged him to prove his allegation. Gladstone stuck to his guns and continued to attack the residential school system as anachronistic.

Similarly, when he advocated equal liquor rights for Indians in Manitoba, he was swamped with criticisms. The *Edmonton Journal* editorialized that the Indians weren't ready and there were far more important matters to be considered. Letters to the editor also questioned the wisdom of the suggestion, some writers preferring instead that general prohibition be reintroduced.

Not surprisingly, Laurie reacted strongly to the news that the senator was supporting the liquor question. During his years with the Indian association, Gladstone was known to favor the change, but when the organization voted to remain neutral on the subject, he had avoided making any public statements. "The Stonies are quite worked up about it," confided Laurie. "It would be wise if you could possibly arrange to go up there, meet them, and definitely deny that you support liquor privileges. I would suggest that you approach the matter from this way: It would be breaking the original Treaty to support any measure which would open liquor to Alberta Indians."[12]

Gladstone had the opportunity to make either a rebuttal or retraction at the general meeting of the IAA, which was held at Morley, but for diplomatic reasons, he decided to do neither. Instead, as personal representative of the prime minister, he simply brought greetings from Ottawa and advised the gathering to remember that he was trying to do what was right for the Indians in whatever area he was visiting. "I hope you will remember this if you read about me in the newspapers," he added.[13]

The question of alcohol also had some amusing sidelights. In spite of the prohibition still in effect in some provinces, Gladstone often was served liquor at social functions and, if the circumstances were right, he accepted it. About four months after his appointment, he was invited to open the Calgary spring horse show and, because of his family's interest in horses, he invited Fred and his wife, and Pauline and me to join Janie and him in the special box.

After the ceremonies, which were complete with flags and scarlet-coated Mounted Policemen, we were escorted to a lounging area below the grandstand. When we walked into the room, one of the Mounties went to the small bar, picked up a glass and turned to Fred.

"What'll you have?"[14]

As a treaty Indian, Fred liked to drink, even though it was illegal. He had become accustomed to getting drinks from pals in the cab of a pickup, from bootleggers in the backyard of a dingy house, or from one of the brightly lit bars in Montana. But never before had he been offered a drink by a Mounted Policeman in full dress uniform.

"Ah . . . a rye and ginger, I guess."

The policeman obligingly poured the drink and when he handed it over, Fred expected either the door to be burst open by the liquor squad or the Mountie himself to pull out his handcuffs. But nothing happened. As Fred saw the rest of us take our drinks, he slowly relaxed, but could never quite get over the shock of the experience.

Three months passed between the time of the senator's appointment and his swearing-in ceremony, and it was another three months before he gave his maiden speech. That provided plenty of time for him to continue his visits across Canada, including places like Saskatoon, Prince Albert, and the Six Nations Reserve at Brantford, Ontario. But as soon as he moved into his office in the Parliament Buildings, he found there was a tremendous amount of paper work to be done. Not only did he receive scores of letters from Indians seeking help, but there was a veritable avalanche of government reports, notices, committee meetings and Senate business which had to be attended to. This was not his forte, but with the help of a Senate secretary, and my wife and me, he was able to maintain reasonable order. As always, his priorities were with the requests from Indians. Some of these he referred to Indian Affairs officials or the minister with his own recommendations, while others he was able to handle personally.

A sampling of letters received during his first few months in office provided some indication of new responsibilities. The Catholic Indian League of Saddle Lake was seeking a semiresidential facility from which children would be bused to integrated schools. A man from the Thunderchild Reserve claimed that the Catholics were running the band and that the Anglicans were ignored. A Sioux from the Birdtail Reserve wanted a copy of the Indian Act to find out how much power a chief really had. An elderly Indian from Moose Lake Reserve complained that his house needed a chimney but no one would help him. In this instance, the senator arranged to have it provided. A U.S. Indian proposed that Canadian and American Indians legally withdraw their reserves from their countries and join the Organization of American States. For a fee of $1,600, he would arrange for the Canadian transfer. In this case, Gladstone notified the RCMP.

In some instances, the complainant did not have a legitimate case, while in other instances Gladstone found himself trying to buck the bureaucracy; regardless of a change in government, the same old crowd still ran Indian Affairs. Sometimes the only way he could resolve a matter was by going directly to the minister. He soon found that if he directed a problem to the officials, he usually got an explanation, rather than action. This was a problem which plagued him during all of his years in the Senate; no matter how justified a situation might be, he could seldom break the wall of indifference and entrenched lethargy in the department. Often, a complaint was taken as a criticism and officials spent more time trying to defend their department's actions than in rectifying the problem it had caused.

In frustration, Gladstone made a public statement at a committee meeting about the problem. "We encounter a cold formality," he said, with the Minister of Citizenship and Immigration at his elbow, "that sometimes makes us wonder whether the officials consider the human aspects of our problems, or just the administrative ones."[15] However, nothing changed.

As the date for his maiden speech approached, there was speculation in the press that Gladstone would enter the Senate chamber in full buckskin regalia. However, when the day arrived, he appeared in a casual grey sports jacket and flannel trousers. His surprise for his fellow senators was not in his garb, but in his opening remarks. "During the weeks that I have listened to the debates here," he said, "I have heard two languages spoken—English and French. To me, these are foreign tongues: therefore I should like to place on the official Debates a few words in the language of my own people, the Blackfoot Indians, as recognition of the first Canadians."[16]

Prior to breaking Senate tradition in this fashion, Gladstone had informed the speaker of his intentions. He knew that some years earlier, Senator Ian Mackenzie had been prevented from using Gaelic in the debates, as English and French were the only official languages. But, as the *Ottawa Citizen* commented, "It's a different thing from that incident. . . . After all, Blackfoot was the original language of at least part of Canada before French or English stepped to the shores of the St. Lawrence."[17]

His speech, delivered in a "soft voice trembling with mixed nervousness and emotion," the new senator made a plea for better education, economic development, and placing more controls in the hands of the Indians.[18] Using examples from the Blood Reserve and his own experiences, he showed how repressive legislation had held the Indians back. He believed that the time had come when they should be given a chance to make decisions on their own, instead of being at the mercy of the Indian agents and government policies.

Judging from newspaper articles and letters from all across Canada, the speech was well received. Editorials praised the firm but moderate approach, urging Canadians to examine the way that Indians had been treated in the past and to find ways of improving their lot for the future. Gladstone repeated his attack on residential schools but this time, instead of being villified by the clergy, he was praised by a Micmac priest who endorsed the idea of self-determination. Gladstone was particularly elated by this letter; during his years with the IAA he had worked closely with Catholic Indians and was concerned that attacks from the clergy might give him an anti-Catholic reputation. While he admittedly was strongly pro-Anglican and had opposed Catholic activities on his own reserve, his relations with individual Catholic Indians was generally good. To him, they were Indians first and Catholics second. Only if religion itself became the issue did his prejudices begin to show.

Someone coined the term "the gentle persuader" which fitted him perfectly. He was a novice in politics, an unpolished speaker, and a neophyte in the Senate, but he revealed the ability to adjust in each of these fields as he continued to pursue a goal that was so important to him, the welfare of Canada's Indians.

CHAPTER FOURTEEN

DIEFENBAKER YEARS

When Jim was appointed to the Senate, his youngest son Horace was working for Indian Affairs as an assistant superintendent at the isolated community on the Upper Hay River in northwestern Alberta. The first time Horace came home, he mentioned casually to his dad that the Slavey Indians wanted to work but there were no industries. He said there was plenty of timber but no sawmill close enough to be of any advantage to them.

Some months later, Horace received notice from a transport company that several large crates were on their way to his agency office. When they arrived, he was surprised to find that Ottawa had shipped a portable sawmill to the reserve. Within a few months, the outfit was in operation, providing both employment and lumber for the community.

Of course, he did not need to be told who had made the arrangements. Gladstone wasn't playing favorites; it was just that he saw a need where Indians were involved and was able to do something about it.

Horace was the only child who became a career civil servant, trying to help his people through the programs of the Indian Department. In spite of the fact that he had been denied a formal education after he left the mission school, he had persisted in his career, educating himself where necessary, and gaining promotions through his intelligence, ability, and natural leadership. Horace had the Blackfoot name of Wolf Moccasin, or *Makoyi-itsikin*, and also was called Dark, or *Sikowa'ntsoyi*. He married Aileen Ayoungman, a Blackfoot girl, and they had five daughters.

The senator's other children were doing well and he was proud of them. Fred had found the fine balance among farming, cattle raising, and rodeo. He was becoming more active in IAA business and in the spring of 1959 he was elected to the Blood tribal council. This placed the senator in an awkward situation, for if he continued to lobby for the elective system, Fred could lose his lifetime appointment. Yet the senator was not deterred; he believed that democratic elections were good for the tribe. Fred had three Indian names: Distant Thunder or *Ikai'ista-pokomi;* Woodchopper or *A'sitsaki,* the name once used by Old Glad; and Eagle Wingtips or *Pe'tawinook.* He married Edith Reid and they had four children, two boys and two girls.

Lucy, who had divorced her Blood husband some years earlier, was now married to an Okanagan Indian named Eneas Swite. They moved back and forth between the orchards of British Columbia and Washington, where Eneas was in constant demand for his knowledge of pruning and looking after fruit trees. Lucy was named Three Flashes Woman, or *No-okska-kanatsoyaki,* by her grandfather Joe Healy. Because he had been struck by lightning in 1887, Healy had the right to name anyone after water, thunder, lightning, and water animals.

Nora, while nursing in Victoria, had met and married a former Cardstonite, Ed Baldwin, and they had moved to Kitimat where he had a heating business. Later, they went to Vancouver. Nora, after her exciting trip to the coronation in 1937, had never come back to live on the Blood Reserve; the west coast had become her home. She had been given the name Trouble Singing, *Sawmitsi-inihkyaki,* but was renamed Princess, or *Ninaki,* after the coronation. They had one son.

Doreen had wandered far afield. While nursing in New Zealand, she had married E. Max Hendra and after moving around to Vancouver, the Blood Reserve, and back to New Zealand, they finally settled in San Francisco, where Max followed his profession as a lithographer. She was named Quiet Thunder, or *Ikinokomyaki,* by her grandfather. She was the mother of two girls and a boy.

Pauline, the youngest, had pursued her vocation as secretary in Edmonton until we were married in 1953. Pauline, in particular, worked very closely with her father, typing letters, arranging itineraries, and even accompanying her folks to Ottawa for the swearing-in ceremony. She was named White Mink Woman, or *Apsui'kaiaki* by her grandfather Healy. We have five children—three girls and two boys.

During the early part of 1959, Gladstone outlined his philosophy on his responsibilities as a senator. It was contained in the last correspondence with John Laurie, before Laurie died from heart failure on April 3.

"I am now representing all of my people in Canada," wrote Gladstone, "and that is what I am endeavoring to do. I do not want it to be said of me twenty years or more from today that I did not try to pave the way for Indians to get along in this world alongside of any other inhabitant living in Canada. We cannot go along with what was in our judgment ten years ago to be in the best interest of the Indians of Canada. I cannot do my job right if I did not realize what the situation will be 30 years from now and today what looks to a lot of people as crazy will be accepted as sound some few years hence. Nothing bears me out more than how it has affected my own family, by them going out in the surrounding world and making good. What my family has done can be achieved by any other boy or girl in Canada's Indians, and the sooner Indians are helped to take that kind of thought or stand, the more it will be of benefit to them.

"I do not want it to be said of Alberta in the years ahead, that they chose to be a way behind any part of Canada, nor do I wish them to lose any part of their way of life. I am proud being one of them and already there is a lot of us thinking of ditching the white religion and taking up our own Indian beliefs in a Christian way. I sincerely believe that Indians can and will be able to come out as a very large influencing factor in making Canada a bigger nation than it already is. I believe this sincerely."[1]

As part of his philosophy, Gladstone publicly demanded privileges that many Indians and whites thought were premature. These included the federal and provincial vote in all provinces, full liquor privileges, involvement of Indians in party politics, and integrated education. Much of the Indian opposition was based on the fear that the government would use these measures to force the Indians out of treaty status. Concerns were expressed that the federal vote would mean the payment of income taxes and the eventual breakup of reserves. Non-Indians believed that education should be provided first, with the vote coming later.

As far as the provincial vote was concerned, the Indian Act enabled provinces to extend this privilege if they wished. A number of provinces had done so, but Alberta had remained aloof from any such plans, claiming that Indians were a federal responsibility. In spite of the fact that the IAA was opposed to the vote, Gladstone did everything possible to have it introduced. Early in 1959 he wrote to Alberta's Conservative leader of the opposition, W. J. C. Kirby, suggesting that "it may be a good move for you to present a Bill towards that goal."[2] He pointed out that when Diefenbaker's bill of rights was passed, the vote would have to be provided, and the Conservatives in Alberta would be "stealing a march on the Socreds."[3]

When this did not produce the desired results, Gladstone worked towards encouraging the Alberta government to designate a cabinet minister to chair an advisory committee on Indian Affairs. Although this eventually happened, it took extensive lobbying on the part of Gladstone and others.

A top priority item in the senator's list of problems was the revision of the Indian Act. The legislation passed in 1951 had many shortcomings, compounded by the 1956 revisions which had placed too much power in the hands of the minister, whether Liberal or Conservative. In addition, the abhorrent clauses dealing with income tax and enfranchisement still remained in the Act, in spite of almost a decade of protest.

It had seemed to Gladstone that the Conservative policy over the years had been directed towards the protection of Indian rights while the Liberals were intent on pushing native people into the mainstream of Canadian society as soon as possible, whether or not they were ready. To him, the Liberals' formula for solving the problem was to do away with reserves and the special status for Indians, thus relieving the government of the responsibility for looking after them.

During his political career, Gladstone had known only the Liberal government, a body which had changed the Indian Act to something which in some ways was worse than the old act. Only in the fields of health and education did he believe the revisions had been beneficial. Now, he pinned his hope on the new Conservative government to put things right.

Some of his hopes were realized. Besides the removal of the band membership qualification in 1958, two years later the government repealed parts of the Indian Act and the Canada Elections Act which tied the federal vote to the payment of income tax. In 1961, the controversial Section 112, dealing with the enfranchisement of entire bands, also was rescinded. These were the sections which had been attacked by almost every Indian organization across Canada. In all instances, Gladstone had the pleasurable duty of guiding these changes through the Senate.

The actual extension of the federal vote to Canada's Indians in 1960 proved to be a stormy affair. "This is a trick to rob us of what we have left," protested a Caughnawaga chief.[4] "Would I lose my Indian rights?" a Micmac leader asked suspiciously.[5] Even Gladstone's former IAA associate, Albert Lightning, said that the Indians of his province were "absolutely" opposed to getting the vote at that time.[6] The Mohawks demonstrated at the St. Regis Reserve during which time they carried such banners as "Diefenbaker Drop Dead"[7] and "Senator Gladstone is a yes-man for Ottawa."[8] Even when the prime minister gave his personal assurance that the vote would not jeopardize native rights, the protesters across Canada were unconvinced. Among them was the IAA, which rejected the proposal unless changes were made in the Indian Act.

Gladstone, of course, clearly favored the vote, but he sympathized with those who were suspicious. When he moved the bill in the Senate, he commented, "On behalf of my people, I must express a fear which exists in the minds of many of them. Too often in the past the Government has given with one hand and taken away with the other. It has made the Indians suspicious—and rightly so—of any action which in any way changes their status."[9]

In the end, the measure became law and Indians were left to decide as individuals whether or not they wanted to vote. In the 1962 election, they generally showed that they were no more and no less interested in voting than were their non-Indian counterparts. In that election, approximately 53 percent of the registered Indian voters cast their ballots.

The Indians of Ontario, British Columbia, Manitoba, and Nova Scotia had accepted the provincial franchise by 1960 and a short time later the privilege was extended to Saskatchewan Indians. As soon as the date for that election was announced, Gladstone was asked to campaign on behalf of the Conservatives. Perhaps he had learned something because of his problems during the Manitoba election for, while he was prepared to visit the province and appear with Conservative candidates, he eschewed direct politicking. This was due in part to his reluctance to be seen as entirely partisan, but more out of respect for the NDP government in Saskatchewan, which he felt had done more for its Indians than any other province in Canada.

As a result, when a letter of support was drafted for him on behalf of the Conservative candidate for Athabasca, Gladstone refused to sign it. It was a blatant pitch, saying, "I strongly urge you to support Harry Houghton on election day next week. I would also point out that he is a great friend of the Indians."[10] The senator did agree to make personal visits to Indian reserves throughout the province and to hear their grievances. The tour was well publicized and even though Gladstone tried to stay away from politics, he still gained the ill will of the NDP. Shortly before the election, he received a letter from the premier's office. "Until this week," wrote an official, "there was no doubt in my mind that your role in relation to the Indian was that of statesman rather than politician . . ."[11] He then went on to attack Gladstone's travelling party for straining federal-provincial relations. He had no argument with anything the senator had said, but he believed that local politicians were taking the opportunity to blame the incumbent government for standing in the way of positive federal programs. This, he said, created suspicion and confusion among the Indians.

Gladstone was quick to respond. He described his speech at Loon Lake by saying, "I told them that the Province had passed legislation giving them the right to vote in Saskatchewan, but they weren't being forced to vote; they could use their own judgment on that. I also told them not to sell their vote, but to vote for the man that they could trust."[12] He explained that he personally had answered every question directly and honestly, but made no excuses or apologies for those with him over whom he had no control.

He encountered the same kind of hostility during a later federal election when he ventured into the riding of Frank Howard, the NDP member of parliament from Skeena, who was an outspoken advocate of Indian rights. Howard told the press that he respected Gladstone, but that he was being used as a pawn by the Conservatives. At that time, the government was considering a mandatory retirement age of seventy-five for senators, and as Gladstone had just reached that age, his future was in question. "How, in honesty," said Howard, "can the Tories parade Senator Gladstone before the Indian people as an effective voice for them when they plan to remove him from office if they get elected?" He believed that the party was being neither "fair nor honest" with the Indians.[13]

"I came here to help the Indians," replied Gladstone. "To explain to them what the vote means and also to see how much can be done in the economic development of their reserves. I'm a Conservative but I'm not a pawn of the party."[14]

As soon as the Conservatives were elected in 1957, Indian groups had begun to raise the cry for major revisions to the Indian Act. The Indian Association of Alberta, in particular, was vehement in its demands that a royal commission be established to investigate both the act and the whole question of Indian Affairs administration. Like the government before it, the Conservatives shied away from an investigative commission and decided instead to appoint a joint committee of the House of Commons and the Senate. Although the IAA complained that the move was simply a delaying action which placed no obligations upon the government, Gladstone supported the idea of a joint committee. While he admitted in the Senate that the 1946–48 committee had been a waste of time, he placed more faith in the Diefenbaker government. "I hope," he said, "that as a result of this proposed joint committee we will now be assisted in making the slow and difficult transition from our native life to that of the people around us."[15]

Early in 1959, the joint committee was established, with Gladstone and MP Noel Dorion being appointed as joint chairmen. During the period that the committee met, Dorion usually conducted the hearings, while Gladstone was free to join the usual cross examinations. In fact, the senator considered himself to be more of an observer than a participant in the hearings, believing that as co-chairman his obligation was to preside rather than to participate. He was discouraged by the authoritative role which senior Indian Affairs officials played in the proceedings and found their submissions to be long and tedious defenses of the *status quo* or glowing accounts of the progress being made under government supervision.

Gladstone's role in the joint committee was, at best, mediocre. He easily surrendered his investigative role to his co-chairman and made little or no effort to direct or control the hearings. While he could have been decisive in attacking senior officials and in elucidating additional information from Indian witnesses, he treated the hearings as though his role was more honorary than active.

His only flurry of activity occurred near the end of the first session when he attacked the Indian Department and suggested that no one be appointed to a senior post in Ottawa until he had actually worked among Indians, so that a person would "know Indians from personal contact rather than through official reports."[16] This comment was given newspaper headlines across Canada but was only a pittance in comparison to the opportunities he had during the hearings.

Gladstone's prominence in Canadian affairs made him a target for publicity seekers and promoters, as well as a few scoundrels. It was a new experience for him to be hit up for loans by white people, particularly aggressive men who radiated an aura of confidence and success. He usually managed to overcome his deeply ingrained respect for well-dressed educated white people and learned that good and bad came in all colors and at all levels of society. Only once was he cleverly victimized by a young Conservative university student who managed to arrange "a small loan" at a political convention.

A few Indians, too, believed that Gladstone was now a rich man and, in keeping with their own concepts of sharing, they thought he should distribute his wealth to the needy—usually themselves. Indians wrote to him for loans, clothing, railway fare, and all sorts of imaginative necessities. None of these mendicants was a personal friend or acquaintance and usually their pleas went unanswered.

In one instance, a Blackfoot confidence man used the Gladstone name to raise money in the Edmonton and Calgary districts. Passing himself off as a son of the senator, he would enter a hospital, business office, or other public place, claiming that some tragedy had just befallen him and that he needed a quick loan to get back home, to Ottawa, or to some other appropriate place. Over a period of several months, dozens of complaints were received by the police about the con-artist and, although he was known by name, there was seldom enough evidence to convict him.

His downfall occurred when he neglected the fact that the Gladstones were strong Anglicans. On this occasion, he went to a Catholic church in Calgary and told the priest that he was the senator's son coming out of the north when his wife had suddenly passed away. Now he needed help for lodgings and meals for the night. Sympathetically, the priest loaned him money and then phoned the Catholic mission on the Blood Reserve to give them the sad news. When the message finally filtered back to my wife and me in Calgary, the whole story and religious orientation were so incongruous that we immediately went to see the priest. While we were talking the Indian con-man returned to try to get more money from his "pigeon" but soon found himself in custody and serving three months in jail.

A body which had a certain degree of success with the senator was a quasi-religious group known as Moral Re-Armament. Formed in the 1920s as the Oxford Group, it had been accused of being pro-Fascist, particularly after its founder, Frank Buckman, commented, "I thank heaven for a man like Adolph Hitler, who built a front line of defense against the anti-Christ of Communism."[17] However, during the war years, re-named the MRA, it stoutly defended the Allied cause and in the postwar years amassed huge donations as it launched a world-wide crusade against Communism. In simplistic terms, it claimed that the world had only two choices — Communism or MRA. It based its ideology upon four absolutes — absolute honesty, absolute purity, absolute unselfishness, and absolute love. It believed that once the leaders of the world had adopted those standards, the problems of mankind would be solved.

As part of its program of bringing nations of the world together, MRA produced movies, stage performances, and glossy publications featuring supporters wearing their native costumes. The people of India, Japan, Africa, and Europe, seemingly mingled freely in this ideological unity against Communism. As part of this visual image, the MRA solicited the support of Canadian Indians, whose feathered headdresses and buckskin costumes were an indispensible part of a parade of nations. Two of their most colorful recruits were Dave Crowchild and George McLean (Walking Buffalo) who were long-time supporters of the Indian association. At MRA expense, they were taken with their families to meetings and conferences throughout the world.

There was no question about the sincerity of many MRA adherents. In the unsettling cold-war period, there was a belief that the world was surrendering to creeping Communism and that leaders were doing nothing to prevent it. Moral Re-Armament was one body which seemed to be taking an active role and offering practical solutions. To devout Christians like Crowchild and McLean, the MRA absolutes fitted perfectly into their own philosophies and lifestyles.

The group had paid no attention to Gladstone while he was a local leader, but as soon as he was appointed to the Senate, they began to favor him with visits and invitations. For his part, Gladstone found the MRA beliefs to be appealing. As a good Christian, he could support their ideology without question and could subscribe to any movement which would enhance the honesty and love of peoples for each other. Accordingly, when he learned that his friend Dave Crowchild was at the MRA center on Mackinac Island in northern Michigan, he accepted an invitation to visit him. During that pleasant weekend, Gladstone met with people from various countries and was immersed in the whole ideology of MRA. By lectures, periods of reflection, and friendly comradeship, Jim was drawn into the sphere of the movement.

Then, early in May, 1959, he was invited to attend a world conference of the MRA in Kyoto, Japan. Gladstone's first reaction was to refuse, as the joint committee was in the process of being organized and Indian delegations already were coming to see him. However, when he asked Diefenbaker's advice, the prime minister urged him to go, stating that one of his members of parliament had already accepted. Considering this to be a directive from his leader, Gladstone agreed on the condition that he pay his own expenses over and above the free air passage which an airline company had provided.

Aside from MRA, the trip was an exciting one and the only time Jim was ever off the continent. He found Japan to be a fascinating place, the teeming masses of people and crowded streets unlike anything he had ever seen. His railway trip from Tokyo to Kyoto was an experience in itself, for he had never seen so many commuters jammed into a railway car. In Kyoto he had caused some consternation and amusement when he was leaving a temple and could not find the shoes that he had left at the doorway. A guide soon discovered that he had become turned around inside and was trying to leave through a different entrance.

Most of the trip involved MRA programs and Gladstone's diary reflected the thorough indoctrination that was used. On May 9 he watched a play which showed "the corruption that is going on in the political life of the leaders of Japan and how they gave up these wrong ideas when they put themselves under the guiding principles of Moral Re-Armament."[18] On the following day he heard how "Madame Lason of France . . . helped bring France and Germany towards peace after being enemies for 1000 years. I thought that only God could bring these things to pass."[19] Over the next three weeks, he heard speeches, confessions, and apologies for their countries' behavior from people from Britain, Holland, Philippines, Indonesia, India, and other parts of the globe. At the end of each day, he was encouraged to sit with his notebook to record his thoughts of MRA. Afterwards, a counsellor examined what he had written and, when desirable, made additional comments.

It was a mind-bending experience which had considerable impact on the naive Indian from the Canadian prairies. But as much as their people tried, they could not get the senator to give up smoking as part of absolute purity. The last comment in his notebook before returning to Canada was a statement by Lord Abbott that "I'd like to especially direct to my great friend the Red Indian from Canada to leave smoking alone."[20]

Upon his return, Gladstone had an opportunity to think more clearly about the movement, particularly when he was away from their constant proselytizing. He realized to what extent he had come under their influence in Japan and, while he supported their basic ideologies, he had no wish to be identified as a zealot or a spokesman for MRA. In the months that followed, several attempts were made to induce him to participate actively in their work, but he declined. He became friends with a number of MRA supporters in Ottawa and enjoyed his visits with them, but he would not let his name be used in their promotional activities. His primary concern was that his identification with MRA could weaken his position when dealing with Indian matters.

Over the next few years, he realized he had made the right decision as more and more negative articles on MRA began to appear in the press and magazines. In 1960, H. W. Herridge rose in the House of Commons to brand the group as Fascist and to demand that it be denied tax exemptions as a charitable organization. But the senator was really shocked when the Anglican newspaper, *Canadian Churchman*, came out with two hard-hitting editorials blasting MRA as "a simplified latter-day Gnosticism"[21] which was "bidding for world domination."[22] Other publications questioned MRA's ability to practise its own "absolutes," particularly in the area of absolute honesty.

Jim continued to receive their literature, but considered MRA to be a part of his life which did not involve his work as senator or Indian spokesman.

In the months following his return from Japan, Gladstone was embroiled in a number of controversies over the federal vote and liquor privileges. A further problem arose when the announcement was made that the Anglican and Catholic residential schools would be closed on the Peigan Reserve. The senator had never made a secret of the fact that he favored integrated education, but at the same time he had cautioned the government to consult with the Indians before taking any precipitous action, and to move only as quickly as the people were prepared to accept.

His concern was based upon the fact that the minister, the Honorable Ellen Fairclough, had toured western Indian reserves in the summer of 1959 and had returned to Ottawa convinced that integrated education should be implemented. She received the support of departmental officials who pointed out that, in addition to educational considerations, the program would be less expensive to operate. Then, as had so often happened in the past, the government was ready to launch a massive program without adequately taking into consideration the human factors.

Gladstone had faced this situation before. Often he found that a decision was sound but insufficient preparation and planning went into it, often destroying any good it might hope to attain. In the area of education, he hoped that the government would introduce a system whereby integrated education would be available but not mandatory. He believed that as the more progressive children went through the white school system, they would serve as examples for the others until all Indians would demand that type of schooling. He saw the eventual use of residential schools confined to "orphans and other children requiring institutional residence facilities during their school years."[23]

However, the Peigan decision made it clear that the government was preparing to phase out residential schools as quickly as possible, without regard to the problems this might create. This placed Gladstone in the awkward position of calling on the government to slow down a change which he strongly supported in principle. "The rapid movement toward integration is puzzling to many of my people," he told his fellow senators. "They feel as though they are caught up in a whirlwind and some are fearful of the results. While I agree that we must move ahead, we must at all times consider the feelings of these people and maintain a strong bond of trust between Government and Indian."[24]

For one thing, Jim wanted the churches out of education as quickly as possible. "If our children are to progress," he said, "they should be encouraged to attend mixed schools. If this is not possible, because of distance, location or reluctance on the part of the parents, then I feel that the children should attend Government-operated schools."[25] However, the government ignored this methodical approach and galloped headlong into a program of closing down Indian schools and sending the children off to nearby white schools, whether or not they were ready.

When the Senate recessed for the summer of 1960, Gladstone had no opportunity to take a much-earned rest. Among other matters of business, John Diefenbaker had accepted an invitation to be made an honorary chief of the Bloods and to be inducted into the exclusive Kainai Chieftainship. At the end of June, the Gladstones were on hand in full regalia as the colorful ceremony took place at the Blood timber limit, within the shadows of the Rocky Mountains. They were less than a dozen miles from where Gladstone had lived in a tent while herding cattle almost half a century before. And a few miles further north was the place where the little boy had played among the millpond logs with his brother Steve. How far he had come and how much his world had changed!

The senator's old school friend, Jack Low Horn, now one of the leading medicine men of the tribe, had the duty of inducting the prime minister into chieftainship, giving him the name of Many Spotted Horses. When the ritual was over, Janie led Diefenbaker in an owl dance; press photographs of them (under the headline "Jitterbug John") appeared in newspapers all across the land. Of course, Janie loved all this fuss and fanfare, especially when it happened among her own people. For years she had put up with the jibes and innuendoes about her *Siapikwan* (Cree) husband, but now everyone could see that he was hobnobbing with the prime minister and Janie actually had a dance with him.

Janie still was a fun-loving, outgoing woman but she found the visits to Ottawa very tiring. She was a family person who wanted to be with her children, her grandchildren, her sisters, her cousins, and all her relatives. They were all one big family and when she was away from them she was lonesome and depressed. Mind you, for a few days at the opening of each new session she enjoyed the round of cocktail parties, luncheons, teas, and banquets. She was a good friend of Olive Diefenbaker and the wives of several western members of parliament but after a few days she tired of the tinkling glasses and mindless chatter. For her, Ottawa was nice for only a short visit.

During those times, she was convinced that her residential school upbringing, with its strong British traditions, had been an asset to her. Such matters as etiquette and proper dress had been drilled into them as students, while the school's annual Old Boys' Reunion had stressed proper protocol in social situations. Besides, both she and Jim had met the Queen on several occasions and had become accustomed to being with the great and the near-great.

Yet there was always a bustle of activity when they got ready for a social evening. Janie hauled out Jim's tuxedo and made sure everything was all right while at the same time she usually took the opportunity of the occasion to buy a new dress, a fur, or piece of jewelry. When they were finally togged out in their formal attire, they looked as though they had never seen an Indian reserve or lived through years of hardship. Janie said that Jim looked like a penguin in his formal attire and there was always plenty of light-hearted joking as they prepared for their outing.

The chieftainship ceremony with Diefenbaker had been an exciting affair; as soon as it was finished, Janie and the senator went to Montana to attend the Indian Days in Browning, and then Jim was off to visit the Hurons in Quebec. When he returned, he learned that he had been named the American Indian of the Year by organizers of the All American Indian Days in Sheridan, Wyoming. He was the first Canadian Indian so honored and agreed to be the keynote speaker for ceremonies in early August. The family decided to make an excursion out of it, so when we set off our party consisted of two cars, one containing the senator and his wife, Pauline and me, and a young relative from Lethbridge; the other had Horace, his wife, and his daughters. Janie, the inveterate diary-keeper, recorded the day-to-day events, which started when she arose on the day of their departure and was surprised to find the senator with his old friend Cecil Tallow, sitting in the living room in their underwear. They had been partying since the night before and had not gone to bed.

In spite of this, we set off at 8:15 A.M., stopping in Browning, Montana, for a visit to the local Indian museum. From there we drove to Great Falls, where we toured through the Charlie Russell museum and continued on through the driving rain to the tiny ranching town of Lewiston, where we spent the night. The next day, part of the town was flooded but our little caravan was soon out on the open prairie where tumbleweeds were more common than rainfall. At one point, Janie became quite concerned when I jokingly told her that the rattlesnakes sometimes were so thirsty that they stood upright like fenceposts while they looked for water. Until she realized the prank, she looked anxiously at the few posts which lined the road to see if they were in danger of being attacked by rattlers.

After going through Billings, the party arrived in Hardin, on the edge of the Crow Reservation. Here the women decided to shop for Indian objects—a shawl, rug, some jewelry—while the menfolk retired to the nearest bar. Next morning we drove to the Custer battlefield and continued across the Crow Reservation, arriving in Sheridan just three hours before the opening parade of the All American Indian Days. As recipient of the national award, the senator was expected to take part in the public activities and an open limousine was provided for him for the parade. The event itself proved to be exhilarating, Janie and Jim in full costume being cheered and photographed by Indians and non-Indians alike.

Always the politician, Gladstone met a number of people who were involved with native issues in the United States. One of these was an old friend from the Crow Reservation, Bob Yellowtail, a man who visited the Bloods fairly frequently and kept up regular correspondence with the senator. During their discussions, the senator learned that the whole question of termination had become a contentious issue but that Washington bureaucrats were still pursuing practices of getting Indians to give up their lands and their legal status. Paralleling this program was a policy of moving Indians to the cities, giving them temporary assistance, and then dumping them.

That evening, Gladstone was welcomed onto the stage of the evening's program and was presented with the award by Wyoming Governor J. J. Hickey. Then, to the consternation of a number of U.S. government officials on hand, he bluntly alluded to the termination problem, without actually interfering in American internal affairs. As quoted in several newspapers across the United States, he commented: "In both countries our governments must realize their obligations to our people. It will be many generations before anything resembling a termination policy can work to the benefit of the Indians. Those who speak of ending government responsibility in a few years cannot fully understand the great changes which must take place in our lives. Let us first have education and understanding. Then we can seriously consider our own responsibilities and those of our country."[26] A discernable cheer arose from the grandstand when the statement was made.

During the next two days, we became a part of the All American Indian Days, as we watched the dances, took part in the church services, and visited with old friends and new. There were many impressions: the massive village of white canvas tepees, so unlike the colorfully painted ones of the Bloods; the surprise and pleasure of finding a Blood tepee among the multitude and greeting Stephen and Queenie Fox from the reserve; the impressive sight of a large troupe of feathered and costumed Sioux Indians making an entrance into the evening performance; the sounds of their bells and whistles intermingling with their honoring song; the visual evidence that tribalism was still alive, as indicated by the animosity between Crow and Cheyenne, who shared adjoining reservations; the meeting with wise and respected leaders, including an Arapaho named William Shakespeare; and the friendliness of everyone as a dozen or more tribes joined together for three days of dancing, singing, feasting, competitions, and demonstrations of arts and crafts. The trip was a never-to-be-forgotten experience.

Upon our return to Canada, we discovered that the Blood Sun Dance was in progress and when we went out to the Belly Buttes, we were just in time for the dance of the secret Horn Society. It formed a significant contrast with what we had just seen in Wyoming: one was an almost carnival-like presentation of crafts and dances, while the other was a sacred re-affirmation of the Sun spirit; the first reflecting the joy of being an Indian and the other giving thanks for being an Indian.

At times like this, Jim's Indianness welled to the surface of his conscious thought and was carried beyond the political realm into a strong feeling of being part of a huge family. That was when he sometimes spoke seriously of adopting the native religion himself, although always qualified with the intention of still remaining an Anglican. He was not alone, for there were many Indians who found a comfortable relationship between the two religions, never feeling that one had to be adopted to the exclusion of the other. Gladstone showed his initial interest by giving financial help to the ceremony, but he never did take the ultimate step of actually embracing the Sun Dance religion. Yet the balance was often there. Just after the Sun Dance, he attended an Indian gathering on the Peigan Reserve where my two-year-old son James went through a religious ceremony in which he was given the Indian name *Kitsemonisi,* or High Otter. On the following day, we attended church at St. Paul's.

By the time autumn of 1960 arrived, Jim, now aged seventy-three, had toured reserves in southern Alberta, the Battleford and Prince Albert districts of Saskatchewan, and the Saddle Lake region of northeastern Alberta. He had given speeches in a number of centers, including Calgary, and had spent most of his time travelling or receiving visitors at his home in Cardston.

When he went to Ottawa, Gladstone expressed his concern about some of the problems he had discussed in the United States. He was aware that many of the difficulties which were experienced across the line usually surfaced in Canada as well. In particular, he was worried about the United

States' practice of encouraging Indians to move to the cities as a means of resolving unemployment problems.

The experience of many families had been that of exchanging reservation welfare payments for city welfare payments, but with the added problems of street crime, lack of cultural identity, and a continued unemployment because of limited education and training. Once they had settled into the city routine, it often was difficult to return to the reserve, both because of the costs involved and because the children had adopted the urban lifestyle.

At the time, the native populations in most Canadian cities were relatively small. There always had been Indians living in cities like Winnipeg and Vancouver, but there was no identifiable ghetto or noticeable desire on the part of reserve Indians in Canada to take up urban life. But in the early 1960s, Gladstone was disturbed to notice trends which appeared to be following the American practices.

In his first speech to the Senate following his return from Wyoming, he expressed his concern. "I am entirely opposed," he told his fellow senators, "to any plan of relocation such as is used in the United States, but I believe we should make it more attractive for our people to leave their reserves to improve their situation. I think financial assistance could be offered to enable those who are leaving their reserves to become established rather than being unceremoniously cut off from some of the privileges they enjoy when they stay at home."[27]

After three seasons of hearing submissions, the joint committee on Indian Affairs finally concluded its meetings early in 1961. The legal counsels and officials began to draft the final report and recommendations—a process in which Gladstone took no part. It was further evidence of his disinterest or his lack of concern for the parliamentary hearings. Interestingly enough, when he tabled his copy of the final report and recommendations in the Senate, he made no reference to their contents; he merely urged the government to consult with the Indians before they tried to implement major policy changes.

Privately, however, Gladstone was extremely unhappy with the document. As he complained to Prime Minister Diefenbaker, "The final report seems to be based upon the requests and suggestions of the Indian Affairs Branch, rather than Indians who gave evidence. Certainly there are a number of recommendations which do not appear in any of the briefs from Indian groups. . . . In retrospect, I can see that I could have served my people better if I could have been a member of the joint committee, rather than Co-Chairman. As a member I could have expressed myself much better and more often than I did. It is too bad that the joint committee did not accomplish something more substantial."[28]

However, before any of the recommendations could be implemented, the Conservatives began a life or death struggle for survival in the wake of Diefenbaker's declining popularity. After the storybook defeat of the Liberals in 1957 and the resounding majority in the following year, the charismatic Diefenbaker showed that he was better in opposition than he was in power, that he was a better orator than he was an administrator. As the government moved through its first few years on office, everyone became aware of the fact that the prime minister had two faults which were politically calamitous: he could not delegate authority and he would not make quick and sound decisions. As a result, important business became bottled up in his office while his senior ministers became disillusioned and angry at the way the affairs of government were being handled.

By the time the 1962 election was called, there was no question that the Conservatives were losing support, but they fully believed that they would win with another large majority. As soon as the election date was announced, Gladstone was on the road, attending nominating conventions, greeting Diefenbaker when he arrived in Lethbridge, and accepting invitations to speak in places like northern Manitoba, Sudbury, Penticton, Prince Rupert, Williams Lake, Medicine Hat, Montreal, Three Rivers, and other points. It was an exhausting schedule which seldom saw him at home for several weeks prior to the election. "He sure is getting a lot of phone calls for him to go & attend meetings & campaigning at the same time I imagine," Janie said of her seventy-five-year-old husband. A little later, she commented: "Well, the Senator is off again. Edith drove him down to Lethbridge where he got on the plane to go east to Quebec. I'm sick of being alone & will be glad when the election is over."[29]

When the results were announced on June 18, the Conservatives were returned to power, but with a reduced majority. From 208 seats, the mighty party had fallen to 116, and could continue in office as a minority government only with the support of the 30-seat Social Credit party. However, Diefenbaker's style of leadership did not change with his reduced majority. Through the session of 1962–63, trouble within his own ranks escalated until the public began to compare the events at Ottawa with those of a three-ring circus; Diefenbaker was cracking the whip, but many of his lions were not jumping through their hoops.

The Indians' old friend Douglas Harkness resigned as minister of National Defence early in 1963 when the prime minister reneged on a NATO agreement to permit the Americans to arm nuclear warheads located in Canada. In fact, Diefenbaker's military policy and anti-Americanism so inflamed his cabinet that a virtual rebellion took place and might have resulted in his downfall had the old vanguard not united in the name of party solidarity. Then the Conservatives lost the support of the Social Credit party and in a dramatic vote on February 5, 1963, they were defeated and had to call for an immediate election.

Under these chaotic conditions, any proposed revisions to the Indian Act were shelved as politicians swung into their campaigns. Some cabinet ministers, like George Hees and Pierre Sevigny, decided not to stand as candidates, while Davie Fulton, Ian Fleming, and Ernest Halpenny pulled out of federal politics after the election.

Throughout the controversy, Gladstone had remained blindly loyal to the prime minister. Like many westerners, he saw Diefenbaker as a champion of the little people, particularly the Indian and the farmer of the western prairies. However, he knew that many Indians still were concerned about the federal vote and their possible loss of rights. As soon as the election was announced, he wrote to Diefenbaker, explaining the situation and asking the prime minister to make a statement which would allay their fears. In response, Diefenbaker wrote an open letter to Gladstone, to be read to Indians wherever he went. In it, he promised that an Indian claims commission would be established at the next session, and would have an Indian member. "The government will proceed as rapidly as possible," he added, "with the full revision of the Indian Act, now ready for introduction. After it is introduced, the Minister will visit every part of Canada to discuss with the Indians themselves the proposed Act and to take advice. All Treaty Rights will be fully respected in the new Act."[30]

Armed with this letter, Gladstone started on the campaign trail, visiting Sarnia and Walpole Island in Ontario to hold meetings with Indians on the nearby reserves. However, that trip convinced him that his health could not stand up to the kind of schedule he had maintained in the previous campaign, so when he learned that Pauline and I were driving to California, he decided that he and Janie should go along. He knew he could not refuse the party if they called on him, but if he was out of the country he believed the problem would be resolved.

On the day that we left Cardston, the senator had long distance calls from Ontario, British Columbia, and central Alberta and in my diary I commented, "We are getting away just in time."[31] The journey itself was a pleasant one through Denver, Santa Fe, and Las Vegas to San Francisco, but Jim was not happy. "We find it was a mistake for him to come on this trip," I wrote. "He is unhappy and fretful most of the time, feeling he has run out on the Conservatives. He almost turned back at Denver and maybe he should have."[32] Finally, at San Francisco he could restrain himself no longer and took a flight back to Canada. There he did a limited amount of campaigning in southern Alberta, but his health prevented him from making any of the arduous journeys which he had undertaken the previous year. His seventy-five years were beginning to take their toll.

When the election was held on April 8, the West was the only area which had remained solidly faithful to Diefenbaker. In a resounding rejection of Conservative policies, the party was reduced to 95 seats while Lester Pearson's jubilant Liberals won 129 seats and the right to form a new government. As a journalist noted, the Conservatives had not been completely annihilated but they had become "the English-speaking party of the farm, the village and the small town."[33]

For Gladstone, the defeat was taken as a personal blow. He apologized to Diefenbaker after the election, saying, "It was a disappointment to me that I couldn't do much more at the past election but my health demanded that I take a rest. I have travelled all over Canada since you appointed me to the Senate. This was an honour to me but more important to my people throughout the country. I have always told them that you were inviting the Indians of Canada to pitch in and help govern the country . . . . The Indians all over Canada are (mostly) loyal to our cause and will always say that *you* are their *Real Chief*."[34]

In fact, the defeat of the Conservatives meant that Gladstone had lost the only power he ever held over the monolithic Indian Department. With ministerial influence, there had been some opportunities to break through the wall of apathy and red tape that shrouded the department, but without it he was rendered almost as helpless as an Indian back on his reserve. Only his public voice and his role in the Senate gave him any leverage in continuing the fight for his people.

James Gladstone at the time of his appointment to the Senate in 1958. (Photo by Capital Press Service)

The first time Gladstone wore a buckskin costume was when he appeared on a stage at the Calgary Stampede in 1957 to present a painting to newly elected Prime Minister John Diefenbaker. (Gladstone Papers)

To pose for their first press picture after the Senate appointment, Jim borrowed a costume from friends while Janie used a blanket from her daughter's couch. During his years in the Senate, Gladstone's buckskin costume became almost a badge of office as he participated in ceremonies and meetings throughout Canada. "I am proud," he told the press. (Calgary Herald)

Shortly after his appointment to the Senate, Gladstone went to the Blackfoot Sun Dance, where he addressed the crowd in their native language. (Gladstone Papers)

Jim Gladstone and friend, 1958. (Gladstone Papers)

Senator James Gladstone, with the Parliament Buildings in the background. (Gladstone Papers)

*Shortly after his appointment to the Senate, James Gladstone met Erik
Nielson, Conservative member of parliament from the Yukon. (Gladstone
Papers)*

During his travels, Jim Gladstone posed with Premier T. C. Douglas, right, and Member of Parliament Frank Calder at an Indian conference at Valley Centre in 1958. (Gladstone Papers)

While appearing before the Joint Committee of the Senate and House of Commons on Indian Affairs in 1960, the Blackfoot delegation visited Senator Gladstone in his office. Standing, left to right, are Adam Solway, Chief Clarence McHugh, and Joe Crowfoot. (Gladstone Papers)

Senator and Mrs. Gladstone greet Blackfoot leaders Clarence McHugh (left) and Matthew Melting Tallow during a visit to Ottawa in 1963. (Photo by Newton Photographic Associates)

James and Janie Gladstone participated in a pow-wow at Fort Qu'Ap-pelle during a Saskatchewan tour in 1963. They are seen at center. (Gladstone Papers)

CHAPTER FIFTEEN

DECLINING YEARS

By 1963, James Gladstone had become comfortable in his role as a senator. He could speak easily without notes, charm his audience with his down-to-earth manner, and impress people with the obvious sincerity of his mission. As long as there was no Indian in Parliament, he believed that he had the responsibility to speak for Canada's natives and, regardless of the party in power, he was their representative.

As a result, he was constantly meeting with Indian groups, gaining their viewpoints and trying to discover how they felt about current issues. Usually his public statements reflected a concensus of Indian opinion, except in those areas where Gladstone looked to the future, rather than the present. His unpopular stand on the federal vote proved to be correct when the Indians found they had lost none of their rights. His belief that liquor privileges should be extended to all Indians was hotly refuted, but none could deny that the principle of equality was sound. Disagreements arose only in its application.

The buckskins and feathered headdress which had seemed so strange to Gladstone in 1958 now were part of his ceremonial garb, taken to meetings and functions all across Canada. Where at first he had problems fastening the breechcloth and the leggings, these had now become as commonplace as the zipper. He still insisted, however, that he wear modern clothing under the buckskins.

His curly brown hair was now white, with a strange streak of yellow-brown on the left side. This was the result of his constant habit of placing his left hand beside his chin as he listened — even though there was usually a lighted cigarette in it. Over the years, his hat had a scorched area on the left side while the hair was discolored by the smoke. They were evidence that he spent much of his time smoking and listening.

During his first five years as a senator, he had seen a number of significant changes take place. The Indian Act had been expunged of its most odious clauses, but was still an unsatisfactory piece of legislation. When Canada's Bill of Rights was passed by the Diefenbaker government, Gladstone suggested that the act should be discarded completely, that it was an impediment rather than an asset to the Indian people. However, the purpose of the joint committee had been to study the administration of Indian affairs, and dissolution of the Indian Act had not been one of its recommendations. Instead, the government had proceeded quietly to draft a new Indian Act which would have been tabled at the next session of the House of Commons had the Conservatives been re-elected. What it would have contained was now academic; the Liberals were back in power.

During the election campaign, David Croll, a Liberal senator, proposed that the entire problem be resolved by abolishing Indian reserves. Speaking in Sudbury, he said that Indians should be assimilated into the "Canadian stream of life" and that reserves were "a national slum."[1] During the remainder of the campaign, the senator's comments were circulated by Conservative candidates to reserves all across Canada, to show that the Liberal stance had not changed since the joint committee recommendations of 1948.

During Gladstone's initial five years, the Conservatives had made a few improvements in the handling of Indian affairs. For all its problems, the program of integrated education was having positive benefits, while the extension of the federal and provincial votes had removed another barrier in the Indians' status as second class citizens.

But the Conservatives had been no more successful than the Liberals in gaining control of the Ottawa bureaucracy. "I came to the conclusion a long time ago," Gladstone told Diefenbaker, "that there was no use going to see . . . the Director of the Indian Affairs Branch. He does not seem to have had any experience with dealing with Indians; being a soldier he had always given orders which must be obeyed."[2] Other native leaders felt the same way, but Gladstone was in a position to publicly make the problem known. He did so on various occasions, but with no discernable results.

One of the possible solutions which he frequently recommended was to appoint Indians to senior positions within the department. His son Horace eventually rose to become a district supervisor, but few ever gained responsible positions at the seat of power in Ottawa. Gladstone told the press that "he sees a need for a deputy minister of Indian Affairs. And the deputy should be Indian."[3] He went on to say that he was "satisfied with the calibre of most persons hired by the Indian affairs department, but critical of the few misfits whose bungling has caused serious problems."[4]

Personally, Gladstone had found the first five years fully satisfying. The question of his Indian status seldom arose, except for the expected comments from his detractors on the Blood Reserve. Everyone across Canada accepted him for what he was—a treaty Indian who obviously had white ancestors in his lineage. He made no secret of the fact that his grandfather had been a Scottish fur trade employee or that he was a distant relative of the prime minister of Great Britain. Nor could his mischievous blue eyes be associated with any tribal origins. But his Indian ancestors, his Indian heritage, and his role as legitimate spokesman for the native people were unquestioned.

Gladstone made no pretence of being anything other than what he really was. The buckskins and feathers were worn because they symbolized a proud people, yet when well-meaning friends suggested that he wear face paint to darken his skin, he simply laughed at them.

Shortly after the Liberals came to power, there seemed to be a possibility that they would follow through on revisions to the Indian Act and the implementation of a claims commission. The new minister indicated shortly after the election that the claims commission would be formed, and although a bill was tabled in the House of Commons, nothing was done for several years. Nor was a revised Indian Act brought forward. Instead, the government began to concentrate on the development of programs which did not require changes in the act. One of the most beneficial of these was a massive shift towards economic development to find ways of creating industries and employment on the reserves. This program received the support of Gladstone and Indian leaders across Canada. On the other hand, there were protests when the government began to negotiate with the provinces to transfer social assistance from the federal field. Gladstone and others cried foul, accusing the government of backing down on a promise to involve Indians in any major changes affecting their lives.

The 1960s marked a period of unrest through much of North American society, and Canada's Indians were not excluded. While Americans were going through the trauma of flower children, campus unrest, and antiwar confrontations with the law, the Indians were looking beyond the borders of their reserves for the solutions to their problems. In some instances they were counselled by hippies who had dropped out of society and moved in with the Indians. More frequently, support came from young Indians who were products of an improved educational system and who had been witnesses to campus unrest. These youthful spokesmen, dubbed "angry young Indians," created a whole new public awareness of native problems. Until this time, most public statements had been made by more moderate leaders, like presidents of native associations and Gladstone. The Indian activists on the other hand were erudite, eloquent, and expressive in bringing native problems before the public. Their radical outbursts often were accompanied by demonstrations, while threatened violence was well within the scope of groups like the National Alliance for Red Power. Persons such as Duke Redbird, Wilfred Pelletier, and Kahn-Tineta Horn demanded a whole new approach to Indian affairs. "I tell my Indian agent that I'm the boss and not he," said Chief Richard Pine at a meeting of the newly organized National Indian Council in 1963, "and that things are going to be done as I decide them with my council."[5]

Gladstone supported the principles but not the methods of these angry young Indians, but he was not invited to be a part of their movement. They treated him with respect, but he was from the old school, part of the conservatism that the radicals rejected.

One of the most effective young spokesmen at that time was Harold Cardinal, a student at the University of Ottawa. His father had been a long-time member of the IAA and Harold had attended school at the home reserve at Sucker Creek and in Edmonton before going east for a higher education. While many of the angry young Indians had an urban background and knew little about reservation life, Cardinal had his roots deeply imbedded in Alberta and the politics of the IAA. When he began to gain national attention, he was invited to participate in the association's work and in 1968, he easily won the presidency of that organization.

Within a short time, the IAA had completely changed its direction. Where previously it had refused government monies in order to maintain its independence, it now actively sought funds. Soon it had rented office space, hired employees, and began to pay salaries to elected officers who formerly had served without compensation.

Some of the old guard recalled the warnings of John Laurie about accepting money from the government, but their fears were ignored as Cardinal led the organization into ambitious programs to establish an Indian educational center and to demand control over much of the government spending. In one dramatic confrontation, the government cut off all funding to the IAA for a brief period, almost as a warning, but reinstated it after their differences were resolved.

This rapid shift of power into the hands of young educated Indians, coupled with Gladstone's deteriorating health and a lack of influence with the new government, gradually altered his position from that of active molder of public opinion to one of senior statesman. During the 1960s he continued to speak about current problems and hopes for the future, but now he sounded more like a respected patriarch whose words were heard and accepted, but no one expected him to take any further action. In many ways, he was at last becoming a senator in the way that most Canadians viewed the Senate. Even when he was given an honorary degree from the University of Lethbridge in 1969, it was more in recognition for what he had accomplished rather than an acknowledgement of his current activities.

Gradually, his health became his greatest handicap. Although usually active and busy as long as he paced himself, he was slowly being crippled by arthritis in his arm and hips, and by the effects to his spine of a minor traffic accident a few years earlier. Yet his doctor was able to state that "Senator Gladstone is a very active man for his age. One would not realize that he is nearly 80 years old and I feel that he gets along reasonably well considering the activity that he follows and concerning his age."[6]

During the federal election in 1965, the senator was back in service as a campaigner for the Conservatives. His limited travels took him to a number of places, including Kenora, Ontario, where he complained that "We Indians have been treated as children too long."[7] The Liberals, however, were returned to power.

The two personal projects which Gladstone continued to pursue during this period were the extension of liquor privileges and the vote to Indians in Alberta. On the subject of liquor, every other province in Canada had taken the step, but the Social Credit party used the IAA opposition as its justification for withholding it in Alberta. On the southern reserves, the prohibition had become a farce, as bars in Montana had been supplying unlimited amounts of alcohol to the weekend visitors for almost a decade. Finally, in the spring of 1966, when the Alberta government was drafting human rights legislation, it realized that the prohibition would violate its own decrees, so full liquor privileges were extended to native people.

The results were as bad as many people had feared; however, they were not unlike the experiences of other provinces. Particularly tragic were reserves like the Stoneys, west of Calgary, where a strong Methodist influence had rigidly controlled drinking. When it was no longer illegal, all bans seemed to have been removed, creating problems much greater and more serious than on those reserves where adjustments already had been made to illegal drinking. Through it all, Gladstone was unperturbed. Long ago, he had accepted the fact that liquor privileges would result in social problems, but he hoped that the Indians would gradually adjust to the situation. He believed that equality was the important issue and that the Indians could not be protected and treated as second class citizens forever.

A similar situation existed a year later when Alberta Indians finally were given the provincial vote. At first there was a concern that huge reserves like the Bloods could swing the results of a constituency. Some people believed that Indians would vote in a block as their chiefs dictated, but they did not understand the independent nature of these new electors. Phil Thompson, the only Indian candidate in the federal election, explained that he did not have the Indians united behind him as outsiders might expect, while Gladstone predicted that voting would be light, as most Indians followed a "wait and see" attitude.

In the end, both men were right. Thompson, as an NDP candidate, did not win his predominantly native riding, and the overall results indicated a light turnout. Indians threw most of their votes behind the Conservatives, but they also gave considerable support to the other parties.

After the defeat of the Conservatives in 1963, Gladstone was convinced that his most effective role for the Indians would be through his public speeches, and particularly his statements in the Senate. The upper house was not usually a newsworthy place, so the senator was popular among reporters whenever he arose to speak. The salient points were usually transmitted through the wire services and appeared in most newspapers across Canada. During this time, a reporter described him as a man whose "only weapon is gentle persuasion."[8]

When discussing Canada's program for its centennial in 1967, Gladstone indicated that many Indians did not have much to celebrate. "A century ago," he said, "many of my people were free, independent and lords of vast territories. Then came the white man with his hunger for our land and his disregard for our rights. He seemed to want everything we had."[9]

Then, using the centennial as a springboard, he brought up the old fear that the government wanted to abolish reserves and turn the responsibility for Indians over to the provinces. He pointed out that many Indians were progressing well and were benefitting by improved education, but he was concerned for the many who had not yet made the transition. "I hope, honourable senators," he concluded, "that some of my comments here today do not seem too contradictory. On one hand, I say there is a need for my people to progress and take responsible places in society. On the other hand, I say to the Government: Stop pushing us! What I say is true: My people must progress in order to survive, but we must do this gradually and at our own speed. You cannot force this upon us overnight. Give us the opportunities, and let us take advantage of them as we feel ready for them."[10]

The centennial year in 1967 proved to be one of the senator's busiest and most productive of the decade. With the nation's preoccupation with the past, Indians were taking a prominent role in activities ranging from the Expo pavillion in Montreal to individual activities in towns and cities across Canada. "People complain about the Indians living too much in the past," commented Gladstone during the year. "Why shouldn't they? Very often the only sensible way of life was the one that is now gone, never to return. All that many of them have today are the promises of the treaties and black memories of Government inaction."[11]

Then, as if to confirm the Indians' worst fears about government relations, an announcement was made in 1968 that the long-awaited revisions to the Indian Act would be considered. Instead of looking at the summary of the Conservatives' joint committee, the Liberals had decided to launch their program with a series of hearings and consultation meetings across Canada.

Nothing more was heard until June of 1969, when the minister of Indian Affairs, the Hon. Jean Chretien, tabled a White Paper prepared supposedly as a result of the consultations. As the minister explained to the House, it proposed that the Indian Act be repealed, Indian lands be placed under Indian control and title, most federal services be transferred to the provinces, the Department of Indian Affairs phased out of existence, and any remaining federal responsibilities be transferred to other government departments. It also recommended that $50 million be made available for economic development over the next five years and an Indian claims commission be appointed.

Indian organizations across Canada were astounded by the news. As they interpreted the recommendations, the federal government intended to cancel the Indian Act, get out of Indian Affairs, and abandon the Indians to the mercy of the provinces.

When government teams travelled across Canada to discuss the contents of the White Paper, the Alberta Indians refused to meet the delegation, claiming that they needed time to prepare a rebuttal and to offer alternatives. Harold Cardinal attacked the report with vitriolic comments, stating that "it offers despair instead of hope. Under the guise of land ownership, the government has devised a scheme whereby within a generation or shortly after the proposed Indian Lands Act expires, our people will be left with no land and, consequently, condemning the future generations to the despair and ugly spectre of urban poverty in ghettos."[12]

As the media became flooded with controversy about the White Paper, Cardinal produced a book, *The Unjust Society,* which carried the attack onto the best seller lists. During the months of dispute, the IAA held meetings and began to formulate its own position paper which it dubbed the Red Paper. Entitled *Citizens Plus,* the paper asked for confirmation of a special status for Indians, that the federal government continue to be the responsible level of government for Indian affairs, that the treaties be modernized and updated, and that Indian reserves continue to be held in trust by the crown. It went on to demand a revision of the Indian Act, changing of economic development procedures, and that a claims commission have broader responsibilities than those proposed by the government.

The senator remained silent during the Cardinal–Chretien battle, making no public statements on an issue that seemed to be enflaming Indians all across Canada. His reason for reticence was simple: in principle, he agreed with the White Paper. In spite of the fact that it had been put forward by a Liberal government and that it was the center of suspicion and hostility, Gladstone found it to be a document which paralleled his own thinking. Just as he had favored the vote when many other Indians saw it as a trap, so did he see the positive aspects of the White Paper.

The suggestion that the Indian Act be repealed was identical to his own public statements eight years earlier. Speaking then to the Ontario advisory committee on Indian affairs, he told them: "We are the only ethnic group in Canada with a special act."[13] He believed that the treaties and the Canadian Bill of Rights provided all the protection that his people needed, that the Indian Act was holding them back and not allowing them to engage in free enterprise nor to get the kind of education they required.

"The Indian communities should be governed by the same Act as the municipalities," he told a Dutch journalist shortly after the White Paper was tabled. "In this way the councillors could abide by the general law and have a clear idea of their duties. As long as the treaty rights are respected, I feel that the Indians in Canada would be much better off if they were ruled and governed by the general laws which apply to all Canadian citizens."[14]

His interpretation of the White Paper's stand on reserves coincided with Chretien's contention that the document "does not suggest that Indians, or Indian bands, should be given clear, freehold title to their land within five years—or indeed within any period of time at all."[15] Gladstone felt strongly that the protection of the crown was essential if Indian reserves were to survive, but he saw nothing in the White Paper which made him believe that the government intended to abandon that responsibility. "Personally," he said, "I would not like to see Indians selling their lands to outsiders, because then there would be no Indian land left in a short time. I feel that the United States made a big mistake by giving land deeds to the American Indians, because most of them mortgaged their lands and now more than one half of the younger people no longer have any lands since their parents had either mortgaged it or lost it to the banks."[16]

The area where the senator disagreed with the White Paper and strongly supported the Red Paper related to the general responsibility of the federal government for Indian people. While he agreed that many services could be transferred to the provinces, he believed that the treaties made a federal–Indian relationship a necessity. This was a point which he made to Chretien when he informed the minister that "I'm not going to make any comment at this time, but I think that [certain] questions on the Indians and their plight should be noted."[17] In particular, he expressed a fear that the White Paper was aimed towards the "abandonment by the government of responsibility to the native people." He did not think that the repeal of the Indian Act had to mark the end of federal involvement; rather, he saw the two as entirely separate issues.

Gladstone was sensitive to the attitudes of the leaders of Indian organizations and agreed with some of their proposals which either expanded the scope of the White Paper or placed additional demands upon the government. This was particularly true of the Red Paper, which put considerable emphasis upon better educational services and a broadened claims commission. Therefore, when he was invited to appear with IAA leaders to officially present the document to Prime Minister Pierre Trudeau and his cabinet on June 4, 1970, he did not believe he was compromising his beliefs. He later told IAA members: "How proud I was in the way *Citizens Plus* was presented in Ottawa, and also proud of the way it was received and accepted by the Cabinet. Let us hope they were sincere and if so, a lot of things contained in *Citizens Plus* will come to pass."[18]

When the presentation was made, the senator was in the position of standing with a group of chiefs in full regalia, with Cardinal in a beaded buckskin jacket beside him, as they faced a whole row of government cabinet ministers. Gladstone was both government and Indian, so in a way, the confrontation was symbolic. A half century earlier, he had promised to work for his people and now there he was, giving them support against a sea of white faces. He did not share his group's suspicion about the intentions of the government, but he respected and understood the existence of their fear.

Rather than subscribe to Cardinal's belief that the White Paper was "wrong and that it will harm our people,"[19] he agreed with Chretien's view that "Indian people, because of past experiences, have a deep distrust of government, both federal and provincial, and tend to regard the proposals with suspicion."[20] He accepted the document as a position paper, hoping that the Indians of Canada would accept those sections which they approved and revise or reject others which were unacceptable. However, he realized that the entire subject had become so emotionally charged that acceptance in any form would be impossible. The government came to the same conclusion and shelved the now-disgraced White Paper after *Citizens Plus* had been received.

Had he been in better health, Gladstone likely would have pursued the parts of the White Paper which he agreed with—and the Red Paper too, for that matter. However, to add to his miseries, he was hospitalized in Calgary several weeks before the Red Paper was presented. His trouble was diagnosed as appendicitis, which would have been a simple matter for a younger man, but at eighty-three, any operation was serious. Yet he agreed to the surgery, came through without complications and three days later was fighting with the nurses because of the restrictions they were placing upon him. On the following day, he became angry when they did not respond to his calls for help to take him to the bathroom with his intravenous attachments, so he ripped out the tubes and announced that he was going back to regular food. Resignedly, the doctor put him on a soup and jelly diet, adding solid food the next day. Then, when a physiotherapist insisted on trying to get him to induce coughing to clear his lungs, Gladstone ejected him from the room, saying that he was already coughing on his own and didn't need any help. After that, they left him alone until his incision was healed up enough for him to go home.

In spite of the operation, he still maintained an active schedule, opening an Indian artist's exhibition in Calgary, attending a seminar on Indians in Missoula, Montana, and taking part in the opening of a junior high school in Fort Macleod.

A few years earlier, when his health began to decline, he had started to talk about retiring. The matter first came up when the mandatory retirement age of seventy-five was implemented in 1963, but because the regulation applied only to new appointees, Gladstone was not affected. Two years later, when his old friend Ralph Steinhauer from the Saddle Lake Reserve was defeated as a Liberal candidate in the federal election, Gladstone wrote to the prime minister and suggested that he be appointed to the Senate. In turn, he indicated his willingness to resign. The letter was never acknowledged.

Throughout the period of his appointment, Gladstone expressed the belief that there had to be an Indian in Parliament, either in the House of Commons or the Senate, to speak for the native people. He often expressed the hope that an Indian would be elected as a member of parliament, implying that this would be a good time for him to retire. This finally occurred in 1968, when an Okanagan Indian named Len Marchand was elected as Liberal member for the Kamloops–Cariboo constituency. Gladstone was at home when the election was announced, so he phoned his secretary in Ottawa and asked her to send a letter of congratulations. "For quite some time now," she wrote, "the Senator has been thinking of retiring from political life, but always hesitated to do so because there was no one to take his place either in the Senate or in the House of Commons. The Senator said that now that you have been elected, he can retire in peace, knowing that someone will be there to take care of the problems of the Indians of Canada."[21]

But Gladstone didn't retire, for he did not really want to leave the job which he had come to love. Not only that, his son Fred had taken over all their farming and cattle interests on the reserve, so if he retired he would have nothing to do. Still a relatively active man, he could not visualize himself sitting and vegetating in his little house in Cardston. In fact, during this period he arranged to acquire a piece of land on the Blood Reserve, right across the road from the town of Cardston, and had a new house built to his own specifications. It was a modern ranch-style bungalow, with a car port on one side, a large garden and flower beds for Janie, and a parking area which could accommodate the many friends and relatives who constantly visited them.

None of the children lived at home with their parents. Lucy was with her husband at their orchard near Kelowna, B.C.; Fred was running the home farm; Nora and Doreen were nursing, the former in Vancouver and the latter in San Francisco; Horace was an official with Indian Affairs in Lethbridge; and Pauline had just taken over the directorship of the Indian Student University Program at the University of Calgary.

After the Red Paper presentation, Gladstone finally decided that he could not carry on. He still moved around, drove his car, and was mentally alert, but he simply could not stand the strain of flying back and forth to Ottawa, walking interminable distances in the airports, climbing stairs, and going through the exhausting routines demanded by the job. And because he was so alert and active within limited circumstances, many people assumed that he was capable of almost unlimited activities. He did not want to disappoint them, many of whom came great distances to see him, and he often so over-exerted himself that he had to be confined to his bed.

During the winter of 1970–71, the senator had an on-again-off-again relationship with his own retirement. Finally, in the spring of 1971 when he was eighty-four, he wrote to the prime minister, tendering his resignation. "The Indians have lost much and gained little during the past century," he told Trudeau. "They have given up their land, their way of life, their religion and their culture. Many have not yet learned how to adjust to our fast moving technological age and have fallen behind. It is easy to put them on welfare and forget them, but I pray that men like you will not let this happen. The transition will be slow and painful, but you and other leaders can help by your encouragement and patient understanding."[22]

When the announcement was made to the public, letters and telegrams streamed in from all over Canada. Tributes were paid to him in the Senate by members from both the Liberal and Conservative ranks. Typical was the comment of Senator Allister Grosart who said, "I knew Senator Gladstone before he came here. I well remember, when the decision was made by the Prime Minister, that there should be a representative of the first Canadians appointed to this chamber, that he initiated an investigation of the prominent personalities who might qualify as representatives of the great Indian nations who were the real founders of this country. That took a very short time, because from all sides one name, that of Senator Gladstone, came forward. He was universally recognized then as the great representative of the Indian peoples, and

I know that as he leaves us he remains the great representative of the Indians of Canada."[23]

Gladstone's farewell speech to the Senate touched not only upon the matters that had concerned him during his thirteen years in the upper house, but of his long-standing promise to work on behalf of the Indians. "I am proud of the day my Indian people took me into their tribe," he concluded, "not only by reason of marriage but on my own account. I grew up with them as a child, and it was a blessing that I consented to that adoption."[24]

What had he accomplished during those thirteen years in the Senate? The most important contributions are the most difficult to measure. Unquestionably, the national image of the Indian that he created helped to offset many of the negative attitudes and misconceptions Canadians had about native people. Because of his willingness to appear at innumerable functions, he was constantly in touch with Canadians who had had no personal experience with Indians. The impression he left was of proud and self-reliant people who had been caught up in the maelstrom of acculturation but, like him, they were making the adjustment. They needed patience and understanding, both from the government and the Canadian public.

He was indeed a man with a mission, and his zeal and convictions affected many people around him. He felt strongly about the role of equality for the Indians, particularly in matters of law; he also saw them as a people with a special status because of their treaties. *"Citizens Plus,"* he told a white group, "means what you have neglected to do in the last 100 years should be given to us in whatever form that you have elected; then we can say we are equal."[25]

The work which he had started with the IAA carried over into his senatorial years, particularly in seeking changes to the Indian Act and removing clauses which were seen as unfair or dangerous. This was part of a progressive movement which he envisioned, but one that would move so slowly that he could participate only in its initial phases. He saw the elimination of the Indian Act as the next step in drawing the Indians closer to the mainstream of society, but at the same time maintaining the special status implied in the treaties.

He saw his role essentially as political but, living up to the description of the "gentle persuader" he tried to achieve his goals by convincing Canadians that the needs were justified. His constant efforts to promote better education, employment, and equality under the law were at the forefront of his labors.

When he retired, he was probably the most well known and well respected Indian in Canada. He had realized many of his objectives, but the rest he left to those who would follow him.

In his letter to the prime minister and his speech to the Senate, he expressed a hope that a younger Indian would be appointed in his place. A month later, Len Marchand wrote to Trudeau asking for the same thing, except that he believed that three Indians would be needed to carry on the work. "There is still a lot of work to be done," said the member of parliament, "and that would be a useful place to tackle some of it."[26] However, no such appointments were made.

Gladstone kept busy in the months after his retirement. He attended the annual meeting of the IAA—something he had done faithfully for almost a quarter of a century. His son Fred was an active member of the executive where he was proving to be a steadying influence upon those who hoped to solve their problems overnight. During the conference, Gladstone heard himself described as one of the true heroes of the Indian movement and listened with interest as the new leaders discussed the problems of land claims, educational centers, sports programs, and economic development. From the tightly knit volunteer organization which Gladstone had led years earlier, a well paid native bureaucracy had emerged. With a revenue of almost one million dollars obtained mostly through government grants, the IAA had its own offices, staff field crews, and consultants to carry out the expanding business of the organization.

On July 23, 1971, Jim and Janie celebrated their sixtieth wedding anniversary, with family and friends coming to Cardston for the event. Telegrams came from the queen, the prime minister, and from many others in commemoration of the day.

The two had been together almost constantly in those sixty years. Gladstone's appointment to the Senate had caused a few problems until Janie decided that she would accompany him during most of his extended trips to Ottawa. There they rented rooms and she provided the kind of home and stability that he needed during his sometimes hectic days in Ottawa. Both of them had grown with the responsibilities of office, and Janie had come to enjoy the banquets and conventions, making friends among the wives of Conservative members. She sometimes spoke to small groups of native people, but preferred to be at her husband's side or with her family.

Early in September, we learned that there was a good chance of buying buckskin hides from the Kootenay Indians in British Columbia. That tribe was well known for producing the finest and softest hides of any in the area, the skins being excellent for dresses and men's costumes.

Deciding to make a holiday of it, Jim and Janie, with Pauline and me and our nine-year-old son John, set out from the Blood Reserve with the intention of reaching Ambrose Gravelle's house on the Kootenay Reserve before nightfall. The drive was a pleasant one during the fall day, the foothills being splashed with yellows, oranges, and browns, intermingled with the green fingers of spruce and pine. The mountains were a hazy blue that evolved into a rugged grey as they drew near.

Passing through the town of Fort Macleod we crossed over the trail where Jim had hauled the water wagon more than sixty years before. We went through the Peigan Reserve, dotted with modern houses, neat farms, and a handicraft store at the turnoff to the Indian town. We did not stop at Pincher Creek, but could see the line of trees which bordered the valley above the town where oil was becoming as important as cattle. A few miles away, out of sight, was Mountain Mill, with only a lonely church standing as a sentinel to what had once been a lively village.

Crossing into British Columbia, we stopped at a roadside cafe in Fernie to eat. After the meal, Jim tried walking up some stairs and suddenly collapsed. We half-carried him to our car and rushed to the local hospital where the doctors labored feverishly over him for half an hour. My little son John and I stood in shock beside him as the doctors worked, but we could see that we were too late. He had suffered a massive stroke and died. The date was September 4, 1971.

Numbly we gathered in the waiting room, where we were taken in hand by a kindly Anglican minister. With his help we phoned the Blood Reserve to break the news and then started the lonely trip home. Once we pulled into the driveway and the others rushed out to meet us, the flood of tears started. Then friends and relatives came from all parts of the reserve and took over. For the next two or three days, we found ourselves as guests in our own home as relatives did all the cooking and housework and would not let the immediate family lift a finger. It was tremendous moral support in the face of such tragedy, although nothing could fill that great gap which had suddenly taken place in our lives.

We learned that newspapers and radio stations all across Canada and in the United States, as well as Great Britain, were reporting the death, and soon the house was flooded with telegrams, cards, and letters. In Parliament, Senator Paul Yuzyk declared that "Senator Gladstone will be fondly remembered by all members of this chamber who knew him. He was a pleasant, friendly person, and a dedicated, hard-working parliamentarian who did much both to improve the economic, social, and educational conditions of his people and to gain some recognition of their rights."[27]

Meanwhile, the immediate family was in shock and mourning. It was hard for us to imagine life without the senator. Not only had he been head of a family of five children, eighteen grandchildren, and four great-grandchildren, but his strength of leadership had been such that everyone else paled in his shadow. We cried, but even the tears could not wipe away the personal sense of loss. I was reminded of something an old Blackfoot said at the time of Crowfoot's death: "Men, women, children, mourn over your great parent; you will no more hear his kind voice and its eloquent harangues. In your distress and misery, you will no more rush to his lodge for comfort and charities. He is no more. No one like him will fill his place."[28]

When the funeral was held in St. Paul's Church four days later, the building was not large enough to take the crowds. The dignitaries were there: Hon. Jean Chretien, Hon. Bud Olsen, Len Marchand, Harold Cardinal, and many others. Indians from the reserve, the family, and Indian and white friends from many parts of Alberta and Montana crowded the wooden church for the last rites. Fittingly, the ritual was Anglican but the eulogy was delivered in Blackfoot by Willie Scraping White, a holy man of the tribe and a schoolmate of the senator's at the old mission.

As the mile-long cortege made its way through the reserve to the cemetery, a small herd of horses grazing on the prairie saw the cars and came running over to the fence. There they stood, watching curiously as the hearse passed by, as though they were saying goodbye to an old friend. And, in many ways, they were.

Gladstone had been born in the era of the horse to an environment which should have limited his life to one of poverty and labor. Yet with the help of several people—first his grandfather, then his father-in-law, then missionary S. H. Middleton, and his associate John Laurie—he had risen above his lot to become one of Canada's most distinguished statesmen. But the success was accomplished mostly by Gladstone himself, through his unfaltering desire to be accepted as a member of the Blood tribe. Ever since he had been admitted to the reserve, he had wanted his people to be proud of him. Jim had promised he would work on their behalf, and he spent the rest of his life doing just that. Starting on the reserve, his efforts had carried him farther and farther until they culminated at the upper house of government in Ottawa. There, the "gentle persuader" found the ultimate audience for his message of understanding and compassion for Canada's Indians.

NOTES

Unless otherwise stated, all quotations by James Gladstone or stories told by him are taken from various interviews by the author from 1951 to 1971.

Chapter One: THE RUNAWAY

1. Interview with Jack T. Gladstone, Erickson, B. C., April 12, 1958.
2. Ibid.

Chapter Two: SCHOOL DAYS

1. Interview with Jack T. Gladstone, Erickson, B. C., April 12, 1958.
2. Circular letter, J. D. Maclean, secretary, Dept. of Indian Affairs, Ottawa, to James Wilson, May 29, 1901. Copy in author's possession. (As much of the research was done before the records of the Blood Indian Agency were destroyed or dispersed, they bear no archival numbers.)
3. Letter, R. N. Wilson to secretary, Dept. of Indian Affairs, March 19, 1906. Blood letter-book, p. 742, RG-10, vol. 1725, Public Archives of Canada, Ottawa (hereinafter referred to as PAC).
4. Circular letter, J. D. Maclean, secretary, Dept. of Indian Affairs, Ottawa, to R. N. Wilson, March 8, 1904. Copy in author's possession.
5. Letter, James Wilson to Indian commissioner, July 27, 1901. Blood letter-book, p. 280, RG-10, vol. 1725, PAC.
6. Letter, Mrs. Hilda Balshaw to author, March 24, 1958.
7. *Calgary Herald,* May 27, 1897.
8. Discharge certificate, in author's possession.

Chapter Three: A WANDERER

1. Parliament of Canada, *Hansard,* House of Commons Debates, Ottawa, July 11, 1908, p. 12739. (Hereinafter referred to as *Hansard.*)

2. *The Gazette,* Macleod, April 5, 1906.
3. L. V. Kelly, *The Range Men* (New York: Argonaut Press, 1965), p. 377.
4. *The Gazette,* Macleod, June 13, 1907.
5. Investigation of R. N. Wilson, Jan. 21, 1908, RG-10, vol. 4018, file 274,096, PAC.

Chapter Four: WITH THE HEALY FAMILY

1. Report of W. J. Dilworth in *Annual Report, Department of Indian Affairs for 1914* (Ottawa: King's Printer, 1915), p. 71.
2. Document dated April 26, 1913, in author's possession.
3. Letter, W. J. Hyde to commissioner, April 28, 1913. Copy in author's possession.
4. Letter, W. J. Hyde to Horse Shoe Liquor Store, April 29, 1913. Copy in author's possession.

Chapter Five: OFF THE RESERVE

1. Letter, J. D. Maclean, secretary, Dept. of Indian Affairs, to W. J. Dilworth, May 26, 1915. Copy in author's possession.
2. *The Albertan,* Calgary, June 11, 1912.
3. *Lethbridge Herald,* July 9, 1913.
4. R. N. Wilson, *Our Betrayed Wards* (Ottawa: Private Printing, 1921), p. 5.
5. *Calgary Herald,* Feb. 21, 1918.
6. Mimeographed copy of surrender document, pp. 2 to 4 only. In author's possession.
7. Wilson, *Our Betrayed Wards,* p. 50.
8. Ibid., p. 6.
9. Ibid.
10. Ibid., p. 7.
11. *Hansard,* House of Commons Debates, April 23, 1918, pp. 1047–48.

Chapter Six: INTO TREATY

1. Letter, S. H. Middleton to D. C. Scott, Ottawa, Sept. 12, 1919, file 425,037-3. Copy in author's possession.
2. Letter, J. E. Ostrander to secretary, Dept. of Indian Affairs, March 12, 1920. Copy in author's possession.
3. Mike Mountain Horse, *My People the Bloods* (Calgary: Glenbow Museum, 1979), p. 65.
4. Letter, Indian agent to John Ibey, Cardston, June 27, 1921. Copy in author's possession.
5. Clare Sheridan, *Redskin Interlude* (London: Nicholson and Watson, 1938), p. 257.
6. Ibid.
7. Ibid., p. 175.
8. *Lethbridge Herald,* Dec. 4, 1926.
9. Letter, J. E. Pugh to D. G. MacKerheher, Oct. 15, 1929. Copy in author's possession.

10. Letter, S. B. Phipps, Alberta Pacific Grain Co., to Pugh, Oct. 17, 1929. Copy in author's possession.
11. Monthly report, Pugh to W. M. Graham, Jan. 1, 1930. Copy in author's possession.
12. Letter, Pugh to Graham, Feb. 20, 1930. Copy in author's possession.
13. Monthly report, Pugh to Graham, Feb. 1, 1930. Copy in author's possession.
14. Monthly report, Pugh to Graham, May 1, 1930. Copy in author's possession.

Chapter Seven: THE DEPRESSION

1. *Family Herald and Weekly Star,* Montreal, April 19, 1933.
2. Letter, Gladstone to Canon L. A. Dixon, Jan. 14, 1952. Copy in author's possession.
3. Interview with Suzette Eagle Ribs, Oct. 10, 1979.
4. Esther S. Goldfrank, *Changing Configurations in the Social Organization of a Blackfoot Tribe During the Reserve Period* (New York: J. J. Augustin, 1945), p. 38.

Chapter Eight: THE CORONATION

1. Letter, Gladstone to Nora, May 4, 1937. Gladstone Papers in author's possession.
2. Ibid., May 15, 1937.
3. Ibid., May 15 and 21, 1937.
4. Sheridan, *Redskin Interlude,* pp. 223–24.
5. Ibid., p. 243.
6. Letter, Gladstone to Nora, Feb. 26, 1939. Gladstone Papers.
7. Letter, Anthony McMillan to Middleton, Dec. 18, 1940. Copy in Laurie Papers, A/L385, Glenbow Archives, Calgary.
8. Letter, Janie Gladstone to Nora, Feb. 19, 1939. Gladstone Papers.
9. Ibid., Feb. 26, 1939. Gladstone Papers.
10. Letter, Gladstone to Nora, April 29, 1939. Gladstone Papers.
11. Letter, Janie Gladstone to Nora, June 4, 1939. Gladstone Papers.
12. Ibid.
13. Letter, Gladstone to Nora, Sept. 27, 1939. Gladstone Papers.
14. Letter, Janie Gladstone to Nora, Oct. 8, 1939. Gladstone Papers.
15. Letter, Gladstone to Nora, Oct. 15, 1939. Gladstone Papers.
16. Ibid.
17. Ibid., Oct. 13, 1940.

Chapter Nine: INDIAN ASSOCIATION OF ALBERTA

1. Draft of a letter to J. Blackmore, Feb. 2, 1944. Gladstone Papers.
2. George Yackulic, "Alberta's Bloods," *Western Business and Industry,* October 1953, p. 29.
3. Minutes, Seventh General Meeting, Indian Association of Alberta (hereinafter referred to as IAA), July 4, 1946. Copy in author's possession.
4. Ibid.
5. Ibid.

6. *Minutes of Proceedings and Evidence,* Joint Committee on Indian Affairs, Ottawa, No. 1, p. iii, May 28, 1946.
7. Draft of a letter from chiefs to Norman Lickers, July 24, 1946. Gladstone Papers.
8. "Quoted from Proceedings," undated mimeographed circular based upon an IAA executive meeting of Jan. 26, 1949. Gladstone Papers.
9. Ibid.
10. Ibid.
11. Ibid.
12. Minutes of meeting of Blood local with Bob Crow Eagle, May 15, 1949. Gladstone Papers.
13. Minutes, annual general meeting, IAA, June 23–24, 1948. Gladstone Papers.
14. John Laurie, "The Indian Association of Alberta," p. 29. Undated manuscript in Laurie Papers, Glenbow Archives.
15. Ibid.

Chapter Ten: PRESIDENT GLADSTONE

1. Minutes of council meeting, IAA, Feb. 4, 1950, p. 1.
2. Minutes of Blood Local No. 1, March 29, 1950. Gladstone Papers.
3. Minutes of Blood Local No. 2, April 1, 1950. Gladstone Papers.
4. Minutes of Blood Local No. 1, March 29, 1950. Gladstone Papers.
5. Letter, Gladstone to John Laurie, March 22, 1950. Gladstone Papers.
6. Post card, Laurie to Hugh Dempsey, June 14, 1950. In author's possession.
7. Letter, Laurie to John Callihoo, Aug. 30, 1950. In author's possession.
8. *Hansard,* House of Commons Debates, April 2, 1951, p. 1527.
9. *Special Committee Appointed to Consider Bill No. 79, An Act Respecting Indians. Minutes of Proceedings and Evidence,* Ottawa, April 17, 1971, p. 37.
10. Ibid.
11. Letter, S. C. Knapp to Laurie, July 27, 1951. Gladstone Papers.
12. S. C. Knapp, "Notice to all Chiefs and Councillors," July 9, 1951. Copy in Gladstone Papers.
13. Minutes of meeting, Little Red River Local, IAA, Aug. 25, 1951. Gladstone Papers.
14. Ibid.

Chapter Eleven: ACTIVE YEARS

1. Letter, Gladstone to Hon. Walter Harris, undated. Gladstone Papers.
2. Ibid.
3. Letter, Gladstone to Laurie, March 16, 1951. Gladstone Papers.
4. Telegram, Dan Johnson to Gladstone, Nov. 14, 1951. Gladstone Papers.
5. Minutes of general meeting, IAA, June 12–13, 1952, p. 1. Gladstone Papers.
6. Ibid.
7. *Calgary Herald,* June 13, 1952.
8. Letter, Dempsey to Gladstone, June 25, 1952. Gladstone Papers.
9. Draft of speech, Laurie to Gladstone, undated. Gladstone Papers.
10. Minutes of general meeting, IAA, June 9–10, 1954. Gladstone Papers.

Chapter Twelve: OUT AND IN AGAIN

1. Letter, Laurie to Gladstone, Sept. 2, 1954. Gladstone Papers.
2. Interview with Clarence McHugh, March 5, 1961.
3. Ibid.
4. Ibid.
5. Letter, Laurie to Gladstone, Nov. 11, 1955. Gladstone Papers.
6. Letter, Laurie to Gladstone, May 3, 1955. Gladstone Papers.
7. Letter, Gladstone to Jim Starlight, Oct. 29, 1956. Gladstone Papers.
8. Letter, Gladstone to Laurie, Aug. 8, 1956. Gladstone Papers.
9. Bruce Hutchinson, *Mr. Prime Minister, 1867–1964* (Toronto: Longmans Canada Ltd., 1964), p. 309.
10. *Hansard,* House of Commons Debates, Jan. 21, 1957, p. 435.
11. Ibid., p. 476.
12. *Calgary Herald,* Jan. 22, 1957.
13 J. H. Ferguson in *Hansard,* House of Commons Debates, Jan. 30, 1957, p. 830.
14. *Calgary Herald,* Jan. 31, 1957.
15. Ibid.
16. Letter, John Samson to Gladstone, Jan. 5, 1957. Gladstone Papers.

Chapter Thirteen: TO THE SENATE

1. *Hansard,* House of Commons Debates, March 25, 1955, p. 2393.
2. Letter, Gladstone to Andy Paull, July 26, 1957. Gladstone Papers.
3. *Calgary Herald,* July 20, 1957.
4. *Hansard,* House of Commons Debates, Oct. 29, 1957, p. 507.
5. Diary entry, Janie Gladstone, Feb. 1, 1958. Gladstone Papers.
6. *The Native Voice,* Vancouver, March 1958, p. 3.
7. *The Canadian Parliamentary Guide* (Ottawa: Pierre G. Normandeau, 1959), p. 87.
8. *Liberty Magazine,* August 1958, n.p.
9. Diary entry, Hugh A. Dempsey, June 22, 1958. In author's possession.
10. *Winnipeg Tribune,* June 13, 1958.
11. *Lethbridge Herald,* June 16, 1958.
12. Letter, Laurie to Gladstone, March 19, 1958. Gladstone Papers.
13. Gladstone speech to IAA, June 20, 1958. Gladstone Papers.
14. Diary entry, Hugh A. Dempsey, June 3, 1958. In author's possession.
15. *Calgary Herald,* July 10, 1959.
16. *Debates of the Senate,* Aug. 13, 1958, p. 514.
17. *Ottawa Citizen,* Aug. 15, 1958.
18. Ibid.

Chapter Fourteen: DIEFENBAKER YEARS

1. Letter, Gladstone to Laurie, Feb. 10, 1959. Gladstone Papers.
2. Letter, Gladstone to W. J. C. Kirby, May 4, 1959. Gladstone Papers.
3. Ibid.
4. *Ottawa Citizen,* Jan. 15, 1960.

5. Ibid.
6. Ibid.
7. *Ottawa Journal,* Jan. 19, 1960.
8. Ibid.
9. *Debates of the Senate,* March 17, 1960, p. 358.
10. Draft letter, June 21, 1960. Gladstone Papers.
11. Letter, Ray Woollam to Gladstone, May 27, 1960. Gladstone Papers.
12. Letter, Gladstone to Hon. John Sturdy, June 7, 1960. Gladstone Papers.
13. *Prince Rupert Daily News,* June 5, 1962.
14. Ibid, June 6, 1962.
15. *Debates of the Senate,* Feb. 10, 1959, p. 135.
16. *Toronto Globe and Mail,* July 10, 1959.
17. Cited in *Calgary Herald,* June 19, 1965.
18. Gladstone notebook, 1959. Gladstone Papers.
19. Ibid.
20. Ibid.
21. *Canadian Churchman,* Toronto, April 1960, n.p.
22. Ibid., May 1961, n.p. For further examples see "The Moral Re-Armer," *Time,* Aug. 18, 1961; Jerry Sheeham, "A New Look at Moral Re-Armament," *Calgary Albertan,* Feb. 27, 28, 1962; "How One Student of Moral Re-Armament was Frozen out of Brazil," *Maclean's Magazine,* March 10, 1962; Ken Lefolii, "The MRA Dossier," *Maclean's Magazine,* May 4, 1963; Jamie Portman, "About MRA," *Calgary Herald,* May 14, 1963; and Tom Driberg, *The Mystery of Moral Re-Armament* (New York: Secker and Warburg, 1965).
23. *Lethbridge Herald,* Jan. 7, 1959.
24. *Debates of the Senate,* July 10, 1961, p. 1105.
25. Ibid., Feb. 16, 1961, p. 348.
26. *Sheridan Press,* Aug. 11, 1960.
27. *Debates of the Senate,* Feb. 16, 1961, p. 348.
28. Letter, Gladstone to Diefenbaker, May 15, 1962. Gladstone Papers.
29. Diary entry, Janie Gladstone, May 26, 1962. Gladstone Papers.
30. Letter, Diefenbaker to Gladstone, March 11, 1963. Gladstone Papers.
31. Diary entry, Hugh A. Dempsey, March 20, 1963. In author's possession.
32. Ibid., April 2, 1963.
33. Hutchinson, *Mr. Prime Minister,* p. 348.
34. Letter, Gladstone to Diefenbaker, June 6, 1963. Gladstone Papers.

Chapter Fifteen: DECLINING YEARS

1. *Toronto Globe and Mail,* Feb. 19, 1963.
2. Letter, Gladstone to Diefenbaker, Nov. 12, 1962. Gladstone Papers.
3. *Calgary Herald,* Nov. 15, 1967.
4. Ibid.
5. *Weekend Magazine,* Toronto, No. 45, 1963.
6. Letter, Dr. Van Orman to whom it may concern, Dec. 15, 1966. Gladstone Papers.
7. *Edmonton Journal,* Oct. 12, 1965.

8. *Calgary Herald,* Nov. 15, 1967.
9. *Debates of the Senate,* March 10, 1967, p. 1605.
10. Ibid., p. 1608.
11. Ibid., p. 1606.
12. "Speech of Harold Cardinal as Presented to the Alberta All Chiefs Conference," April 3, 1970. Gladstone Papers.
13. *Toronto Globe and Mail,* Feb. 6, 1961.
14. Letter, Gladstone to H. G. Van Maurik of *Zuidoost-Pers,* Nov. 6, 1969. Gladstone Papers.
15. "Statement by the Hon. Jean Chretien," Oct. 2, 1969. Mimeographed paper. Gladstone Papers.
16. Letter, Gladstone to Van Maurik, Nov. 6, 1969. Gladstone Papers.
17. Draft letter, Gladstone to Chretien, undated. Gladstone Papers.
18. Minutes of the general meeting, IAA, 1970. Gladstone Papers.
19. Indian Chiefs of Alberta, *Citizens Plus* (Edmonton: Indian Association of Alberta, 1970), p. 1.
20. "Statement of the Hon. Jean Chretien," Oct. 2, 1969. Gladstone Papers.
21. Letter, Mrs. D. Bouffard to Len Marchand, June 26, 1968. Gladstone Papers.
22. Letter, Gladstone to Trudeau, April 9, 1971. Gladstone Papers.
23. *Debates of the Senate,* March 31, 1971, pp. 811–12.
24. Ibid., p. 814.
25. "Citizens Plus means that . . . " Minutes of annual meeting, IAA, 1970. Gladstone Papers.
26. *Lethbridge Herald,* May 5, 1971.
27. *Debates of the Senate,* Sept. 14, 1971, p. 1244.
28. Hugh A. Dempsey, *Crowfoot, Chief of the Blackfeet* (Norman: University of Oklahoma Press, 1972), p. 213.

INDEX

ABOUT THE AUTHOR

Hugh Dempsey has written and edited many books on western Canadian history, including *Charcoal's World* and *Crowfoot*. He is the editor of the *Alberta History* quarterly and an executive member of the Historical Society of Alberta.

He has been associated with the Glenbow Museum in Calgary since 1956, as archivist, chief curator, and associate director. He has lectured on ethno-history and western Canadian history in Alberta and Montana. The University of Calgary awarded him a honorary degree in 1974, and in 1975 he became a member of the Order of Canada.

He is an honorary Chief of the Blood Indians and has worked closely as a consultant with Indian groups. He is married to Pauline Gladstone and has five children.